# THE BATTLE FOR MANILA

RICHARD CONNAUGHTON

JOHN PIMLOTT

AND DUNCAN ANDERSON

PRESIDIO

This book is dedicated to the noncombatant men,
women, children and infants who were killed during the
Battle for Manila, February 3 to March 3, 1945.

First published in Great Britain 1995
Bloomsbury Publishing Plc, 2 Soho Square, London W1V 6HB

Copyright © 1995 by Richard Connaughton, John Pimlott and
Duncan Anderson

Published by Presidio Press
505 B San Marin Drive, Suite 300, Novato CA 94945

Library of Congress Cataloging-in-Publication Data

Connaughton, R.M. (Richard Michael), 1942–
The Battle for Manila / Richard Connaughton, John Pimlott, and
Duncan Anderson.
p. cm.
Includes index.

ISBN 0–89141–578–5

1. World War, 1939–1945 – Campaigns – Philippines – Manila.
2. Manila (Philippines) – History, Military. I. Pimlott, John.
1948–    . II. Anderson, Duncan. III. Title.
D767.4.C595 1995    95–11918
940.54′25–dc20    CIP

Maps on pages 9–13 drawn by Keith Chaffer

Typeset by Hewer Text Composition Services, Edinburgh
Printed in Great Britain by Clays Limited, St Ives plc

# CONTENTS

# PHOTO CAPTIONS

1 Internees at the University of Santo Tomás raising the US flag over the main entrance of the campus on February 6, 1945, 48 hours after their liberation by the 1st Cavalry Division. (Ayala Museum – Library and Iconographic Archive)

2 Lieutenant Colonel Toshio Hayashi and his men being escorted away from the University of Santo Tomás on the morning of February 5. The civilian in the white shirt on the right is special agent Ernest Stanley. (Ayala Museum – Library and Iconographic Archive)

3 Gun lines were quickly established in the grounds of the University of Santo Tomás. Here 105mm howitzers are seen firing on February 5. (US Army)

4 Manila's long, straight streets provided excellent fields of fire for weapons like this American .30 Browning machine-gun, which could hit targets at more than 2000 yards. Unfortunately at such distances it was impossible to tell Japanese from Filipinos. (US Army)

5 The burnt-out Bay View Hotel, with the Luneta Hotel in the background, from M.H. del Pilar Street. For three days from February 9 the Japanese imprisoned hundreds of girls and young women in the Bay View and raped them repeatedly. (Ayala Museum – Library and Iconographic Archive)

6 With scarcely a glance at a Japanese corpse, US troops advance deeper into Manila on February 12. (US Army)

7 The Philippine General Hospital, liberated by the Americans on February 17. Familiar with the sight, soldiers and evacuees are unconcerned about this dead Japanese soldier lying near the front steps of the hospital. Note that looters have already stolen his shoes and personal belongings. (Ayala Museum – Library and Iconographic Archive)

8 The ruins of Manila's New Police Station. This two-storey, reinforced-concrete building, the focal point of Japanese resistance to the east of Intramuros, came under attack by the US 129th Regiment on February 13. A week later it had still not been taken. Veterans of the 129th described it as 'the most formidable obstacle the regiment encountered during the war.' (Ayala Museum – Library and Iconographic Archive)

9 A US 240mm howitzer firing into the walls of Intramuros on February 19. (US Army)

10 At 8.40 a.m. on February 23, troops of the 3rd Battalion 129th Infantry scramble ashore on the south side of the Pasig River near the Government

Mint, and dash for the breaches the artillery barrage has made in the walls of Intramuros. (Ayala Museum – Library and Iconographic Archive)

11 Between February 23 and February 25 US troops cleared the Japanese from Intramuros. Here an American soldier uses a flamethrower to eliminate an enemy strongpoint in the wall. (Ayala Museum – Library and Iconographic Archive)

12 Women and children killed by bayonet and rifle fire in Intramuros. (US Army)

13 Soldiers of the US Infantry, supported by an armored bulldozer, mop up resistance in the streets of Intramuros. (US Army)

14 The ruins of the Legislative Building, scene of intense fighting between February 25 and February 27, seen from the northwest. (US Army)

15 A view of the Quezon Bridge and the devastated south bank of the Pasig, looking toward the east. (US Army)

16 Alaistair ('Shorty') Hall with his children (from left) Ian, Consuelo, Alaistair and Roderick outside the gymnasium of the University of Santo Tomás internment camp, in February 1945, shortly after the reunion.

17 US General of the Army Douglas MacArthur, commander of Allied forces in the South West Pacific, broadcasts, on February 26, 1945, his address in Manila restoring to the Commonwealth government the administration of liberated areas of the Philippines. Sergio Osmena (right), President of the Commonwealth, and US officers stand behind General MacArthur. The general said: 'My country has kept the faith. Its soldiers come here as an army of free men dedicated, with your people, to the cause of human liberty, and committed to the task of destroying those evil forces that have fought to suppress it by brutality of the sword.'

18 A photograph believed to show Rear Admiral Sanji Iwabuchi, commander of Japanese forces in Manila.

19 Major General Robert S. Beightler, commander of the 37th Infantry Division. (US Army)

20 General Tomoyuki Yamashita, Commander-in-Chief of all Japanese forces in the Philippines, led away to Bilibid prison after signing the surrender document on September 3, 1945. (US Army Military History Institute)

21 The Memorial of the Philippine Liberation, Corregidor Island. It bears no mention of the Liberation of Manila.

# FOREWORD

The authors wish to record their thanks and appreciation to the many people who have made available anecdotes and diaries and have given interviews. We are particularly grateful to Señor José Olbes and Señor Enrique Zobel, who, at very short notice, gave freely of their time and submitted themselves to extensive interrogation. Special thanks are due to the members of the Memorare-Manila 1945 Committee, notably His Excellency Juan José P. Rocha and His Excellency Miguel Perez-Rubio, but particularly to the Committee's historian, Edgar Krohn Jr. While many people have helped with the research and writing, the book could never have been produced without the imagination, persistence, and unflagging energy of Mr Roderick Hall. He got the project off the ground and supported it through to the end. Special thanks should also be given to Roderick Hall's sister, Consuelo H. McHugh, who generously supported the project and devoted considerable time to reading the manuscript. The authors are grateful to them both. Thanks are also due to the Ayala Museum, Manila, Library of Congress Office, South East Asia, and to the Director and Staff, US Army Military History Institute, Carlisle, Pennsylvania.

The authors found that the re-creation of the destroyed city posed many difficulties, not the least of which was the correct use of place-names. Street names appearing in this work are those which were in use at the time. Many have subsequently changed. In addition, a number of streets appearing in the narrative do not feature in the maps. To have done so would have led to congestion and confusion. Where this is the case, the streets appear for the record.

The authors set out on this project with a detachment that American, Japanese, or Filipino historians may have found difficult. However, as we met more and more survivors of the battle it was impossible to remain emotionally neutral; at various times we all experienced feelings of horror, revulsion, disgust, anger, pity and guilt. We also felt hatred. How, then, did the people who survived the destruction of Manila come to terms with the experience? The behaviour of Elpidio Quirino, a former President of the Philippines, is a guide. Here was a man whose family was massacred either by the Japanese or by American artillery. When he became President in 1949, one of his first official acts was to issue a Presidential Proclamation pardoning all the Japanese war criminals tried, convicted and incarcerated in the Philippines. People around him were perplexed. 'How,' they asked, 'after all you have been through, can you pardon these people?' He replied: 'I cannot live the rest of my life harbouring hatred towards our former enemies.'

RMC, JLP, DA
Camberley, England
January 1995

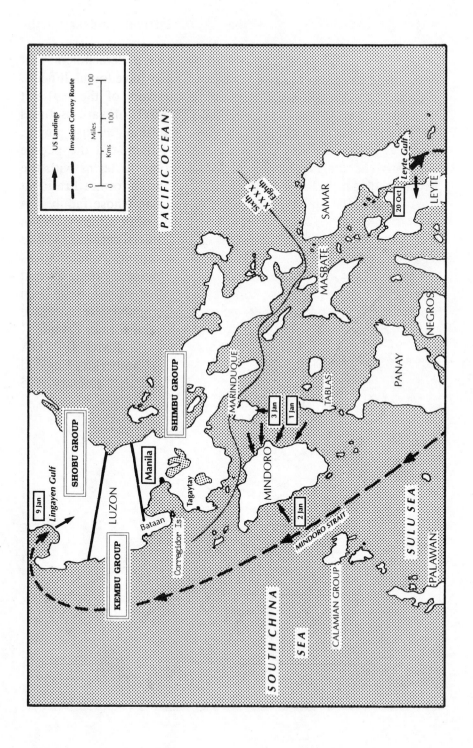

PACIFIC OCEAN

SOUTH CHINA SEA

SULU SEA

LUZON

Lingayen Gulf

9 Jan

SHOBU GROUP

KEMBU GROUP

SHIMBU GROUP

Manila

Bataan

Corregidor Is.

Tagaytay

MINDORO

MINDORO STRAIT

MARINDUQUE

TABLAS

PANAY

NEGROS

MASBATE

SAMAR

LEYTE

Leyte Gulf

20 Oct

Sixth
XXXX
Eighth

1 Jan

2 Jan

3 Jan

CALAMIAN GROUP

PALAWAN

US Landings

Invasion Convoy Route

Miles
100

Kms
100

0

0

9

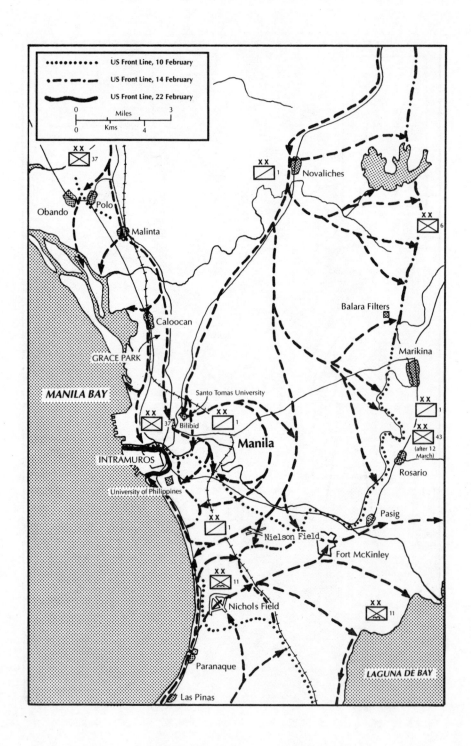

US Front Line, 10 February
US Front Line, 14 February
US Front Line, 22 February

Miles 0 — 3
Kms 0 — 4

Novaliches

Obando
Polo
Malinta

Caloocan

Balara Filters

Marikina

GRACE PARK

MANILA BAY

Santo Tomas University

Bilibid

Manila

Rosario
(after 12 March)

INTRAMUROS

University of Philippines

Pasig

Nielson Field

Fort McKinley

Nichols Field

Paranaque

LAGUNA DE BAY

Las Pinas

# MAPS

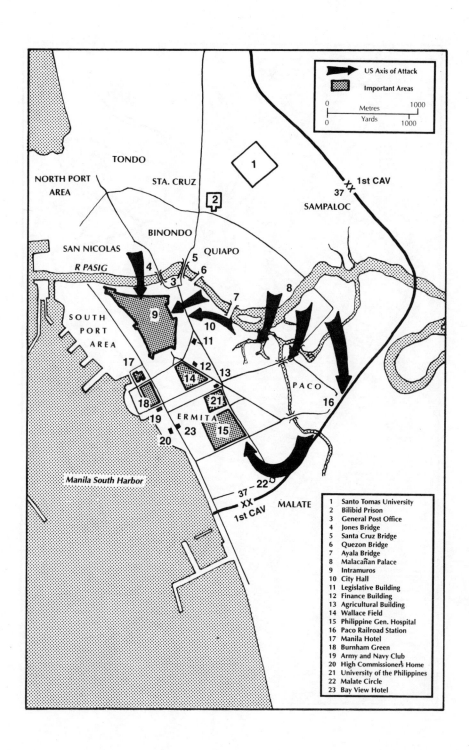

- 1 Santo Tomas University
- 2 Bilibid Prison
- 3 General Post Office
- 4 Jones Bridge
- 5 Santa Cruz Bridge
- 6 Quezon Bridge
- 7 Ayala Bridge
- 8 Malacañan Palace
- 9 Intramuros
- 10 City Hall
- 11 Legislative Building
- 12 Finance Building
- 13 Agricultural Building
- 14 Wallace Field
- 15 Philippine Gen. Hospital
- 16 Paco Railroad Station
- 17 Manila Hotel
- 18 Burnham Green
- 19 Army and Navy Club
- 20 High Commissioner's Home
- 21 University of the Philippines
- 22 Malate Circle
- 23 Bay View Hotel

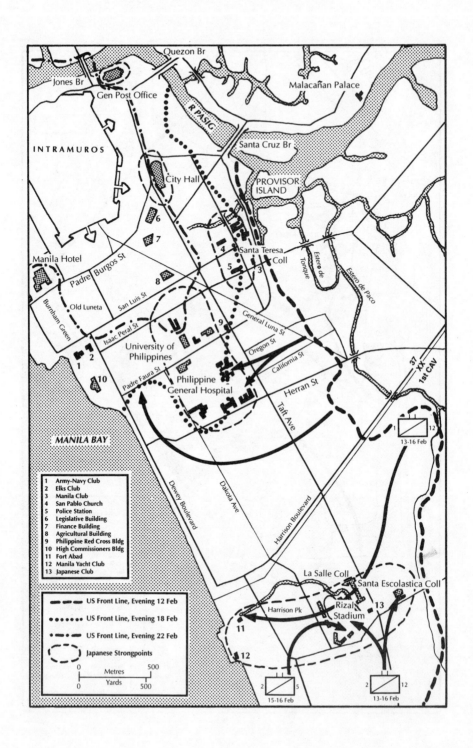

Quezon Br

Jones Br

Gen Post Office

Malacañan Palace

R PASIG.

INTRAMUROS

Santa Cruz Br

City Hall

PROVISOR ISLAND

6

7

Santa Teresa Coll

Manila Hotel

4

5

3

Estero de Tonque

Estero de Paco

Padre Burgos St

8

Old Luneta

San Luis St

Burnham Green

General Luna St

Isaac Peral St

9

University of Philippines

Oregon St

California St

37 XX 1st CAV

2

Padre Faura St

Philippine General Hospital

Herran St

1

10

Taft Ave

1 | 12

13-16 Feb

MANILA BAY

Dewey Boulevard

Dakota Ave

Harrison Boulevard

1   Army-Navy Club
2   Elks Club
3   Manila Club
4   San Pablo Church
5   Police Station
6   Legislative Building
7   Finance Building
8   Agricultural Building
9   Philippine Red Cross Bldg
10  High Commissioners Bldg
11  Fort Abad
12  Manila Yacht Club
13  Japanese Club

La Salle Coll

Santa Escolastica Coll

Rizal Stadium

13

Harrison Pk

— — —   US Front Line, Evening 12 Feb

• • • • • •   US Front Line, Evening 18 Feb

—•—•—   US Front Line, Evening 22 Feb

⟋⟍   Japanese Strongpoints

11

12

0          Metres          500
0          Yards           500

2 | 5

15-16 Feb

2 | 12

13-16 Feb

# MAPS

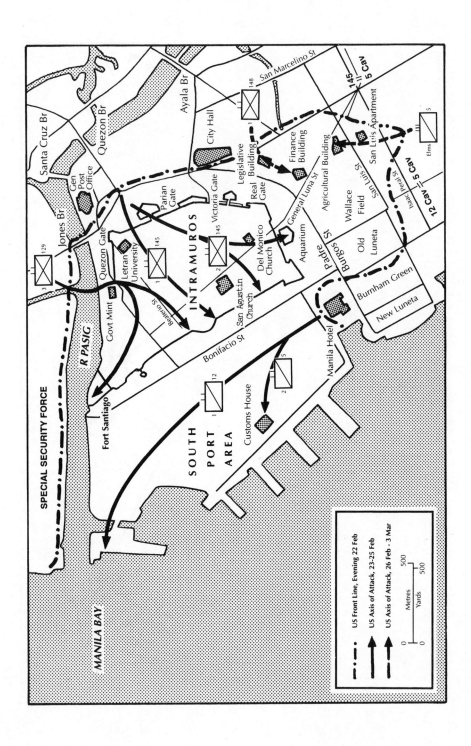

13

# 1

# PEARL OF THE ORIENT

Between July 1941 and March 1942 the Japanese overran and occupied the great cities of Southeast Asia – Saigon, Hong Kong, Singapore, Batavia (Djakarta), Rangoon and Manila. In most places the occupation lasted for less than four years. When the British Fourteenth Army advanced on Rangoon in May 1945 the Japanese evacuated the city; four months later they surrendered Singapore, Batavia, Hong Kong and Saigon to British forces. But Manila was different. The Japanese defended Manila against the advance of the American Sixth and Eighth Armies. During the month-long battle which followed between February 4 and March 3, 1945, the city was completely destroyed: all that remained by the end were heaps of smouldering rubble. The charred bodies half-buried in the ruins bore terrible witness to a massacre beyond the nightmare of any Manileño. An estimated 100,000 Manileños had been killed. The Battle for Manila occupies a unique place in the history of the Pacific War. It was the only occasion on which American and Japanese forces fought each other in a city and it was the largest battle of its kind yet fought by either the American or the Japanese armies. The destruction of Manila was on the same scale as the destruction of Warsaw (August 1–October 2, 1944), and smaller only than the battles of Berlin (April 20–May 2, 1945) and Stalingrad (September 13, 1942–February 2, 1943).

The Manila which lay in ruins that spring of 1945 was a unique blend of three different cultures which had shaped its recent and past history: the indigenous Tagalog Filipino culture of Luzon overlaid by 330 years of Spanish spiritual and intellectual colonization and 40 years of American control and influence. This eclectic mixture contained yet further ingredients: Chinese and Japanese settlers had lent an East Asian flavor, and the Scots and the Germans, those great 19th-century traders of Southeast Asia, had brought with them their own cultural and economic legacy. Other great cities – Shanghai, Singapore and Istanbul – have married elements from two continents. But Manila, quite singularly, embraced not only Southeast and East Asia, Europe and North America, but, thanks to Spanish influence, significant elements of Latin America. It was a city which (as a Manileño of 1940 might have said) felt equally at home with the tango, the flamenco, the waltz, the jive, and Balinese dancing. Spiritual fascists in late-1930s Tokyo viewed Manila's cultural heterogeneity with mistrust: a multi-colored blot on a pure Asia. To most others, including the Manileños themselves, this very diversity was a source of celebration, like some rich tapestry or mosaic.

Manila was uniquely beautiful: she was universally known as the Pearl of the Orient, a jewel beyond price. Many cities were destroyed between 1942 and 1945 – a long list in which the names of Stalingrad, Hamburg, Warsaw, Dresden, Berlin, Hiroshima stand out prominently. Lives were shattered, and the cultural damage to their mother nations in each case was irreparable. Yet in the case of Manila, something rare, and something irreplaceable, was destroyed. The Philippines had lost their capital, but the world had lost a city whose very evolution, drawing upon the cultures and histories of four different continents, had made it part of the international heritage. The tragedy of the destruction of Manila lies deeply engraved on the hearts of all Filipinos, and in the memories of the inevitably diminishing band of US Pacific War veterans. Yet the tragedy goes on, for to most people in the world outside, the story in its entirety has never been fully told.[1]

What was life like in Manila in its heyday? One of the few Americans who did not love the city and its people was Major Dwight D. Eisenhower, who arrived in Manila as chief of staff to General Douglas MacArthur, the newly appointed head of the American Military Mission to the Philippines, in October 1935. Apart from a tour in the Canal Zone and a year working for the US Battlefield Monuments Commission in France (1928–9), the

45-year-old Eisenhower had never lived outside the United States. There is a photograph of the two men taken on their very first day in Manila: the pair are standing in front of the Manila Hotel just to the south of their point of disembarkation at Pier 7 in the South Port district. Both wear the customary white drill suits and white panama hats. MacArthur's face also wears a jaunty smile, as if to acknowledge the greetings of the Manileños pressing forward against the barriers. Eisenhower's expression is totally different. He seems in pain – perhaps it is the heat, for which he had a low tolerance – yet also strangely apprehensive: the look of a man who is beginning to realize he may have made a serious mistake.[2] Eisenhower, who embodied the sober virtues of the Pennsylvania Dutch (the family originally came from the Rhineland and spelled their name 'Eisenhauer') found the rhythms of Manilan life infuriating. To his diary he confided: 'we have learned to expect from the Filipinos with whom we deal a minimum of performance from a maximum of promise. Among individuals there is no lack of intelligence, but to us they seem . . . unaccustomed to the requirements of administrative and executive procedure.'[3] The methodical, prosaic, protestant clerk ground against the Latin-Asian culture of the Manileños.

Eisenhower initially worked in an office near MacArthur's inside the air-conditioned splendor of the Manila Hotel, the most modern in the city. Then President Quezon offered him an office next to his own in Malacañan Palace, about a mile and a half northeast across Manila's Pasig River, in order to improve liaison between the Military Mission and his government. Thereafter Eisenhower split his day between working alongside MacArthur in the Manila Hotel and working alongside Quezon in Malacañan Palace. His diary and private correspondence from this period recite a litany of complaints. Things which should have been done were left undone, and there was no judgment in the Filipinos. Progress was always too slow. Revealingly, he shows no interest in the sights or events he must have witnessed on his daily journey to and from work.[4]

Eisenhower's drive from the Manila Hotel to Malacañan Palace would have taken him east and then north along Padre Burgos Street. This tree-lined boulevard skirted around the walls of the old Spanish city of Intramuros, whose 400 acres of narrow, cobbled streets, churches, and fortresses had been built on the site of the old Muslim stockade. This was the heart of Manila, seized by the Spanish in the 16th century, attacked by the Chinese in the 17th, besieged and briefly occupied by the the British in the 18th, and taken by the Americans at the end of the 19th century.

On the right-hand side of Padre Burgos toward the intersection with Taft Avenue Eisenhower could witness a sight more appealing to his own utilitarian tastes: modern construction work. His stay in Manila coincided with the gradual implementation of an American architect's plans for a new administrative center. This monumental project, conceived as early as 1904, owed more to necessity than to modernist aesthetics. Manila was in a notorious earthquake zone – the city had suffered dozens of major earthquakes – and any new public buildings would have to be guaranteed quake-proof. The designs called for extremely deep foundations and the widespread use of reinforced concrete with a tolerance far greater than that demanded of similar buildings in most parts of the United States. One block south of Padre Burgos, the Agricultural Building was already finished; to the right, just before the intersection with Taft Avenue, stood the new Finance and Legislative Buildings.[5] Just beyond the intersection with Taft the vast outlines of City Hall were beginning to emerge: a monolithic building which offended the aesthetic sensibilities of many Manileños. The Manila journalist Nick Joaquín was to refer to it as something which 'vaguely looked like a prison.'[6]

The most interesting route to Malacañan Palace involved driving on for another 500 yards or so up Padre Burgos to where the grandiose General Post Office now dominated the southern bank of the Pasig. To the left, across Calle Aduana, lay Jones Bridge, which led into the district of Binondo, the historical China Town. Straight ahead lay Santa Cruz Bridge, from which Rizal Avenue ran due north through the district of Santa Cruz toward Grace Park on the northern outskirts of Manila. To the right was the Quezon Bridge. At the bridge's foot stood the Plaza Miranda, dominated by the newly completed neo-Renaissance Quiapo Church, the most recent in a series of churches on this site dating back to 1592. Quiapo was downtown Manila, its main shopping and entertainment area. Due north from the Quezon Bridge, construction was in progress of a new highway, Quezon Boulevard, which ran due north more or less parallel to Rizal Avenue. This project was causing a great deal of discontent in the mid-1930s since it involved the demolition of parts of Quiapo, an area second only to Intramuros in historic interest.[7] Eisenhower's journey took him right at the Plaza Miranda and then east following the line of the Pasig along Aviles Street, through an area graced by the elegant mansions of the mestizo aristocracy, to the district of San Miguel. Here, in a spacious 40-acre garden by the banks of the Pasig, stood Malacañan Palace, the elegant late-18th-century country house which had been home to both Spanish and American governors, and was now the center of government of the President of the Commonwealth.

Few majors in the American army of the 1930s could boast better working conditions: Malacañan Palace was rather grander than Abilene or Fort Leavenworth. But Eisenhower still managed to complain. He misunderstood the nature of Filipino hospitality and made no concessions whatsoever to Filipino feeling. When Quezon wanted to make Eisenhower a general in the Philippine Army and MacArthur a field marshal, Eisenhower protested vigorously to his chief: 'General, you have been a four-star general. This is a *proud* thing. There's only been a few who had it. Why in the *hell* do you want a *banana* country giving you field-marshalship?' Eisenhower recalled that at this point MacArthur exploded in rage.[8]

Eisenhower might have found his years in Manila more tolerable had his wife Mamie, who joined him in 1936 with their son John, been happier. But Mamie found the climate oppressive and disliked the food. She was unwell for most of her three and a half years there, spending nearly all her time at home in the company of a small circle of American officers and their wives. One of the few Mileños with whom the Eisenhowers socialized was Captain Joseph McMicking, then a reserve pilot of the infant Philippine Air Force, who taught Eisenhower to fly. McMicking, with his tall, dark good looks, moustache and ready smile, resembled a casting director's version of a war hero. He came from a prominent Scots-Filipino trading family, headed by his father José McMicking. The lifestyles and values of the Scots Mileños made them acceptable to the Eisenhowers. Their son John, who now attended the exclusive Bishop Brent School in Baguio, was far more enthusiastic about Manila and the Philippines. His parents' re-creation of a little America within a foreign environment was not unlike their earlier experience of Paris. During their 15-month spell in that cosmopolitan city, the couple had similarly excluded themselves from exposure to foreign people, experiences and culture.[9]

An American who did not like Paris life was unlikely to enjoy Manila. But the Eisenhowers were exceptions: most Americans who ended up in Manila took to it quickly. Major Richard Sutherland, his wife Josephine and his daughter Natalie, who arrived there in July 1938, were in this respect characteristic. Josephine loved Manila and rapidly became good friends both with Douglas MacArthur's wife Jean (both women were from Tennessee) and also with Aurora Quezon, wife of the Philippines' president. Sutherland's background (his father had been a senator for West Virginia) contrasted sharply with Eisenhower's stolid Pennsylvania Dutch upbringing. Unlike most American officers, Sutherland had studied history at Yale rather than engineering at West Point. The Sutherlands moved into a house on Dewey Boulevard in the southern part of the district of Malate overlooking Manila Bay, one of the city's most desirable up-and-coming residential areas. Life in Malate was good. Nearby were the exclusive Manila Polo Club and the Manila Yacht Club. But Sutherland was more interested in golf than he was in polo or sailing. He would drive a mile further east of Nielson Field to Fort McKinley and one of the finest golf courses in Southeast Asia.

Sutherland struck up a particular friendship with Alaistair 'Shorty' Hall, a six-foot-four Scottish stockbroker, with whom he played golf at least once a week. The Sutherlands often visited 'Shorty Hall and his wife Consuelo. Their eldest son, Roderick, remembered one especially joyous occasion in 1939 when his father and Sutherland celebrated the American's promotion to the rank of full colonel. It was through families like the Halls that the Sutherlands steadily expanded their social contacts. Consuelo Hall's maiden name was McMicking, and she soon introduced the Sutherlands to her family, including her brother, Joe McMicking.[10] The Sutherlands also made friends among Manila's Spanish population, both 'Peninsulares' (Spanish-born) and 'Insulares' (Philippine-born) like the Olbeses. Many of the Insulares shared Sutherland's passion for golf; it was unsurprising that after the war their families took the lead in developing Spain's magnificent golf courses.[11]

For a time Sutherland worked in tandem with Eisenhower, but when Eisenhower returned to the United States in November 1939 Sutherland took over as MacArthur's chief of staff. Sutherland's daily journey to his office in the Manila Hotel was so exotic it could scarcely count as commuting: it was the ideal route for any tourist who wished to see the main sights of Manila. His drive took him north along the coconut-palm-lined Dewey Boulevard, skirted on the left by the sea wall and with Manila Bay stretching out beyond, its waters crowded with ships of all sizes, from great ocean liners to interisland schooners. Beyond, to the northwest and west, rose the outline of the mountains of the Bataan Peninsula and the fortress island of Corregidor, an outline dramatically defined by the Manila sunset of pale yellow light rapidly deepening into dark crimson. Lining the right side of the boulevard, with spectacular views across the bay, stood the imposing mansions of the wealthy and powerful, the embassies and consulates of foreign governments, a few expensive high-rise apartment houses, and Manila's more exclusive nightclubs, like the Silver Slipper.

After about a mile Malate gave way to the district of Ermita. Dewey Boulevard continued north but the coast curved to the west. Here on the left was the residence of the US High Commissioner to the Philippines, Francis B. Sayre, an office which was frequently in conflict with both the military mission and the President of the Commonwealth, while on the right stood the Bay View Hotel, one of the most modern and expensive in Manila. Two hundred yards further on the right was the intersection with Isaac Peral Street, and immediately on the left, by the shore of Manila Bay, stood the most visible symbols of the United States' presence: the Elks and the Army and Navy Clubs, both of which were exclusively for Americans. The Elks, of course, was even more exclusive, banning women of any nationality or race.

The last part of Sutherland's journey took him north through the green stretch of the Luneta, Manila's version of Hyde Park, Central Park or the Tuileries. The Luneta occupied an area of little more than a half square mile, and since the American occupation it had been subdivided into four roughly equal parks, running west to east: New Luneta, Burnham Green, Old Luneta and Wallace Field. It was here that the Manileños held their fiestas and some religious festivals. Padre Burgos marked the northern boundary of the Luneta; to the northeast loomed the walls of Intramuros; to the west stood the Manila Hotel. The drive usually took Sutherland about ten minutes but sometimes longer. The picturesque horse-drawn *calesas* were steadily giving way to the *auto-calesa*, the father of the 'jeepney,' and the majority of Manila's 20,000 or so privately owned cars were owned by the residents of Ermita, Malate and Pasay. By the late 1930s traffic jams were becoming increasingly common.[12]

American officers like Sutherland enjoyed life in Manila to the full. So did most American enlisted men. After a long voyage from San Francisco in unpleasant conditions aboard the US Army transport *Tasker H. Bliss*, 20-year-old Private Paul P. Rogers arrived in Manila on October 24, 1941. Rogers, a touch-typist, was assigned to MacArthur's headquarters. These were currently being expanded, and had recently been moved from the Manila Hotel into the headquarters of the Philippine Department, the name given to the US garrison of the islands. This HQ was housed in Fort Santiago, the old Spanish citadel which occupied a triangle where the wall of Intramuros ran down to where the Pasig River emptied into Manila Bay. The barred cells and dungeons of Fort Santiago bore mute testimony to generations of suffering, but in 1941 these were only historical curiosities. Rogers remembered the details of his first meal at Fort Santiago:

> Next morning I sat down for my first breakfast at a table set with linen, good china, and flatware. Filipino mess boys served breakfast: platters of papayas, bananas, and oranges; biscuits, rolls, and toast; eggs, fried and scrambled; ham, sausage, and bacon; and milk, coffee, and juice. As they ate, the soldiers complained of the poor quality and poor service . . . So it was at lunch and dinner: relative elegance, great abundance, and constant complaints.[13]

The young Rogers suddenly found himself enjoying a standard of living wildly beyond that then possible in the United States. He ordered five new uniforms from Sung Lee, a Chinese tailor in Intramuros, walked down through the Luneta and across Isaac Peral into the Ermita district and the University of the Philippines, founded by the Americans in 1910. Here he enrolled in a Spanish-language course, and spent his spare time in cultural tourism. There was much to interest Rogers in Intramuros, the oldest city he had ever seen. The Spanish had bequeathed scores of churches to Manila but they had also given the city the San Juan de Dios Hospital, originally founded in 1577 by the Franciscans, but taken over in 1656 by the Order of the Hospitallers of St John of God. In 1941 Juan de Dios was still ministering to the sick: it was the city's second largest hospital after the modern Philippine General Hospital. A short distance away through the narrow, cobbled streets overlooking the Pasig was the Church of Santo Domingo, the fourth to be constructed on the site since Dominican friars had consecrated a small wooden chapel in 1588. In the early 17th century a Chinese convert sculpted an image of the Virgin Mary for Santo Domingo. Over the next century this image, in her role as Nuestra Señora del Rosario de la Naval de Manila, became the most popular of all of Manila's Madonnas, and the centre of Marian devotion in the city. Rogers' cultural tourism would also have taken him to Quiapo, along much the same route that Eisenhower had driven. Here in Quiapo Church on the Plaza Miranda was the most famous of Manila's objects of devotion: the Black Nazarene, a statue of a Meso-American Christ falling under his cross which had been carved by a Mexican artist in the 18th century. Every Friday huge crowds jammed the church and the surrounding plaza, while the festival of Nuestro Padre Jesús Nazareno on 9 January each year brought downtown Manila to a standstill. Rogers recalled that he visited such places cautiously, 'as befitted a young Protestant who was uncertain whether they might not house the devil.'[14]

Rogers, a serious-minded young man (by his own admission something of a prig) avoided the more obvious delights of Manila. On November 10 his sergeant took him 'out on the town' to Manila's night spots. The once infamous Gardenia district up in Sampaloc, north of the Pasig, was by now just a shadow of its former self, but new night spots had developed. The most popular were only a short walk south from Intramuros in the university district in Ermita. Here bars and nightclubs had grown up along M.H. del Pilar and W.H. Harrison Streets, developments which had spilled westward toward Dewey Boulevard and the Bay View Hotel. Here was the Silver Slipper and the Santa Ana Cabaret, the largest in the world. Rogers' sergeant set to work on the young man, but without much success. Rogers remembered that he 'turned down liquor, cigarettes, and a woman in that order.' The sergeant promised his buddies 'We'll get some whiskey in that son of a bitch if we have to put it in with a syringe,' but they didn't. In any event, they had a good time making the attempt.[15]

The affection in which most Americans held Manila had deepened into love: this, at least, was the view firmly held by the Field Marshal of the Army of the Philippines (and after July 1941 Commander in Chief of US Army Forces Far East), Douglas MacArthur. Manila was where his father, Arthur MacArthur, had reached the pinnacle of his career as military governor in 1900; it was where he himself, as a second lieutenant, had first come under fire in 1903, and it was where he had developed his friendship with Manuel Quezon when he returned to command the Philippine Department in 1922. Quezon saved his friend MacArthur from an embittered retirement when, in 1935, as President of the new Commonwealth, he asked him to head a Military Mission to the Philippines, the object of which was the creation of the island's armed forces.

So in the late 1930s, instead of retiring to Milwaukee with his aged and doting mother, MacArthur became Field Marshal of the Army of the Philippines, holding court in his penthouse apartment in the Manila Hotel. It was here that he forged links with the business community and made investments which ensured that he would not be poor once he ceased to be head of the Military Mission. These links were strengthened by his growing prominence in the Masonic lodge which met on Taft Avenue. It was in Manila that MacArthur at last achieved a degree of personal happiness with Jean Fairbrother and their newborn son Arthur. Unlike the Sutherlands, the MacArthurs did not socialize a great deal. They attended state functions and the occasional semiofficial dinner at the Manila Polo Club or the Army and Navy Club, but they preferred going together to the cinema in Quiapo, rather like any ordinary couple in the late 1930s. MacArthur would sit through any movie, but he preferred westerns and war movies. It was in Quiapo that they saw John Ford's *Stagecoach*, Cecil B. DeMille's *The Buccaneer*, and Raoul Walsh's *They Died with Their Boots On* – all of which may well have influenced the style of command MacArthur chose to adopt at the end of 1941.[16]

Manila gave MacArthur a power and a status he could not have enjoyed in the United States: for this he was suitably grateful. He believed it to be his mission to create a viable defense for the entire Philippine archipelago. His ideas differed radically from those held by the United States War Department and Navy, who, since the start of the century, had viewed America's possession of the Philippines not as an asset but as a strategic liability: a liability made more onerous by Japan's acquisition in 1919 of German islands in the North Pacific which dominated communications between Hawaii and the Philippines. The series of Orange (Japan) War Plans (WPO) developed by Washington steadily reduced the role of the United States garrison, the 'Philippine Department,' from an active to a defensive one. In the event of war the garrison would merely 'hold' the Bataan Peninsula and the forts dominating the entrance to

Manila Bay while the United States Navy battled across the Pacific to the rescue. MacArthur's plans were far more ambitious. His national Philippine Army – some 200,000 men, annually trained and backed by a small air force and a substantial force of torpedo boats – would be able to defend all the islands of the group. He continued to urge Washington to abandon the WPO concept, but he got nowhere. All updated war plans were based on the assumption that the Philippines neither could nor should be defended.

On July 2, 1941 the situation changed dramatically. Japanese forces landed in southern Indo-China: this was to have far-reaching implications. The Japanese occupation of that region threatened not only the British and Dutch Asian empires but also the United States' supplies of rubber, tin and bauxite. On July 27 President Franklin D. Roosevelt announced a sudden hardening of American policy toward Japan. All Japanese assets in the US were to be frozen – a move which essentially cut off Japan's supplies of oil. On the same day the US Army's chief of staff, General George Marshall, recalled MacArthur to the United States Army and appointed him Lieutenant General commanding a combined Philippine Army-Philippine Department command, the United States Army Forces Far East (USAFFE). On August 1 Marshall told MacArthur of the official change in the United States' Pacific policy – the Philippines were now to be defended – and promised him substantial help. From then on, until well after the Japanese attack on December 8, Marshall continued to reassure MacArthur that help was on the way.

MacArthur went to his grave believing that he had prompted Washington's change of policy – an opinion which, given the debacle which was to overwhelm USAFFE in the early months of 1942, Marshall was quite willing to foster. But the real agent for change was the United States Army Air Force's new Air War Plans Department, whose chief, Colonel Harold L. George, had served as an observer with Britain's Royal Air Force during the Battle of Britain in 1940. George's department produced a blueprint for a defense of the Philippines by aircraft operating without the assistance of land or naval forces. What he called a 'strategical defensive' could be established by the deployment of 340 heavy bombers and 130 fighters to Luzon. The commander of the Air Force, General 'Hap' Arnold, and the Secretary for War, Henry Stimson, took up the plan enthusiastically and on July 25 secured

Roosevelt's approval for the dispatch of large numbers of heavy bombers and fighters to the Philippines.[17]

Between August and early December 1941 an eight-million-dollar airfield improvement and construction program gave the Philippines some 40 completed and semi-completed airfields, and the largest concentration of war planes outside the United States. The first B-17s flew over Manila on their way to Clark Field on August 25 – three tight V formations, each of three aircraft, their enormous silver wings glinting in the sun. The effect of this and subsequent flights on many Manileños was dramatic: 'Keep 'em flying!' became the catchphrase of the teenagers who gathered along Dewey Boulevard in the evenings, a phrase which had much the same meaning as the 'Stay cool, man' of their children's generation. MacArthur was equally delighted when Brigadier General Lewis Brereton, commander of the new Far Eastern Air Force, landed on November 3. MacArthur greeted him warmly with the words: 'Lewis, you are just as welcome as the flowers in May.'[18]

Land reinforcements began arriving too, and MacArthur made the most of them. On October 19 the M-3A1 Stuart tanks of the newly disembarked 194th Tank Battalion paraded through the streets of Manila to reassure the population that American help was on its way. Forming a long column in the port district, the tanks followed Padre Burgos around Intramuros, past the monolithic City Hall, where MacArthur stood on a specially erected podium taking the salute. The column then passed over the Pasig at Jones Bridge and proceeded north up Rosario Street through Binondo until it met Azcarraga Street, the major east-west throughfare in northern Manila. Turning west, the column sighted packed rows of small timber-frame houses not unlike those found in the 'colored' areas of New Orleans or Charleston. These marked the southern outskirts of the Tondo district, the most heavily populated area of the city. The route through the city had been lined with spectators but as the tanks neared Tondo it seemed that the entire population had turned out, forsaking for the moment their cockfights and their bands. Azcarraga was packed 20 deep with people gaping in amazement and cheering; they had never seen anything like it and it was wonderful free entertainment. Then the tanks neared their final destination, the Tondo classification yard and the flat railroad cars which would carry them north, initially to Fort Stotsenburg.[19]

By this time the citizens of Manila were becoming quite used to seeing soldiers in the streets. MacArthur had ordered the initial mobilization of one regiment from each of the Philippine Reserve Divisions on September 1, with additional regiments being mobilized in early November. At the same time the Reserve Officer Training Corps (ROTC) at the universities was called out. Visitors remember watching the young men in ill-fitting uniforms and papier-mâché helmets drilling with ancient rifles on the grass verges at the foot of the walls of Intramuros.[20] It was clear that they still had a long way to go, but MacArthur did not believe that a Japanese attack was imminent. At a Thanksgiving dinner at the Manila Polo Club on November 20 MacArthur assured guests that although the conflict was inevitable, 'the time and place will be our choosing.'[21] Intelligence in both Washington and Manila indicated that April 1, 1942 would be the earliest date possible for a Japanese attack. This should allow enough time for the vast amounts of equipment MacArthur had ordered – 125,000 steel helmets, 84,000 Garand M-1 rifles and several thousand machine-guns – to arrive from the United States so that the training of the Philippine Army could be completed.[22] Even if the Japanese did attack before April 1, MacArthur thought that his Philippine Divisions, albeit ill-equipped and under-trained, would acquit themselves well against the Japanese. All that he had heard about Japanese soldiers pointed to their weakness and inefficiency: they had been unable to defeat the peasant militias of China after more than three years of war, and had been humiliated by the Soviet Army in the border clashes of 1938 and 1939, the same Soviet Army which had in turn been humiliated by the militia of Finland in November 1939. In November 1941 the odds facing the Filipinos seemed far more even than they did later.[23]

Manileños and their American allies spent the night of Sunday, December 7, 1941 in an unusually festive mood: the feast of the Immaculate Conception, due to take place the next day, was one of the most important holy days in the Philippine calendar. Some inhabited the 'groovy world of the boogie and the conga,' in the words of Nick Joaquín, who wrote a graphic account of middle-class youth enjoying the last hours. 'From the Luneta to Casa Mañana on the Vito Cruz corner [the boulevard then ended on Vito Cruz, at the corner where stood Casa Mañana, a nightclub where the sounds were mostly Latin] Dewey Boulevard nightly offered a vast jam session of youngsters stomping in frenzy right on the sea wall to the music of portable phonographs.'[24] Another Manila journalist,

Carmen Guerrero Nakpil, remembered that she had been at the big dance at the University of the Philippines. The rest of Manila was doing the same – cocktail parties in Malate and backyard dances accompanied by guitars and bongos up in Tondo.[25]

The Americans, too, (with the exception of Private Rogers, who had gone to bed early with an improving book) were having a ball. The biggest party of all – perhaps the biggest in the history of Manila – was being held in the Manila Hotel by 1200 men of the 27th Bombardment Group to celebrate the birthday of Brigadier General Brereton. Because it was such an important occasion, the airmen had delayed implementing an order from MacArthur to fly B-17s stationed at Clark Field down to Mindanao, where they would be out of range of Formosa-based Japanese bombers. The party began to break up at about 3 a.m., with many of the Americans, including the hard-drinking Brereton, a little the worse for wear. Sutherland had been at the party but had left about an hour earlier.[26] The phone rang shortly after 3 a.m. with the news of Pearl Harbor. By 5 a.m. the USAFFE were swinging into action; aircrew were racing back to Clark and their B-17s, while other airmen were manning their P-40s at Nichols Field, to the southwest of Manila. In the city the Philippine Constabulary were coming into barracks, receiving briefings on rounding up enemy aliens – for the moment Japanese, but the list would soon be extended to include Germans and Italians – and discussing preliminary plans for the commandeering of trucks and buses for military purposes.[27] Everything was moving with surprising efficiency.

Sunrise came shortly before 7 a.m. and the morning was a cool 70°F; it would soon become hot and then unseasonably oppressive. Cooler weather was due in the next few weeks. Most people heard the news of Pearl Harbor while listening to Manila's commercial radio station, KZRH. Down in Ermita and Malate many of Manila's Spanish elite, both Peninsulares and Insulares, were getting ready to go to what promised to be the biggest society wedding of 1941 at the exclusive Nunciatora Apostolia chapel on Dewey Boulevard. One of the guests, José Olbes, a 27-year-old Insulare insurance broker regarded by many of the society girls as a major catch, heard the news while shaving. If his razor did not slip, it was only because the Japanese attack was not entirely unexpected – only the time and place were unknown. The wedding was one of the casualties of Pearl Harbor. Although it still went ahead, only a handful of guests, mainly those living within walking distance along Dewey Boulevard, managed to attend the ceremony. Still fewer attended the subsequent reception at the Manila Polo Club. There was simply too much to do.[28]

At their rambling mansion on the southern outskirts of Manila, Constance Prising, wife of the American tobacco millionaire Frederick Prising, had not heard the news. She set off with her adopted eight-year-old son Robin in her chauffeur-driven car to attend mass at Our Lady of Lourdes in Intramuros. The drive up Dewey Boulevard became etched on young Robin's memory: the street was strangely deserted. When the Prisings reached the church mass was already underway and it was not until the congregation began to disperse that young Robin picked up snatches of conversation – 'hit . . . Roosevelt . . . this morning . . . battleships . . . two waves . . . radio.' Running over to a group of Filipino boys, Robin was told 'Los Japanese – they bomb – make bombs at Pearl Harbor. All ship – American ship – burn, burn, burn – no more ship.'[29]

Although there was an almost universal confidence that despite Pearl Harbor the United States would quickly defeat Japan, Manileños had seen newsreels of Warsaw, Rotterdam, London and Coventry and fully expected their city to be bombed. Precautions had to be taken. Robin Prising remembers a British Embassy attaché outside Our Lady of Lourdes advising a Filipino friend: 'Stock up with tins, old boy, before the blitz.'[30] Alaistair Hall's 9-year-old son Roderick had gone as usual that morning to Pasay's American School. He was surprised to see the family chauffeur ariving at the school to pick him up, his father's seven-seater Chrysler filled to window level with canned goods.[31]

Such precautions were prudent. The other precaution, enjoined by the example of many Chinese and European cities, was the evacuation of as many of the non-essential civilian population as possible. A Civilian Emergency Administration had been set up at the beginning of the year and had attempted trial evacuations but had received little cooperation.[32] Consequently the evacuation of Manila which now got under way was partial and chaotic. Expensive private cars loaded with personal belongings drove down Dewey Boulevard and Taft Avenue, heading for the relative security of hotels in the area of Tagaytay. These were the fortunate few. In the Manila that few Americans ever visited – the predominantly blue-collar and lower-middle-class suburbs south of the Pasig and east of Ermita and Malate, districts like Pandacan, Paco and Singalong – the railroad stations were crowded with women and children cramming themselves onto trains to Lipa, Batangas and points south. By the middle of December an estimated 200,000 people had left Manila.

The activities of one small group of Manila's citizens were being closely monitored. On the morning of December 8 the Philippine Constabulary rounded up 300 of the city's Japanese community – gardeners, storekeepers and businessmen, many of whom later proved to be Japanese intelligence agents – and incarcerated them in Bilibid prison on Azcarraga Street. Four days later they were joined by members of Manila's German and Italian communities. The Germans found they had little in common with their new allies. Having arrived first, the Japanese had set up a kitchen and invited the Germans to share their meals. One German inmate described Japanese fare as 'just plain lousy – half-cooked rice, some vegetables and water to drink.' The Germans complained to American and Filipino guards, who took pity on them and allowed some of them to work in the kitchens. Things soon got better. A German internee recalled: 'In the morning we had ham and eggs, like the American guards. For lunch and dinner we had canned potatoes, canned meat, and canned vegetables.' The stay of the Axis internees in Bilibid was going to be short but already an obvious moral had emerged: it was better to be fed by the Americans than by the Japanese.[33]

The first Japanese bombing raids were directed not at Manila, but at Clark and Iba airfields. Japanese air strikes hit both bases just before midday on December 8, destroying much of USAFFE airpower. Rumors of the disaster were soon circulating around Manila.[34] The blackout came into force on the night of December 8, but it did not deter the Japanese. The shoreline of Manila Bay and the Pasig served as navigational beacons. Bombers hit Nichols Field to the southeast of Manila in the early hours of December 9, some bombs landing in Pasay and Malate. The following day Japanese bombers devastated Cavite naval base and Cavite township on the southern shore of Manila Bay. Cavite burned for days, the fires clearly visible from Dewey Boulevard. More than 1500 were killed and many hundreds more were injured. The wounded were evacuated in boats across the bay and disembarked near the yacht harbor on Dewey Boulevard, where they were placed in rows amid the coconut palms along the sea wall while awaiting transport to the Philippine General Hospital. The bombers returned on December 13, their target this time Manila's port districts. These areas were raided again on December 15, 20, 21 and 24, and badly damaged.[35]

Despite the damage and the evacuation, morale generally remained high during the middle two weeks of December. Since the 8th, Manileños had watched thousands of troops moving north. Fourteen-year-old Enrique Zobel, grandson of the senior partner of Manila's Ayala y Cia, remembered standing outside the family home on Dewey Boulevard and watching the long columns of the 26th Cavalry, the last horse unit in the American army, ride north along the boulevard from Fort McKinley. More than 50 years later he still thought it one of the most moving sights he had ever beheld. Robert Allen, an American engineer, witnessed the same sight, and was moved almost to tears. For a generation brought up on Hollywood movies, this was the way to go to war.[36]

Most of the newly mobilized reserve divisions made the journey north in far less romantic style. In the three days after Pearl Harbor the Philippine Constabulary, assisted by American and Filipino military police, commandered virtually all the trucks and buses in the city, and drove north via the Quezon Bridge and Quezon Avenue through the district of Sampaloc to España Street and the University of Santo Tomás. This was the most famous educational institution in the islands, the alma mater of the Philippine leadership from Rizal to Quezon. Though the present campus dated from only the 1920s, Santo Tomás had been founded in 1611, making it the second oldest university outside Europe. The grounds now became an enormous motor pool where vehicles were repaired, serviced, and then fueled before taking the young troops north. Seemingly endless columns of buses and trucks moved up Calle Andalucía and Rizal Avenue, their ultimate destination the shores of Lingayen Gulf.[37]

In the two weeks after December 8 stations like KZRH and papers like Carlos P. Romulo's violently anti-Japanese *Manila Herald* poured forth optimistic predictions and supplied accounts of great (and imaginary) victories. The Philippine divisions deployed around the head of Lingayen Gulf – the only possible landing point on the Luzon coast with the exception of heavily defended Manila Bay – and waited. None of the Filipino soldiers had had more than four months' training, some as little as ten days'. They were to fight well in the favorable terrain of Bataan and later still many would make fine guerrillas, but in the flat, relatively open land at the head of Lingayen their inexperience placed them at a considerable disadvantage.

The convoy carrying Lieutenant General Masaharu Homma's 43,000 veterans entered Lingayen Gulf on the night of December 22, opposed only by sporadic and ineffectual American submarine attacks. The Japanese started landing before first light. The high winds and pounding surf capsized a large number of craft, and many of the invaders were forced to swim ashore without arms or equipment. The initial advantage was with the defenders: had they been given a few more weeks' training and a few thousand of the rifles and machine-guns still on their way from the United States, the landing at Lingayen Gulf would have been a great Filipino victory. As it was, the Japanese soon gained the upper hand. By dawn Filipinos were streaming southeast around the head of the Gulf. MacArthur's commander at Lingayen, Lieutenant General Jonathan Wainwright, attempted a counterattack, throwing the 26th Cavalry, elements of a provisional tank battalion, and Brigadier General Clyde Selleck's 71st Division of the Philippine Army, against the Japanese. Never having trained together, the tanks and cavalry were unable to coordinate their activities. The Japanese drove the units back and by early afternoon of December 23 their patrol probes had produced widespread panic and chaos in Selleck's division.[38]

In his *Reminiscences* MacArthur claimed that his decision to reactivate WPO 3, the withdrawal to Bataan, was made when he received news of a second Japanese landing at Lamon Bay on the east coast of Luzon, only 40 miles southeast of Manila. He apparently suddenly realized that Homma intended 'to swing shut the jaws of a great military pincer, one prong being the main force that had landed at Lingayen, the other the units that had landed at Antimonan.'[39] In fact the country between Lamon Bay and Manila was so rugged that it took the Japanese advancing from this direction more than ten days to reach the city, even though only lightly opposed. The southeastern jaw of the 'great military pincer' swung shut so slowly that it did not present a significant military threat.

MacArthur was familiar with the Philippine terrain, and certainly no fool. This rather disingenuous account in his *Reminiscences* suggests that even 23 years later he still found it hard to face the collapse of his Philippine Divisions at Lingayen and the consequent decision to abandon Manila. It was an admission that his Military Mission had failed in its primary task. He was deserting the city he loved and the home in which he had found happiness in accordance with the demands of a policy against which he had protested since 1935.

On December 24 radio and newspapers declared Manila an 'open city.' Manileños remember the sense of profound shock they felt at the sudden realization that the Americans had abandoned the city to the Japanese. Placards appeared in the streets proclaiming the city's new status, streets which were soon crammed with USAFFE forces retreating from southern Luzon towards Bataan. There were touching parting scenes. Carmen Guerrero Nakpil had many friends in the USAFFE, the boys she had grown up with, cousins, beaux, friends of her brothers. As they retreated towards Bataan, 'the boys telephoned from every stop, from McKinley and from Caloocan. From San Miguel de Mayumo, they said, "We're blowing up the bridge and going in. You won't hear from us for some time."'[40] On Dewey Boulevard Enrique Zobel was sitting down to a Christmas Eve lunch with his mother when a staff car drove up. It was his father, Colonel Jacobo Zobel, whose division had been stationed in the south. There was time for a few hurried farewells and then Colonel Zobel sped off up Dewey, to join the columns withdrawing towards Bataan.[41] It was about this time that Captain Joe McMicking also said goodbye to his family. He had been mobilized during the summer, flown some daring reconnaissance missions in an increasingly hostile air environment, and been seconded to MacArthur's headquarters staff as an assistant to Colonel Charles A. Willoughby, MacArthur's intelligence chief. He was now on his way to Corregidor.[42]

Manila may have been declared an open city, but this did not stop the Japanese bombing it. The editor of the *Manila Herald*, Carlos P. Romulo, now a colonel on MacArthur's staff, had been detailed to remain with the rear-echelon headquarters in Manila, after the bulk of the HQ withdrew to Corregidor. On December 27 Japanese bombers devastated Intramuros. Romulo, watching from a window in Fort Santiago, described the scene: 'They were streaming over the city from every direction. The thudding jar of explosions came in from the riverfront district. Great billows of smoke began rising up from the old Walled City.' After the raid Romulo went to inspect the damage. The Church of Santo Domingo, the adjoining convent, Santa Rosa College, and Santa Catalina College, all of which formed the spiritual heart of Manila, were burning furiously. Romulo walked into the shopping area along the Escolta, which had also been hit. Here some of the stores were festooned with Christmas decorations, their front windows piled high with gifts. There were also two Santa Clauses standing on the Escolta, 'complete with long white whiskers and red cotton-trimmed suits. One was walking up and down in front of a toy store, as though dazed. The other was more practical. He was helping pile sandbags in front of the entrance of his shop.'[43]

The following day, December 28, American engineers began blowing up the oil-storage depots in the Pandacan district to the east of the city. Columns of black, oily smoke rose thousands of feet into the sky, blocking out the morning sun, and creating an apocalyptic backdrop for the last hours of American Manila. On the same day the American administration threw open the food stores in the warehouses in the South Port district to all comers.[44] They did not want to see these vast stocks fall into the hands of the Japanese, and envisaged a relatively orderly removal of food in Filipino hands. But law and order soon broke down after the withdrawal of the troops. The Philippine Constabulary, armed only with bamboo staves, proved no match for looters, whose activities soon spread to areas well away from the Port district. They ransacked the cold-storage depot at the foot of Quiapo Bridge, a mile to the east of the Port district. For a short time Paco market overflowed with commodities being sold very cheaply. Enrique Zobel recalled that his mother 'stocked up with toilet paper, Lucky Strikes in tins for father, and a sack of cracked wheat from which we later had to pick out the bugs.'[45] José Olbes heard of one group delighted with their 'liberation' from the cold-storage depot of what looked like a containerful of something valuable – a large, heavy crate bound with steel straps. They dragged it two miles northwest to Tondo, managed to break it open, and discovered – a coffin. It contained the body of an elderly American being shipped back to the United States for burial.[46] By New Year's Eve gangs were marauding Manila's wealthier suburbs. Alaistair Hall wrote in his diary for Thursday, January 1: 'Looting spread from Piers to Grocery Stores and Sari Sari (corner shop). One near [by] House forcibly broken into and everything taken including Frigidaire.'[47]

The work of the rear-echelon headquarters was almost done. On New Year's Eve Carlos P. Romulo drove along Dewey Boulevard to his home on Vermont Street in Malate to say goodbye to his wife Virginia. The boulevard was deserted: 'the Yacht Club, the night clubs, and hotels . . . all looked like funeral parlors. Their windows were blanketed in blackout curtains.' To the right curved the sweep of Manila Bay, from which 'the funnels of sunken ships stood up like tombstones.' In the early hours of January 1 Romulo drove back up Dewey toward the landing stage on the Pasig near Fort Santiago, the embarkation point for Corregidor.

Mobs of looters were roaming the streets, the ill-armed constabulary having abandoned the attempt to maintain order. To the northeast the oil depots of Pandacan continued to spew spectacular fireballs into the night sky, while directly north the port area was in flames. The Manila Hotel lay on Romulo's route and he stopped off in the hope that he would be able to pick up some extra supplies from the hotel's kitchens. The surreal scene described by Romulo might have come straight out of a Buñuel movie. In the lobby a band was playing while elegantly dressed couples, largely Americans and British, clung to each other in a last slow dance. It was the final night of American Manila.[48]

# NOTES

1 Eighteen years after the battle, the US Army Center of Military History produced the history of the Philippines Campaign, January-August 1945: Robert Ross Smith, *United States Army in World War II. The War in the Pacific: Triumph in the Philippines* (Washington DC, 1963). This is an excellent campaign history, but the destruction of Manila is treated as an almost incidental by-product of other operations. In biographies of MacArthur, Manila is treated as a tragic incident for which MacArthur was in no way culpable: William Manchester, *American Caesar* (New York, 1978), pp. 413–420; D. Clayton James, *The Years of MacArthur, 1941–1945*, Vol. II (Boston, Mass., 1975), pp. 631–648. In more recent histories, the destruction of Manila receives less than a page: Ronald H. Spector, *Eagle Against the Sun. The American War with Japan* (New York, 1985), p. 524; Lieutenant-General E. M. Flanagan, *Corregidor* (Novato, CA, 1988), pp. 101–102. The Philippines have now produced a detailed account of the destruction of Manila, written from the victims' perspective: Alfonso J. Aluit, *By Sword and Fire. The Destruction of Manila in World War II, 3 February-3 March 1945* (Manila, 1994). Aluit's compilation, published by the Philippines Commission for Culture and the Arts, provides invaluable source material for a new generation of historians hitherto confined to American sources.
2 D. Clayton James, *The Years of MacArthur, 1941–1945*, Vol. I (Boston, Mass., 1970), p. 362ff.
3 Robert Ferrell (ed.), *The Eisenhower Papers* (New York, 1981), pp. 19–20; Stephen E. Ambrose, *Eisenhower The Soldier* (New York, 1983), p. 105.
4 Ibid., pp. 106–107.
5 Aluit, *By Sword and Fire*, p. 85.
6 Nick Joaquín, *Manila my Manila* (Manila, 1990), p. 173.

7   Ibid.
8   Ambrose, *Eisenhower The Soldier*, p. 107.
9   Ibid., p. 108.
10  Paul P. Rogers, *The Good Years: MacArthur and Sutherland* (New York, 1990), pp. 52–55; author's interview with Roderick Hall, London, June 28, 1994.
11  Author's interview with Sr. Enrique Zobel, Sotogrande, Spain, June 21, 1994; author's interview with Sr. J. Olbes, Sotogrande, June 22, 1994.
12  Aluit, *By Sword and Fire*, p. 123.
13  Rogers, *The Good Years*, p. 9.
14  Ibid., p. 12.
15  Ibid., p. 13.
16  James, *The Years of MacArthur*, Vol. I, p. 559.
17  General H. H. Arnold, *Global Mission* (London, 1951), p. 159; W. F. *Craven and J. L. Cate, The Army Air Forces in World War II*, Vol. I (Chicago, 1948), pp. 139–145; Mark S. Watson, *Chief of Staff: Pre-War Plans and Preparations* (Washington DC, 1950), pp. 438–440.
18  Eric Morris, *Corregidor. The Nightmare in the Philippines* (London, 1982), p. 29; Joaquín, *Manila my Manila*, p. 174; Lewis Moreton, *The Fall of the Philippines* (Washington DC, 1952), p. 67.
19  Morris, *Corregidor*, p. 35.
20  James, *The Years of MacArthur*, Vol. I, p. 616.
21  Morris, *Corregidor*, p. 43.
22  James, *The Years of MacArthur*, Vol. I, p. 613.
23  Duncan Anderson, 'Douglas MacArthur and the Philippines,' in Brian Bond (ed.), *Fallen Stars* (London, 1991), p. 174.
24  Joaquín, *Manila my Manila*, p. 176.
25  Carmen Guerrero Nakpil, *A Question of Identity. Selected Essays* (Manila, 1973), p. 197.
26  Morris, *Corregidor*, p. 70; Rogers, *The Good Years*, p. 93.
27  Edgar Krohn and Walter Kühne, *The German Club 1906–1986. A History of the German Community in the Philippines* (Manila, 1986), p. 51.
28  Olbes interview, June 22, 1994; Zobel interview, June 21, 1994; Renato Constantino, *Under Japanese Rule* (Manila, 1993), p. 69.
29  Robin Prising, *Manila, Goodbye* (Boston, Mass., 1975), p. 50.
30  Ibid., p. 51.
31  Hall interview, June 28, 1994.
32  James, *The Years of MacArthur*, Vol. I, p. 617.
33  Krohn and Kühne, *The German Club*, p. 53.
34  Lewis H. Brereton, *The Brereton Diaries: The War in the Air in the Pacific, Middle East and Europe, 3 October 1941–8 May 1945* (New York, 1946), pp. 34–44.

35  James, *The Years of MacArthur*, Vol. I, pp. 16–20.
36  Zobel interview, June 21, 1994; Robert Coleman Allen, *Philippine War Diary. A Prison Camp Saga* (Washington DC, 1991), p. 4.
37  Constantino, *Under Japanese Rule*, p. 135.
38  Anderson, 'MacArthur and the Philippines,' p. 175.
39  General Douglas MacArthur, *Reminiscences* (New York, 1964), p. 124.
40  Guerrero Nakpil, *A Question of Identity*, p. 197.
41  Zobel interview, June 21, 1994.
42  Hall interview, June 28, 1994.
43  Carlos P. Romulo, *I Saw the Fall of the Philippines* (London, 1943), p. 77.
44  Victor Buencamino, *Memoirs of Victor Buencamino* (Manila, 1977), pp. 264–265.
45  Constantino, *Under Japanese Rule*, p. 75.
46  Olbes interview, June 22, 1994.
47  Unpublished diary of Alaistair 'Shorty' Hall, entry for January 1, 1942.
48  Romulo, *I Saw the Fall of the Philippines*, p. 88.

# 2

# THE JAPANESE IN MANILA: JANUARY 1942-JANUARY 1945

The first Japanese entered the southern outskirts of Manila on the evening of January 2, 1942. Manileños awaited their arrival with mixed feelings. Victor Buencamino, head of the National Rice and Corn Corporation (NARIC), went to bed that night after a day spent trying to defend his warehouses from looters. Exhausted but unable to sleep, he scribbled in his diary: 'I can hear the trample of marching feet with heavy shoes. It must be a battalion. The Japs prefer to move at night. What is it that they are singing? It is a strange, weird hymn. Only last night I could still hear the boogie-woogie music from the San Juan cabaret at a distance.'[1] Robin Prising later remembered his parents talking in hushed voices about the Rape of Nanking, though, aged only eight, he had no idea at all of what that might be. As a precaution Frederick Prising drove his wife and son to the Assumption Convent, where, along with other women and children, they had been offered sanctuary.[2] The Halls were equally worried. Alaistair Hall's wife, Consuelo, dressed the family's Chinese amah in Western clothes, hoping she would pass for a Filipino.[3]

Hall's first encounter with the Japanese came after 10.00 p.m. His father-in-law, José McMicking, had suddenly suffered a massive hemorrhage. Hall immediately packed himself and his mother-in-law into their car and set off for Pasay to get the family doctor. They ran straight into the advancing Japanese Army. Hall had almost certainly heard rumors about the appalling Japanese massacres in Hong Kong only the previous week, so his drive was as brave as it was foolhardy.

At first he was stopped and frisked at bayonet point by Japanese on Vito Cruz Street. Turning right on Taft, he was stopped again. The Japanese wanted to commandeer the car but Hall managed to talk them out of it, even securing a military escort by inviting the Japanese to drive with him. At last he managed to summon the doctor: but sadly his father-in-law died the next morning. It had been an extraordinary night.[4]

By January 3 Manila was under new management. The city's American and British population were the very first to feel the effects of occupation. The Japanese kept in their posts those employed to maintain essential services – the telephone system, electricity and water – until Japanese or Filipino replacements could be found. Some were still at work in the summer of 1942. One of them, Miss Edna Brown, chief operator for the Manila Telephone Company, spent a very short time in internment: she was released as soon as the Japanese realized that without her the city's phone system would cease to function.[5] But the Edna Browns of Manila were the exception. The Japanese had on their hands some five thousand American and British civilians, far more than they had taken on Christmas Day in Hong Kong, or, indeed, were to take six weeks later in Singapore. They also had to handle the growing number of American and Filipino military prisoners. The national penitentiary at Bilibid was an obvious solution. The Axis civilian prisoners – Germans, Japanese and Italian – had already been released. The Japanese began trucking in American civilian and military prisoners. Bilibid, a typical example of forbidding American prison architecture, consisted of a central hub from which wings extended like the spokes of a wheel. The Japanese divided the jail into separate military and civilian sections, holding 800 and 700 prisoners respectively.

Bilibid was soon filled to overflowing. There were still nearly four thousand Allied civilians left to intern, and the number of suitable establishments was limited. The Japanese chose the campus of Santo Tomás University, which until recently had functioned as the motor pool for the Philippine Army. The high walls encircling its grounds could keep people in as well as out, and the elaborate wrought-iron railings topped by spearheads proved functional as well as decorative. The new inhabitants were less likely than former generations of students to appreciate the aesthetic niceties of their new campus surroundings. From January 5 trucks began arriving at Santo Tomás, disgorging Manila's American and British expatriates. Many of them had married into Filipino families, had half-Filipino children, and could not envisage a separate existence of the kind now forced on them. Terrible scenes of separation followed: fathers taken from wives, wives taken from husbands, parents taken from children. José Olbes' American brother-in-law was imprisoned: his sister was inconsolable.[6] On January 5, only the day after the sad occasion of his father-in-law's funeral, Alaistair Hall was made to report to the Rizal Stadium in Malate, on the corner of Dakota Avenue and Vito Cruz Street. Alaistair Hall had been born in Scotland, while his wife and children had been born in the Philippines. The Rizal Stadium, which had been specially erected for the Asian Games of 1934, now witnessed very different scenes. Hundreds of Manila's expatriate elite milled round the stadium as the Japanese soldiers attempted to impose order on chaos by drawing up lists. It took five hours for the transport to Santo Tomás to arrive.[7] Robin Prising and his mother were among those taken there, and their different nationalities almost led to tragedy. Constance Prising's passport was American but her son's was British. When the Japanese tried to carry off eight-year-old Robin to a different section his mother protested violently. A Japanese officer, unused to arguing with women, hit her in the face and kicked her to the ground. Thirty years later Robin could remember every detail of the scene: the way the officer's face had twisted into a convulsion of hate, the way his lips went shooting out when he spat on her.[8]

After much initial confusion the inmates subdivided the lecture halls and dining rooms inside the Santo Tomás complex into separate annexes and dormitories. The gymnasium, for example, functioned as the dormitory for 300 of the 3700 internees, many of whom were elderly. The younger internees looked after the old, but the severity of a prison's regime depended in large measure on the goodwill of its commandant: thus conditions in the different prisons varied widely. The commandant of Santo Tomás, Lieutenant Colonel Toshio Hayashi, was not an ogre: he was capable of showing both compassion and – most unusual in a Japanese officer – a sense of humor. Even though one sadistic warder, Lieutenant Abiko, proved a persistent threat, most prisoners could learn to tolerate, if not to respect, their Japanese mentors. They soon learned to conceal, at least publicly, the opinion of the Japanese later voiced by one former internee: 'They were generally regarded as an army of coolies, slit-eyed, bandy legged, misbegotten little monsters of an inferior race – we had been captured by a tribe of monkeys that had just leapt out of the trees.'[9]

For their part the Japanese regarded the American and Allied internees as a third-class, defeated people, from whom they demanded a bow from the waist as a mark of respect and subservience. If prisoners obeyed the rules their lives were tolerable. If not, they were punished. Americans and Britains took a secret pride in finding ways to avoid the hated bow of servility: Robin Prising got caught out on one occasion and earned a severe beating from Lieutenant Abiko.[10]

Attempts to escape resulted in execution. A few weeks after internment, two Britons and an Australian scaled the wall but were quickly recaptured. The Japanese used them to teach the rest of the camp a lesson. The guards dragged them back into Santo Tomás, kicking them and beating them with their rifle butts. They then took them off to be tortured, choosing a room just off the main hall in the central building. From here their screams of pain reverberated round the entire prison. The internees must have winced at each cry, but managed to distance themselves through an ethic of self-preservation. The escapees, they said, had been insane to make the attempt, and had jeopardized every prisoner's welfare. The punishment was grave, but they should have thought of it beforehand. Then the unspeakable occurred. The three men were sentenced to death, shoved onto trucks and taken to the Chinese cemetery, where they were forced to dig their own graves as other prisoners stood witness. On February 15, 1942 their sentence was carried out: they were killed by multiple pistol shots.[11] These were the first of several executions. As the guerrilla movement in the Philippines gained sway in the months after summer 1942, some internees inevitably fell under suspicion. On one occasion the camp tannoy summoned by name three men to report at the front of the main building. They were then taken to Fort Abad and executed. One of the murdered men had a namesake, a newspaperman imprisoned in Santo Tomás. Not for the first time, the Japanese had executed the wrong man.[12]

In the early days of internment the regime in Santo Tomás was notably relaxed. The young, old and infirm were allowed out on parole as long as they wore red armbands to denote that they were Japan's enemies. Their daily life was closely monitored by the Kempeitai, the Japanese equivalent of the Gestapo, who frequently interrogated the trustees to discover how they were funding themselves and who was helping them. Inside the camp, authority to maintain discipline had been delegated to the internees, a function they exercised diligently through an Executive Committee and subcommittees such as the Parents' Committee. The hierarchy was very like that found in British boarding schools: headmaster, housemasters and masters. They had their own camp police force and a jail for those who broke the law. The internees were not entirely comfortable with this system: but at least it meant that by disciplining themselves, they could avoid the Japanese imposing discipline on them. One of the most distinctive (and to later eyes faintly absurd) bodies was the 'Moral Patrol.' The patrol checked that no girls older than ten wore shorts – all women were to wear proper skirts and dresses. This was more to do with the internees's desire to protect their womenfolk from the hot eyes of the Japanese guards than it was with Japanese moral standards. Standing orders also prohibited bodily contact between the different sexes and forbade couples to wrap themselves in blankets. 'Demonstrating affection,' read the orders, 'should be prohibited and the internees' attention should be called to the fact that such displays are frowned upon by the Japanese authorities.' It is not impossible that the moral standards of the American Bible Belt found a useful formal endorsement in the Japanese camp authorities. The internees also ran a Day and Night Patrol, for which there were orders and guidelines. Crowded conditions could make noise a serious problem at night; especially noise from the ablution blocks. The patrol was instructed to 'please enter men's toilet when necessary and ask people to be quiet. Where ladies are concerned, rap on the door and ask for less noise.' A loudspeaker controlled daily routine, giving and repeating orders to guards and internees alike. It also supplied the morning reveille – the incongruously breezy tones of the Andrews Sisters' song 'Good Morning, Good Morning' played on a worn-out record.[13]

Out in the grounds the flag of the Rising Sun flew from the flagpole in front of the building. A belt of acacia trees ran down from here to the gate, presided over by a bamboo watch-tower designed to spot any would-be escapees. A shantytown of lean-to huts of planks and bamboo with nipa thatching had grown up among the acacias, providing a home of sorts (at least during the daylight hours) for the fortunate few. Yet privacy was still limited: the Japanese guards and the Moral Patrol made regular checks to ensure that three sides out of four remained open to view. Primitive as they were, the huts provided some relief from the oppressive sense of crowding enforced by a prison regime. Internees grew vegetables in small gardens between the lean-tos. Soon these provided welcome supplements to increasingly meager diets.[14]

Manila's American and British citizens endured 37 months in the internment camps. They may not have appreciated it at the time, but the tragic course that events were to take made them the lucky ones. Some Manileños felt no more enthusiastic about the Japanese than did the captives inside Santo Tomás. Carmen Guerrero Nakpil remembered being distinctly underwhelmed by her first sight of the Japanese on January 3, 1942. 'The morning light revealed a whole detachment of soldiers, squat, unkempt and ragged, camped along the sidewalks of Mabini. Their stench rose to the shuttered windows behind which we watched. They washed at the fire hydrants, sprawled on the pavement in their loin-cloths and shouted gibberish to each other.'[15] Pedro Picornell, a Malate teenager who went on to do much distinguished work in the Remedios Hospital, had a similar memory. The Japanese came up Taft Avenue, at the corner of Herran, riding bicycles. They were generally well behaved 'except for running around in G-strings and bathing naked in fire hydrants.'[16] During this period, the customary street wear in Manila was still collar and tie, though some young men had begun to wear loose-fitting Hawaiian shirts. But naked buttocks would never be acceptable to the largely Catholic population of Manila: it was hard to adjust to the sudden invasion of young men from a society where mixed nude bathing was perfectly natural and the Christian concept of sin unknown.

The Japanese who cycled up Taft Avenue in early January 1942 were filled with a sense of mission: they were liberating Asia from the physical, intellectual and spiritual domination of the West. Some Manileños did indeed see the Japanese as liberators, but the greeting they received in Manila was far cooler than that given them in cities like Batavia and Rangoon a little over two months later. There was much to be done – an Asian people corrupted by a total of 370 years of Spanish and American colonial rule had to be redeemed. Allied propaganda derided this sense of mission as a crude cover for exploitation, but in early 1942 it was very real. Certainly a majority of officers understood what they had to do, and probably a majority of the other ranks believed they were on a crusade, not just for the aggrandizement of the emperor of Japan, but for the redemption of Asiatic peoples.

The Japanese quickly established control in the city. General Masaharu Homma still had a battle to fight (it would not be over until May and would destroy his career). For the time being, real authority devolved to Colonel Seichi Ohta, the commander of Kempeitai forces allocated to the Philippines. Ohta set up his headquarters in Fort Santiago; it had been the focal point for MacArthur's authority. The dungeons and torture chambers were not a consideration at this point. Japan was winning everywhere, and had little need to intimidate. On April 8 eight leading Manila businessmen and officials, including Victor Buencamino, the head of NARIC, were ordered to report to Fort Santiago at 11.30 the following morning. Buencamino endured a terrible, sleepless night. The next morning he said what he was convinced would be his final farewell to his wife and children, and reported to Ohta. It turned out to be a Kempeitai public relations exercise. Buencamino recorded in his diary that Ohta had greeted them with the words 'We want to show you that Fort Santiago is not a place of torture.' There then followed a guided tour. 'We were taken around and shown the cell of Dr. Rizal. Games and exhibitions were performed before us. One Japanese officer, a Lieut. Koeki, took a bale of hay and hacked it in two parts with one swift stroke of his samurai sword. We had quite a luncheon, too.'[17]

Ohta liked Manila; he could speak English and within weeks of his arrival was trying to learn Spanish. Thanks to the internment of Manila's American and British expatriates there were desirable residences lying empty in the better areas of the city. Ohta led the rush. He toured the city and commandeered the Marsman mansion in Pasay, a few blocks from where the Prisings had lived.[18]

Had General Homma, his commanding officer, been given the same opportunity, he would also have enjoyed Manila. Homma's own English was perfect: he had served with the British Army in 1918 in France, where he earned a British decoration for bravery. But the campaign had not gone as planned. Homma's inability to take Bataan and Corregidor while other commanders conquered Malaya, the Dutch East Indies and Burma, led to his removal from the Philippines and his relegation to the retired list. His successor as commander of Japanese forces in the Philippines was General Shijuichi Tanaka, who arrived in the summer of 1942. Tanaka had a terrifying reputation, having carved out a very successful career as a military policeman in civil affairs in Manchuria and China. In September 1940 he had been appointed to command Japan's military police forces, in effect becoming the Kempeitai's top man. But Tanaka was no Heinrich Himmler. Compared with the head of the Gestapo, and indeed, compared with most Japanese officers, Tanaka was a man of some cultural breadth. He was certainly well travelled: as a young officer he had spent three years in London, followed by two years as military attaché in Mexico City and two years in Washington DC. Tanaka could speak both English and Spanish and, like Colonel Ohta, he enjoyed Manila. He moved into the American High Commission at the north end of Dewey Boulevard, only a short walk across the Luneta to Fort Santiago.[19]

Tanaka's stay in Manila was cut short in May 1943 when he was promoted to the Army General Staff in Tokyo. His replacement was General Shigenari Kuroda, a 56-year-old military bureaucrat who had managed to avoid active service throughout his career. Kuroda could speak perfect English. He had served as resident officer in Britain between 1922 and 1925 (where he developed his passion for golf) and as military attaché in New Delhi between 1935 and 1937, when he had renewed some old acquaintances. He was known throughout the British Indian Army as a delightful and cultured if rather lazy man. The appointment to Manila was like a posting to paradise. He took over Tanaka's quarters in the High Commission and was frequently seen with club in hand practising his swings on the Luneta or on the grass verges around Intramuros. Whenever he could he got onto Manila's golf links, where he became as much a fixture as Richard Sutherland had once been. Kuroda also enjoyed the company of beautiful women; of these Manila had more than its fair share, and Kuroda was reputed to have enjoyed a succession of attractive and charming mistresses. Unlike Tanaka he was prepared to leave the day-to-day administration of the occupation to Colonel Ohta. None of the Japanese who ruled Manila wanted MacArthur's penthouse on top of the Manila Hotel. This was preserved in exactly the state in which the MacArthurs had left it and became a major tourist attraction for visiting dignitaries.[20]

After Wainwright surrendered Corregidor on May 6, 1942, Manila became a strategic backwater until the summer of 1944. The city's chief military importance was as a transit centre for personnel and aircraft moving southeast to the battlefields of the Solomons and New Guinea. The Japanese rapidly scaled down the number of troops in the Philippines until by the summer of 1943 there were just over 40,000. Of these 25,000 were stationed on Luzon, of whom some 15,000 were in the Manila area, the largest concentration being at Fort McKinley.

Japan may not by this stage have attached any military significance to the Philippines: but in political terms the islands were still vital. The reasons for this are clear. Elsewhere – Indo-China, the East Indies, Burma – there was real substance to Japan's claim to be liberating the peoples of Asia from European colonialism. But the Philippines were different. They did not obviously need 'rescuing' in quite the same way, since they already enjoyed a considerable degree of autonomy. America (unlike France, the Netherlands and Britain) was not a colonial power: and indeed independence was only four years off. Any 'liberation' of the Philippines would have to be of a different kind: a liberation of the Filipino soul from the shackles of Western ideology by returning it to its true, oriental self. Only then could it play its part in the 'new order.' The battle for the spirit of the Philippines would thus take place in that heartland of Western cosmopolitanism, Manila.

When Homma's army entered Manila on January 2, 1942, it was accompanied by a large, well-trained propaganda corps: cultural warriors with a mission to win the hearts and minds of the Filipinos. The 'corps' was about a battalion in strength, not unlike a modern American civil affairs unit, and drew on men from a very diverse range of professions. Since Manila's population was largely Christian, the corps included about a platoon's worth of clergymen, composed equally of Catholic priests and Protestant ministers. The propaganda corps needed media outlets: radio and newspapers would have to be restored as soon as possible. Thus the corps came fully armed with a platoon-sized group of print and radio journalists and technicians, and photographers. Cinema and theatre would obviously prove important in influencing the population and so the corps included about a platoon's worth of cine-cameramen, and cinema and theatre people. With the long-term intellectual conversion of the population in mind, the corps included squads of novelists, poets, and painters. Japanese newspapers, radio stations and newsreel companies needed to be supplied with stories. Homma

THE BATTLE FOR MANILA

included more than 100 correspondents in his propaganda corps, and detailed some 300 officers and men to assist them.[21]

The Japanese entered Manila with some very precise objectives. Before returning to Japan, Homma had given an address unfolding his vision of the 'New Philippines' within the Greater East Asian Co-Prosperity Sphere. Unlike most other Asian peoples the Filipinos – particularly the Manileños – had been spiritully colonized, first by the Spanish and then by the Americans. They had slavishly imitated the American way of life and a society had evolved that was characterized by the worst aspects of Latin and North American culture, a society which was at once easygoing and obsessed with material possessions. The Philippines now had an opportunity to regain the oriental virtues of honesty, fortitude, diligence, hardwork, frugality, and thrift.[22]

The task of the Japanese was made easier by the disillusionment with the United States which spread throughout Manila during the first six months of 1942. The Manileños were badly shaken by the collapse of the Lingayen Front, the retreat to Bataan, and the abandonment of Manila. Then they waited with bated breath for the arrival of the American fleets and convoys which the Voice of Freedom had promised them. They did not come. In the final week of March the Voice of Freedom announced that General MacArthur had escaped to Australia, where he was to take command of American forces for a counteroffensive. On April 8 the Voice of Freedom announced that Bataan had fallen. Over the next few days rumours began circulating in Manila about emaciated columns of Filipino and American prisoners – later known as the 'Bataan death march' – staggering from the peninsula to railheads north of the city. The Japanese countered any accusations of brutality by pointing out that the prisoners were so weakened by the last weeks trapped on the Bataan Peninsula that they would have died anyway. They also spread the rumour – one widely believed – that American logistics officers gave priority to feeding American soldiers, to the point where Filipino troops starved. So although news of the Bataan death march did not generate a flurry of pro-Japanese sentiment, it helped fan the embers of Filipino resentment. The last blow came on the night of May 5–6. The Voice of Freedom went off the air and early on May 6 MacArthur's successor, General Jonathan Wainwright, surrendered not just Corregidor but all US forces in the Philippines. Many Philippine and American units, particularly those operating in the south of the islands, chose to ignore this order and carry on a guerrilla campaign, but in Manila the psychological impact of the surrender was profound.

On May 7 convoys of Japanese barges landed some 6000 exhausted, unkempt American and Filipino prisoners at the yacht harbor on Dewey Boulevard. From here they were marched up the boulevard and through the city to the rail transport which would take them to the camps north of Manila. When Australian and British prisoners had walked through Singapore they had been jeered at: so had the Dutch in Batavia. The Manileños did not jeer at these ragged troops, but their very raggedness seemed to symbolize something more profound: the fraying of American confidence, and of Manila's confidence in America. Many Manileños ran behind Japanese guards and offered the prisoners cigarettes and food – it was like a sentimental gesture to an old friend leaving, perhaps never to return.[23] In early summer 1942 even the most optimistic and pro-American Manileños must have harbored real doubts about whether they would ever see that friend again.

The new Japanese occupation intended life in Manila to return to normal as quickly as possible: only then would long-term cultural conversion start to take place. Radio KZRH came back on the air on January 14 under new Japanese management, its first task to counter claims of American victories and Japanese atrocities made by the Voice of Freedom.[24] Carlos Romulo had set up that radio station as soon as he had reached Corregidor, leaving behind in Manila his newspaper, the *Manila Herald*. When the paper started to roll off the presses once again, editorial policy had changed dramatically. 'US Aircraft Carrier Sunk' screamed the banner headline. Articles included accounts of an American submarine sinking a Japanese hospital ship, the beginning of the reconstruction of Hong Kong, and the return of normality to Manila. Readers were assured that 'Downtown Manila is regaining some of her former liveliness. More business establishments are re-opening and more people are being seen in the streets. Coffee shops, snack counters and restaurants are crowded most of the day.'[25] On February 1, 16 of Manila's 48 theaters reopened, showing hurriedly censored American movies. By Easter the bookshops had also opened their doors, their shelves now free of all those texts which the propaganda corps deemed ideologically offensive.[26]

The propaganda corps knew that a sudden assault on Filipino

values would be counterproductive. Cleverly, they emphasized the similarities between Japan and the Philippines. Homma's officers were at pains to prove that being a good Asian was not incompatible with being a good Catholic. The propaganda corps secured the permission of the Archbishop of Manila, Archbishop Michael J. O'Doherty, for Japanese priests to officiate in Manila's churches. On Sunday January 11 a Japanese priest, Father Tukamuto, presided over a friendship mass at the Santa Cruz Church. The following Sunday Japanese priests conducted services throughout Manila, including one at the cathedral. On March 5 the Archbishop of Osaka, Monsignor Taguchi, arrived in Manila on a nine-month goodwill mission. The highlight came in September 1942 when Archbishop Taguchi and Archbishop O'Doherty co-officiated at a ceremony honouring Tabuyen Ukon, a Japanese Christian of the early 17th century who had fled to Manila to escape Tokugawa persecution.[27]

The Japanese began their 'reeducation' of the Philippines in an obvious place – the schools. On February 17 new basic principles of education were announced: fostering of pro-Japanese and anti-Western sentiments and encouraging a renewal of Filipino culture, both to be aided by the eradication of Hispanic and American influences. Early in the summer many schools reopened, students returning to find a new history syllabus, new Japanese-language lessons, and throughly revised textbooks.[28]

Conversion would take place far more readily if the Japanese could work through Philippine institutions. Quezon had already laid the groundwork for this in his final days in Malacañan Palace, when he had created new city boundaries for Manila – the city of Greater Manila – so that the area which could be declared 'open' would be enlarged. The exact boundaries of Greater Manila remained vague but extended roughly eight to nine miles from Grace Park in the north to Pasay in the south, and to the new Manila Heights and Quezon City subdivisions some five to six miles east of downtown. Quezon chose as mayor of Greater Manila his former executive secretary, Jorge B. Vargas, who was instructed explicitly to cooperate with the Japanese in order to spare Manila unnecessary suffering.[29]

Homma soon realized that a man of Vargas' standing should be running more than a city. Thus Vargas was appointed to lead a new interim government for the islands, the Philippine Executive

Commission. He in turn appointed as mayor of Greater Manila his old political ally, Quezon's former private secretary and secretary for labour, Leon G. Guinto.[30] Guinto reorganized the administration of the city on corporatist lines, which in fact owed very little to Japanese traditions of local government, and much more to Italian and Spanish Fascist and Falangist systems. He divided Manila into four districts, each headed by a district chief. The district chief in turn organized the various districts into neighbourhood associations each headed by a president, whose job was to list the names of each resident in an association book, and to record births and deaths and movements in and out of the neighbourhood. The efficiency of the neighbourhood associations varied widely. A task which would be quite easy in Malate would prove difficult in Ermita and impossible in Tondo, even if the presidents approached their jobs with enthusiasm.

The Japanese intended the political reorganization of Manila to be but the prelude to a political reorganization of the entire Philippines. Like the Americans, the Japanese promoted the Philippines' independence – but an independence on their own terms. On August 8, 1942, Vargas, as chairman of the Philippine Executive Commission, issued Executive Order No. 109, which created an all-embracing, Falange-type organization, the Association for Service to the New Philippines – in Tagalog the Kapisanan sa Pagiliingkod sa Bagong Pilipines (usually shortened to 'Kalibapi'). According to Vargas the Kalibapi 'will aim at the mental education, moral regeneration, physical invigoration and economic rehabilitation of the Philippines under the guidance of the Japanese Military Administration.' Existing political parties were incorporated into the Kalibapi and by the early summer of 1943 it had about 40,000 members in Manila.[31]

On May 6, 1943 Japanese premier Hideki Tojo arrived in Manila for what amounted to a state visit to Vargas. Roderick Hall, then attending St Paul's convent school in Malate, remembers the day well. All schools had been ordered to send students to the gathering. Representatives from each school marched up Dewey Boulevard to the Luneta, joining a growing column. The Luneta was packed with more than 100,000 drawn from the Kalibapi and its youth organizations and Manila's schools. As Tojo mounted the podium, flanked by Tanaka and Vargas, Hall recalls joining in the shouts of 'Banzai!' which filled the park.[32] After Tojo's visit, momentum towards independence accelerated rapidly. In June the Kalibapi selected a Preparation Committee for Philippine Independence. By September it had produced a preliminary constitution, and on the 23rd of that month it elected a national assembly. On October 14, 1943 the Philippines became an independent republic, with one of Quezon's former acquaintances, José P. Laurel, as president. Laurel moved into Malacañan Palace, established a presidential guard, and began issuing decrees.[33]

The formation of the Laurel government was the highpoint of Japanese influence in the Philippines; an influence that thereafter began to wane. Not because the Americans were any closer to returning to the islands: this possibility seemed remote since MacArthur's counteroffensive in the South West Pacific and Nimitz's drive across the Central Pacific had barely begun and the nearest American forces were still down on the Huon Peninsula in Australian New Guinea. The deterioration in Japan's position in the Philippines owed nothing to the Americans, and everything to Japanese occupation policies. Back in December 1941 the German internees had noted that it was better to be fed by the Americans than by the Japanese. During the course of 1942 this was a lesson the entire archipelago, but particularly a big city like Manila, was to find out for itself.

At the very heart of Japan's problems lay an apparently insoluble economic dilemma. The Japanese offensives of 1941–2 had been conducted on a logistic shoestring. Tokyo planners had given priority to munitions, relying on the troops' ability to forage for themselves to relieve pressure on already extended supply lines. When the Japanese arrived in Manila they had virtually no reserves of food. Nor would there be much coming from Japan: Tokyo's policy was to make Japan's garrisons as self-sufficient as possible. The Japanese Army would have to depend on supplies grown in the Philippines. The problem was that the five days of looting which preceded their entry into Manila (December 28–January 2) had massively reduced centrally located food stocks in the city. Most people had enough for a few weeks – indeed, for a short time the Paco market was glutted – but when these stocks ran out serious problems would arise. The planting season in the rich rice lands of northern Luzon ran from early December through January; but the troubled military situation had drastically impaired the customary level of planting.[34]

As the looted food supplies gave out in the early spring of 1942 a major food crisis developed. It was exacerbated by Japanese policies. The Quezon government had established a centralized storage and marketing institution, the National Rice and Corn Corporation (NARIC), which was supposed to stimulate food production and iron out price fluctuations. In keeping with their corporatist philosophy, the Japanese attempted to establish a controlled economy, fixing prices for rice and making the sale of rice through NARIC mandatory. Decrees of the Japanese military administration, backed up by decrees from the Philippine Executive Commission, made it illegal for farmers to sell food direct to the markets.[35]

No policy could have been better designed to dry up food supplies to NARIC and establish a thriving black market. The official NARIC price for rice was pegged at 14 centavos per kilo, with the January 1942 ration pegged at 1.25kg. Steadily diminishing supplies of rice to NARIC forced a lowering of the ration. By December 1942 it stood at less than a quarter of the January ration – 0.3kg – and in early 1943 fell to 0.24kg. Meanwhile a black market flourished. By late 1942 rice could be bought in the Paco market for 50 centavos a kilo, more than three times the official price, with the disparity widening all the time.[36]

The problem of feeding Manila preoccupied both the Japanese military administration and the Vargas Commission. They tried out two complementary policies: exhortation and coercion. The first consisted of encouraging greater land cultivation. Extra publicity was given to the new strains of rice introduced from Formosa – a kind of 'super rice' designed to revolutionize agriculture in the Philippines – and to the arrival of grain ships from Saigon intended to alleviate existing shortages. In fact little land was brought into cultivation and the Formosan rice failed to thrive. The Saigon grain ships sailed confidently into the cinema newsreels but somehow never made it as far as Manila Bay.[37] Coercion proved no more effective. The Kempeitai and the Philippine Constabulary conducted periodic drives against profiteers and black marketeers. They set up iron cages outside the City Hall – 'looters cages' – in which offenders were exposed to public opprobrium. But, as usual, the small fish were caught while the big ones escaped the net. A chain of corruption developed which involved a number of highly placed NARIC officials and certain members of the Japanese military administration.[38]

A steadily worsening food shortage was matched by equally

great shortages in other areas of the economy. The Japanese commandeered most motor vehicles during their first weeks in Manila, and motorized buses and taxis were soon running on gas bags fueled from burning charcoal. Major shortages soon developed in clothing, shoes, cigarettes, and soap. By late 1942 virtually all consumer items were in short supply. Manila followed the classic pattern of a city under occupation. Shortages of food and consumer goods led to general impoverishment, a flourishing black market, and massive inflation. In January 1942 the Japanese had introduced an occupation currency, paper notes ranging from one centavo to ten pesos. As goods became scarcer prices rose. The Japanese dealt with the problem by printing more money in ever larger denominations – first 50-peso and then 500-peso notes. Within months Manila was in the grip of an inflationary spiral. Japanese notes rapidly became worthless: they were universally known as 'Mickey Mouse money.'

Soaring inflation meant that in rural areas a money economy virtually ceased to exist. Villages simply bypassed currency and returned to a barter system. Such a system also operated within Manila, though here it could never entirely replace money. Manila's sophisticated financial institutions found it increasingly difficult to function. The insurance company for which José Olbes worked was inundated with requests for life policies, for which the premiums would be paid in currency which was worthless. Olbes and his colleagues got round the difficulty by refusing to issue policies for more than a year at a time.[39] Similarly the Zobel family's Ayala y Cia refused to sell land for occupation currency, confining their transactions to short-term leases.[40]

The impact of inflation varied. Some traders made enormous paper fortunes. Middle-class Manileños on fixed incomes, and the Filipino families of Allied internees, found life particularly difficult. Consuelo Hall assured her husband Alaistair, who was now confined to Santo Tomás, that in order to buy food 'I have sold a lot of junk I was happy to get rid of.'[41] But she was putting a brave face on what was, in reality, a brutally necessary and in some cases poignant transaction. José Olbes recalled that families like the Halls 'started selling good things – beautiful pieces of jewelry and table were – Limoges china, paintings . . .'[42] Frederick and Constance Prising, who had been moved to the Remedios Hospital in Malate, sold all their silver to a Syrian merchant: but within three months galloping inflation had consumed the entire proceeds.[43]

But it would be wrong to depict these families as helpless victims of circumstances beyond their control. They may not have been able to change the course of war, but most were built of stern stuff, the stuff of survivors: after all, they were direct descendants of a long line of the smartest and toughest traders in Asia. The younger generations in particular rose to the challenge, some with evident relish for the opportunities the occupation offered them to display their entrepreneurial skills. Alaistair Hall's second son, Ian, began making high teas for young men who gathered at the Hall household for poker sessions. With the money they paid him he bought cheap Filipino cigarettes wholesale, and then sold them at a handsome profit to the young men of Manila. He was nine, but he was the son of a stockbroker.[44] Thirteen-year-old Oscar Ocampas, the eldest son of recent immigrants to Manila, followed Ian's example, dealing in cigarettes at Plaza Lawton. Ocampas discovered that banana-peel fibres were excellent for shining shoes, and branched successfully into the shoe shine business. Fortunately by the time the flies had started to descend on their shoes, the customers would usually be a block or two away.[45]

Fourteen-year-old Enrique Zobel reveled in adversity. He had last seen his father on Christmas Eve on his way to Bataan, but then there was silence. Ayala y Cia's assets were frozen and the Zobels literally had no money. Enrique noticed that motor vehicles were rapidly disappearing from Manila's streets, and the germ of an idea began to grow in his mind. He sold his father's stamp collection, some of his mother's silver, and his own Rolex watch. With the proceeds he leased two *carretelas* – the open, horse-drawn carriages which had once been a distinguishing feature of old Manila. Enrique next went to the polo club, now the quarters of a Japanese cavalry unit, and demanded that the Japanese return to him his family's six polo ponies. The audacity of his request caused a heated altercation. He soon found himself in Fort Santiago being interrogated by a major in the Kempeitai. Luckily, Colonel Ohta became involved in the proceedings: he took a shine to Enrique and invited him to lunch in the house he had commandeered in Pasay. It transpired that Ohta was anxious to learn Spanish. Sensing a potential conversationalist in the young Zobel, he arranged for him to visit his house every Thursday to give him lessons. In return, the Japanese would give him back his horses.

Very soon the Zobel *carretelas* were a regular sight as they carried their passengers between Pasay and Binondo, while every Thursday Enrique took Ohta through the complexities of Spanish grammar. In September 1942 the friendship between them was such that Ohta sent Enrique in his staff car to the prison camp at Capas. Here the teenager met his father for the first time since Christmas Eve. Colonel Jacobo Zobel had survived the Baatan death march but had succumbed to dysentery and now weighed only 86lb. Enrique carried his father into Ohta's car and they sped homeward. It was well into 1943 before Colonel Zobel had fully recovered.[46]

Food shortages, economic dislocation, hyperinflation, a flourishing blackmarket, the emergence of teenage entrepreneurs – all these factors would have spelt disaster even for a popularly elected government of any society. In Manila, the mess was blamed entirely on the Japanese occupation. The situation was aggravated by the serious culture clash between the Japanese and the Manileños. The Japanese may have claimed that they were helping the Filipinos recover their Asian dignity, but they seemed to take a perverse delight in publicly humiliating them. The first step was their insistence that Manileños bow down from the waist to Japanese soldiers on sentry duty, and even to every Japanese officer and soldier passing in the street. To the Japanese this did not seem strange; it was a mark of courtesy standard within their own army and society. José Olbes remembered a group of off-duty Japanese soldiers on M.H. del Pilar Street preoccupied with watching girls. They failed to notice a staff car with a full colonel drive by. The car screeched to a halt, the furious colonel leapt out and immediately began screaming abuse at the men and slapping them in the face. Virtually all Filipinos witnessed such incidents and many were themselves the victims: as José Olbes remarked laconically, the Japanese 'were very free with their hands.'[47]

Thirteen-year-old Tony Moncupa was one of the first to experience a Japanese blow. Shortly after the start of the occupation he was cycling furiously on an errand when he cut in front of a Japanese truck, forcing the driver to brake violently. As the truck again accelerated, the driver 'reached over and conked me on the head with his fist. Boy! did I see lots of stars!'[48] In any society the behaviour of teenage boys will provoke violence: such an incident could have happened just as easily in Los Angeles. But the Japanese did not confine themselves to hitting teenage boys. The military administration moved Japanese supervisors into

NARIC's headquarters and soon they were slapping senior Filipino office staff for minor misdemeanors. NARIC's director, Victor Buencamino, protested to the Japanese manager but the slapping went on. Buencamino finally issued an instruction that any Filipino slapped by a Japanese was to slap the Japanese right back. He told his personnel: 'If they take you to Fort Santiago I'll go with you.'[49] When roused to anger the Japanese could be completely indiscriminate. In one incident outside the German Club a Japanese NCO struck a European civilian in the face. This was no paroled Allied internee but a senior official of the club, a citizen of Japan's ally, the Third Reich. The result was a minor diplomatic incident and a serious deterioration in relations between Manila's German community and its Japanese allies.[50]

Many Filipino women found Japanese behavior particularly humiliating. By the standards of contemporary Asian societies, women in the Philippines, particularly in Manila, enjoyed a very high status. This was the paradoxical result of the interaction of two different legacies. The traditional notion of the chaperoned madonna provided a degree of security and protection while the newer image of the educated North American working girl enabled a liberation from the characteristic domestic role often expected of Asian women. During this period, it seems that the women of Manila enjoyed the best of both worlds. In 1941 many of them went to university and then became lawyers, doctors, journalists, and a thousand other things, but the men still treated them chivalrously. Japanese soldiers came from a very different society: the proper place for women was at home, in the kitchen, or in bed. Although the streets of Manila were not as dangerous for women as parts of New York or Los Angeles, there were real risks. Sometimes it was worse than the usual nuisance of catcalls, whistles and eyings-up. Seventeen-year-old Carmelina Demerin was stopped by Japanese sentries on Vito Cruz. As she bowed from the waist a sentry slapped her on the bottom, and then frisked her. Fifty years on she could remember every sensation. 'His hands roamed all over my body. Numbed with fright, I couldn't anymore feel the things he was doing to me.' Other Manileños passing the checkpoint kept their eyes firmly ahead, refusing to notice an incident which before January 1942 would simply not have happened on a Malate street.[51]

In offices and factories Japanese managers and supervisors subjected Filipino girls to the same sort of physical violence they inflicted on male workers. The situation in some factories where the work force was overwhelmingly female seems to have become increasingly bad, particularly when there was no Victor Buencamino to stand up for the employees. Here Japanese supervisors employed systematic beatings to encourage correct attitudes to work. Marcela Sayo Talusig stitched baseball gloves at the Goodrich factory in Paco. She recalled that her Japanese supervisor punished the slightest mistake by pulling the girls' hair and beating them.[52] Japanese girls slaving in factories in Nagoya and Kobe may have grown used to such treatment; in Manila it caused massive resentment.

All Manileños who lived through the occupation never forgot the frequent sight of angry Japanese, shouting and slapping. The continual fear of violence flaring up produced an atmosphere tense with uncertainty. Episodes were so sudden, and apparently random, that Manileños could never feel secure when the Japanese were around. One night in the summer of 1942 Marcela Talusig's teenage brother did not come home from an errand. Some days later her parents discovered that he had been arrested while passing the Masonic Lodge on Taft Avenue and taken to Fort Santiago. There had been a burglary the previous evening and a Japanese sentry thought he recognized young Talusig as one of the thieves. It was a case of mistaken identity but it took two years to rectify and secure Talusig's release.[53]

Like all big cities, Manila had its share of pickpockets; but pickpockets who stole from the Japanese put every innocent bystander at risk. One *calesa* driver, Tony Amando, was arrested and locked up in Fort Santiago when a Japanese civilian passenger discovered his briefcase was missing and accused Tony of the theft. Fortunately Tony's father worked for NARIC; strings were pulled and he was released after a few days.[54] José Olbes remembered one occasion on a crowded bus when he watched in horrified fascination as a pickpocket deftly removed a Japanese passenger's wallet. Olbes was not the only person who witnessed the incident. At the next stop he and everyone else got off the bus, leaving the victim alone to discover his loss.[55]

Sometimes people didn't have a chance to get away. A Thursday afternoon in Malate's Gaiety Theater almost ended in tragedy for Enrique Zobel and some of his teenage friends. They were watching an old Buck Rogers serial when suddenly the lights came on. Japanese soldiers with rifles and fixed bayonets ran down the aisles, shouting at the audience to get out and line up on the pavement. Here soldiers held the audience at bayonet point while an officer, furious to the point of incoherence, demanded the return of his sword. He too had been watching the movie when he discovered that his weapon had been stolen. The afternoon was hot, but Zobel remembers feeling ice-cold. No one moved. After what seemed like an eternity but was probably ten minutes, the Japanese grabbed about a dozen young men at random and bundled them into a truck for the trip to Fort Santiago. A Japanese officer had been dishonoured – a far more serious offense than stealing a wallet or a briefcase – and someone had to pay.[56]

That same summer José Olbes faced an even more serious situation. A Japanese officer quartered in a neighboring house was found one morning by his aide-de-camp lying in a pool of blood, stabbed to death with his own sword. The Kempeitai sent a message through the president of the neighborhood association. Unless the murderer was discovered within forty-eight hours, hostages would be taken to Fort Santiago. As a young, unmarried man living next door to the murdered officer, Olbes would have been an obvious choice for a hostage. Several anxious hours passed before the murderer, a Filipino houseboy who had been slapped once too often, was arrested and carried away for summary execution.[57]

Even without the food shortages and economic problems the Japanese did not behave in ways calculated to win Filipino love or respect. That they had failed even in the early stages is suggested by the fact that the Manileños went out of their way to give special treatment to the few Allied internees still at large. 'Shorty' Hall had been assigned to work among very old internees – some of them veterans of the Spanish-American war – who had been moved to the lunatic asylum on Proviso Island in the Pasig. Hall was allowed limited movement around the city. He found that the red armband he was required to wear, identifying him as an enemy of Japan, ensured free travel in *calesas*. Although some of the drivers were desperately poor they refused to take his money and some even pressed cigarettes on him.[58] In the summer of 1942 Constance Prising had a similar experience. By this time she was on parole with her husband and son at the Remedios Hospital in Malate. Fearing the Manileños' hostility, she tried to make herself look Spanish before taking her son Robin shopping in Paco market. Her efforts to haggle with the traders in what sounded like a dainty Castilian lisp seemed to provoke their anger. She dropped her disguise, spoke in English, and a miraculous transformation came over the vendors. 'Here, please – I don't sell to you, please – you take,' said one, as he thrust handfuls of calamansis at her. Another rushed up with a big papaya: 'Please – my present to you. I am Narciso. You tell if your houseboy comes that Narciso will make a good price.' Robin remembered his mother so choked by emotion that she could scarcely speak.[59]

Manileños had a reputation for being warm and generous to old friends who had fallen on hard times: thus these incidents might not in themselves seem politically significant. But in August 1943 opinion was tested by one particular episode about which there could be no misunderstanding. Six months earlier a Japanese movie company had arrived in Manila to shoot a 'no expenses spared' epic, *The Dawn of Freedom*. This movie was ostensibly about the 'liberation' of the Philippines but the subtext was clearly the liberation of Asian culture and the Asian intellect from the shackles of the West. The director, Abe Yutaka, insisted that real Americans be employed for the final climactic sequence in which MacArthur's forces abandon the city. The Japanese commander in the Philippines, General Kuroda (then having an affair with one of Yutaka's leading ladies) was happy to oblige. He arranged for thousands of American POWs to be trucked into Manila so they could suffer the humiliation of reenacting for the cameras their defeat of 18 months earlier.[60] Manileños turned out in their thousands to watch the final scenes. There was an extraordinary outburst of spontaneous emotion, quite unlike the stage-managed mass sentiment extorted from the Filipino crowds drilled to greet Tojo at the Luneta three months earlier.

When the Americans arrived, the Manileños cheered themselves hoarse, ignoring the furious Japanese. Groups of girls in their late teens and early twenties, most of them from prosperous districts like Ermita, Malate and Pasay, broke through the Japanese cordon and threw packets of cigarettes and food parcels to the Americans. The Japanese guards arrested many of them, some none too gently, and bundled them off to Fort Santiago. One of the girls was Señorita 'Chibi' Ortigas, José Olbes' fiancée. Olbes spent a sleepless night phoning everyone of political importance he could think of. His fiancée's uncle knew José Laurel, and this phone call worked. Early the following day the Japanese released the girls with little more than a slap on the wrist.[61]

The scene on the movie set may have said more about the

Manileños' anti-Japanese sentiment than it did about their pro-American sentiment. On that occasion, the girls showed their feelings – to the point of recklessness. But (as usual) it was the male adolescents who translated resentment into action, often with considerable success. There were many things boys could do to make the Japanese feel unwelcome: small things that would accumulate and annoy them over time. Throughout Luzon the Japanese were referred to as the 'sakang,' which is Tagalog for 'bowlegged'. So peculiar was the gait of some Japanese that Filipinos also adopted the Anglo-American term of abuse, 'monkey-men.' The Japanese knew this and were sensitive about it. Librado Nery, an apprentice draftsman who worked in Quiapo, took special delight in playing on this sensitivity. On one occasion he passed a sentry while eating a bag of peanuts. Perhaps his bow was not low enough because the Japanese glowered at him. A beatific smile suddenly lit up Librado's face. He walked up to the sentry and offered him some peanuts. The sentry looked puzzled as he ate the offering; he knew that something had been done to him but he couldn't quite work out what.[62] Librado's act of defiance was small but it could easily have resulted in his death. Another technique was to exploit the similarities between certain Japanese and Tagalog words. Boys passing sentries would smile, bow low, and utter what the soldiers interpreted as 'oheyo,' which is Japanese for 'good morning.' But what their friends (within earshot and straining not to laugh) would hear was the Tagolog 'layop ka,' which means 'you are an animal.'[63]

Japanese soldiers enjoying an evening on the town were particularly vulnerable. The Japanese had established a 'comfort house' for officers opposite Malate's Assumption Convent, only half a block from the Hall's house. Like all boys on the threshold of their teens, Rod and Ian were fascinated, often hiding under a hedge between the brothe and the road, watching the girls sitting on the veranda, combing their hair and putting on make-up. On one occasion the boys ran into a group of extremely drunk and violent Japanese sailors. The men shouted at them, exposed themselves and by this and other gestures indicated that they wanted women. The brothers pointed the sailors to the only comfort house that they knew and, well aware of what would happen when the drunken ratings were confronted by officers, ran like fury. [64] The Hall boys were unaware at the time that they were witnessing a tiny part of a story that is only now being unfolded – that of the enforced shipment of thousands of

Chinese, Korean and Taiwanese women to the comfort houses of Manila and various other cities of Southeast Asia.

Most Japanese soldiers in Manila were probably on the receiving end of this covert guerrilla warfare. Each episode may have been only a pinprick, but over time the pinpricks grew very sore; and such subversive activities among the young did not suggest promising young orientals in the making. A far more public means of expressing anti-Japanese hostility was the theater, a medium which (ironically) the Japanese propaganda corps had done much to stimulate. Filipino scholars rightly regard the occupation period as the golden age of indigenous theater; Hollywood movies were unobtainable and the Japanese and Filipino industries produced only a trickle of major features. In these circumstances live theater was reborn.[65] Manila under the occupation had nearly fifty playhouses, most of which could boast a performance every night, with matinees on Saturdays and some weekdays. The propaganda corps sponsored Tagalog plays, the most overtly political of which was *Dawn*, the story of a Filipino guerrilla who comes to realize that Filipinos and Japanese are friends and brothers and that they should build the new Asia together. *Dawn* backfired badly. To make the guerrilla chief's disillusion with the USA believable he had to be given lines which portrayed him as a pro-American fanatic. Each time he uttered the words 'the Americans will come back. They'll never forsake us,' audiences broke into a storm of applause.[66]

Most plays were not like *Dawn*. Manileños were no different from Londoners, Parisians or Berliners in their tastes. They went to the theater to escape. Entrepreneurs like Joe Chimaco, the Ziegfeld of the Far East, reconstructed the lavish reviews which had characterized entertainment at the turn of the century. The most popular show during these years was Chimaco's *Philippine Review*. Manileños flocked to it not for the dancing girls but to see two of Chimaco's great comic creation – the famous Pugo and Togo. These two stand-up comedians, the painfully thin Mariano Cantreas and the rotund Andrés Solomon, were an inspired comic combination, like Laurel and Hardy, or the vaudeville stars Gallagher and Sheen, or Mutt and Jeff from the newspaper comic strips.[67] Togo could bring the house down by waddling bandy-legged across the stage and pulling back his right sleeve to reveal an arm festooned with wristwatches, items which Japanese soldiers were reputed to value highly. In another skit Pugo came on stage leading a dog. Togo waddled by, bowed low to Pugo, and then even lower to the dog. Pugo then asked Togo why he was bowing, to which Togo replied: 'I am democratic. I bow to all God's creatures, the two-legged, the four-legged . . . the bandy-legged.' It never failed to have the audience rocking in the aisles.[68] Skits like this earned Chimaco 31 days' incarceration in Fort Santiago. He was released through a combination of political pressure and the good sense of Kuroda, who realized that Pugo and Togo served as an important safety valve for the Manileños.[69]

It was only a short step from harassing and ridiculing the Japanese to active military resistance. In some parts of the Philippines American and Filipino units had ignored Wainwright's surrender of May 6, 1942, and had gone to ground, to emerge later as guerrillas. As economic conditions worsened and as Japanese behavior alienated more and more Filipinos guerrilla resistance spread. In Manila a group of Philippine Army reserve officers formed the Manila Intelligence Group, and devoted themselves to monitoring and recording Japanese air and naval movements through the area. They considered this activity the most valuable contribution they could make, a view which both MacArthur and his intelligence chief, Major General Willoughby, heartily endorsed. MacArthur was anxious that guerrillas did not go off half-cocked, kill a few Japanese, and then leave innocent civilian populations exposed to Japanese reprisals.[70]

Some ex-Reserve Officer Training Corps students who had been demobilized at Christmas 1941 found the caution of the reserve officers irksome and formed the Hunters, usually known as Hunter's ROTC Guerrillas. They generally came from the right side of the tracks. A very different group was formed by the ex-boxer and ex-bus driver Marcos Augustin and his mistress, the former journalist Yay Panlilio. They called themselves Marking's guerrillas, a word formed from the elision of the first letters of their leader's first name with the last letters of his surname. The Hunters and Markings squabbled with each other and until the summer of 1944 confined themselves to producing and disseminating anti-Japanese propaganda, though it is doubtful they could have done more in this respect than the Japanese were doing themselves.[71]

In May 1943 MacArthur's South West Pacific Area (SWPA) HQ in far-off Brisbane had established a subcommand, the Philippine Regional Section (PRS) under the prominent Manila lawyer,

Courtney Whitney, who now held the rank of brigadier general. The PRS organized regular submarine supply runs to the Philippines, often under the command of a US Naval Reserve officer, Lieutenant Commander 'Chick' Parsons, who before the war had been an executive of the Manila-based Luzon Stevedore Company. From the summer of 1943 submarines were dropping intelligence agents off the coast of Luzon, some of whom made it to Manila.[72] One of the most successful trips was that of Major Emigidio Cruz, a Philippine Army surgeon who had served on Bataan, and had subsequently escaped to Australia. The submarine USS *Thresher* dropped Cruz off Los Negros on July 9. He then made his way north using interisland shipping and after many hair-raising adventures eventually arrived in Manila by train from the south on October 22. Cruz stayed in Manila until November 8, making contact with guerrilla groups and with members of the Laurel government, all of whom assured him of their continued loyalty to the now ailing President Quezon. The impact of the Cruz mission was dramatic: it provided an extraordinary boost to morale, for it was a clear indication that MacArthur was indeed going to return. On no one did it have a greater impact than Cruz's wife. He wrote of their first meeting, in the heart of an enemy-occupied city after a separation of nearly three years, in a rather matter-of-fact way – he was, after all, a doctor: 'My wife was shocked, too, when she saw me, but after praying for a few minutes to the Image of our Holy Virgin, she became composed. She was speechless, keeping a tight hold on me and trying to convince herself that I was not a product of her imagination.[73]'

Inhabitants of Manila like Señora Cruz had lived so long under the Japanese, with no sign of an American counteroffensive, that they had come to believe it would never happen. In Tokyo the view was different. There it seemed all too clear that the Philippines was indeed the objective of a great US counteroffensive. In Imperial Headquarters planners used small red flags to trace the American advance on a huge wall map of the Pacific. On October 2, 1943 they put a red flag on Finschhafen, on the northern coast of Australian New Guinea, the first indication that MacArthur's SWPA forces were on the move. Thereafter the flags traced a remorseless advance westward along the New Guinea coast; Saidor on January 2, 1944, Madang on April 1, Hollandia on April 22, and Sansapor, at the westernmost point of New Guinea, 1200 miles from Finschhafen, on July 30. MacArthur's forces were now only 800 miles south of Mindanao. The advance of Nimitz's forces westward from the Central Pacific was equally remorseless. Tokyo's planners put red flags on Tarawa Atoll in the Gilbert Islands on November 24, 1943, on Eniwetok in the Marshalls on February 17, 1944, on Saipan in the Marianas on June 15, on Guam on July 21 and on Tinian four days later. From here the Americans were only 1000 miles east of Luzon.

By this time much had changed in Manila. In May 1944 transport aircraft began arriving at Nielson and Nichols Fields from Saigon, carrying Field Marshal Count Hisaichi Terauchi and the numerous staff of the high command of Southern Army to their new headquarters.[74] The Tokyo planners believed they had divined the American master plan, a converging drive by Nimitz and MacArthur onto the Philippines. Overnight Manila was transformed from a strategic backwater into a bustling nerve centre from which Terauchi was to supervise the conduct of what Tokyo called 'the decisive battle.' Reinforcements began arriving. Manila Bay filled with troopships, no longer in transit to New Guinea but destined for the defence of the Philippines. At the end of July, with the Americans at Sansapor, and on Saipan, Tinian, and Guam, Imperial Headquarters produced its counter-stroke, the Sho (Victory) Plan, which envisaged climactic naval, air and land battles with the Americans throughout the Philippines.

Terauchi had been in Saigon for three years and resented the move to Manila. Saigon was a charming French provincial city where the population was quiet. Manila was a teeming metropolis, where the population was increasingly hostile. Lieutenant General Kuroda did his best to introduce Terauchi to the delights of Manila, but the 65-year-old field marshal found Kuroda's pastimes tiring. Terauchi was worried about the atmosphere in Manila. He soon had real doubts as to Kuroda's ability to command 'the decisive battle.' Officers on Terauchi's staff reported that they had heard Kuroda say, on more than one occasion, that the task of defending the Philippines was impossible. When shown the Sho Plan, Kuroda had told Terauchi that although the concept was good you couldn't 'fight with concept alone. Words will not sink American ships and that becomes clear when you compare our aircraft with theirs.'[75] To Terauchi this sounded dangerously like defeatism. The field marshal had noticed that Kuroda's mood was often one of amused, cynical detachment. Moreover, there had been occasions when Terauchi needed to contact Kuroda urgently and had been told that the general was not available. It transpired that at such times Kuroda was usually on the golf links.[76]

Terauchi urged Imperial Headquarters to change the commander in the Philippines. There was one obvious candidate for the job, General Tomoyuki Yamashita, who early in 1942 had secured spectacular victories in Malaya and Singapore. But Japan's most victorious general had been too successful for his own good. Yamashita's popularity had aroused the enmity of his arch-rival, Prime Minister Tojo, who had managed to secure his transfer to the backwater of Manchuria. The disasters which befell Japan in the Central Pacific in the summer of 1944 led to the resignation of the Tojo government on July 18. Such were the ways of Tokyo's military bureaucracy that Imperial Headquarters did not send a formal instruction ordering Yamashita to the Philippines until September 25, 1944. Eleven days later Yamashita's aircraft landed in Manila.

Yamashita had been used to the serenity of Mutankiang. In Manila he sensed the same atmosphere which had perturbed Terauchi. Everywhere there was a feeling that something was about to happen. More than 200,000 Japanese personnel had now arrived in the Philippines and more were arriving each day. Manila now played host not only to Terauchi's headquarters, but also to the headquarters of General Kyoji Tominaga, commander of 4th Air Army and of Vice Admiral Gunichi Mikawa, commander of South West Area Fleet. Yamashita inherited Kuroda's old headquarters, and also brought in some trusted associates like Lieutenant General Akira Muto, who was to serve as his chief of staff.[77] During the course of 1944 the demand for accommodation suitable for officers of staff rank and above became progressively more intense. The Olbeses (José had married his fiancée in February 1944) found setting up home in a conventional sense impossible. They were lucky enough to find a large house but very rapidly it filled up with relatives and friends whose own homes had been commandeered. By the autumn of 1944 they shared their home with no fewer than five extended families.[78] They were not alone; throughout the better areas of Manila it was now the rule to find several families crammed into a single house. The McMicking-Hall house, for example, was now filled to overflowing; Rod shared a bedroom with his grandmother, his aunt and a family friend whose home had been requisitioned. Every other bedroom was filled with relatives or staff, with some staff living in a flat over the garage.[79] There were advantages in overcrowding. José Olbes dissuaded Japanese Air Force officers from commandeering his house by showing them the number of women and children they would dispossess. The officers offered Olbes another house near Nichols Field, which he declined politely but firmly, on the grounds that the airstrip would be bombed if the Americans were to return. In the event the houses around Nichols Field survived, whereas Olbes' neighbourhood was entirely destroyed.[80]

Overcrowding was inconvenient but was the least serious of the problems confronting Manileños. Guerrilla attacks, which had been something which happened in the provinces, now took place in Manila. On June 16, 1944 saboteurs set fire to a tanker in Manila Bay, which burned spectacularly. A month later they set ablaze Piers 5 and 7 in the South Port district. They struck again on July 25, setting fire to a steamer in the Pasig, which was loaded with rice, crude oil, and other supplies.[81] And then on the morning of September 21 came an event which many Manileños scarcely believed possible. Robin Prising had been transferred back to Santo Tomás a month earlier and was at his lessons on the roof of the main building, from where he had a good view of the city and the harbor. The morning was hot and he let his mind drift from arithmetic:

> There was a dull, indefinite humming in the air and a low vibration. The sound began to grow. And as it swelled into a roar the windowpanes trembled till the concrete building started to shake. Out of the massy surge of clouds, the American bombers came, tier upon tier of them, flying high, flying low, an earth shaking armada of aeroplanes, glistening silver-white in the sun as they rode the air . . . As we began to count them, black bombs dropped from their bellies, smashing the harbor and airfields of Manila.[82]

The effect on the prisoners in Santo Tomás was dramatic. Internees who kept a chronology of events of the imprisonment typed after the date September 21, 1944 'THE AIR RAID.'[83] The effect on the Japanese was equally profound. On October 9 they took over the whole front campus of Santo Tomás and began stockpiling arms and ammunition.[84] The Japanese could not deny the raid had taken place; instead the press on September 22 carried banner headlines: 'Great Manila Air Battle: US Bomber Fleet Wiped Out!' At the Gaiety Pugo and Togo responded:

Pugo: 'What can shoot down more American aircraft than all the guns in the Combined Fleet?'

Togo: 'Search me? A new secret weapon?'

Pugo: 'No – the *Manila Herald*![85]

As well as being funny, Mariano Cantreas and Andrés Solomon could be very brave. By the autumn of 1944 Japanese tolerance, never great even in a quiet time under the amiable Kuroda, was becoming increasingly strained. American propaganda now appeared everywhere, handed out by guerrillas or dropped from aircraft. Children turned up at school with an impossible luxury, chocolate bars with wrappers bearing the words 'I Shall Return – MacArthur.' The slogan 'Warning – the Americans are Coming' was found on billboards, inside toilets in the theaters, and in streetcars and buses. Most spectacularly, it was chalked up on a bulletin board inside Fort Santiago.[86]

On October 13 in Santo Tomás, Alaistair Hall received a letter from his mother in Scotland, which she had posted five months earlier. Restricted to the standard 25 words, Mrs Hall had written: 'Joe happy to receive your letter. He is well and very optimistic but sorry cannot write. Hopes to celebrate next birthday, March 23, with his family.'[87] 'Joe' was Uncle Joe McMicking; the only way that Colonel McMicking could spend his next birthday with his family was if he came with a liberating army.

A week later, on October 20, José Olbes knew something was happening; throughout the day a constant stream of Japanese aircraft flew south over Manila while others took off from Nichols and Nielson Fields to join them.[88] Shortly after 2.00 p.m. rumors started circulating. The Voice of Freedom had been picked up on some long-wave frequencies (sets with short-wave capability had been banned by the Japanese since 1942), which meant the signals were coming from somewhere close to Luzon. Carlos P. Romulo had been heard on the air, along with President Sergio Osmena, the successor to President Quezon, who had died the previous year. And MacArthur had also been heard. Guerrillas were soon circulating the text of the message: 'People of the Philippines, I have returned! By the grace of Almighty God, our forces stand again on Philippine soil . . . Rally to me![89]

In Tokyo that day planners at Imperial Headquarters congratulated themselves; the Americans had done exactly what they had predicted, and now the Sho trap could be sprung. Over the next four days Japan's Combined Fleet did precisely this and paid the price. Enrique Zobel had left Manila in the summer for the family hacienda in the south; here he quickly linked up with local guerrillas. In the last week of October he saw an incredible sight along the beaches of the San Bernardino Strait: between the low- and high-water marks there were literally thousands of drowned Japanese sailors, casualties in the Battle of Leyte Gulf.[90] By the evening of October 25 the American Navy had broken the back of Japan's Combined Fleet; it had sunk four aircraft carriers, three battleships, ten cruisers and eleven destroyers. And yet in Manila Vice Admiral Okochi assured Yamashita that although Japanese naval losses had been grevious those of the Americans had been just as bad. Excited Japanese pilots had reported six burning American auxiliary carriers (small ships carrying few aircraft) as the destruction of six major fleet carriers. On October 27 the Americans pulled back their fleet carriers to bases in the Central Pacific for refueling and maintenance. The sudden disappearance of these ships convinced even the sceptical Yamashita of the validity of Okochi's claims – at least for a couple of weeks.

While the Americans continued to pour ashore on Leyte, guerrillas struck throughout the Philippines. Reports of atrocities flowed into Yamashita's headquarters; guerrillas had hacked half-drowned sailors to pieces as they struggled ashore on the southern coasts of Luzon after the Battle of Leyte Gulf while elsewhere guerrillas had murdered innocent Japanese civilian women and children. About a week after Leyte Gulf, patrols around Yamashita's headquarters at Fort McKinley discovered machine-guns and grenades hidden in the grass. A search of huts near the headquarters uncovered 100 rounds of ammunition. And around the end of the first week of November engineers located a bomb buried under the floor of the officers' mess at Fort McKinley.[91] It was clear to Yamashita that Ohta's Kempeitai was losing its grip on the situation in Manila, and needed help. On November 10 General Artemio Ricarte, a leader of the Philippine nationalist revolt against both Spain and the USA, who had spent nearly 40 years in self-imposed exile in Japan, presided over a meeting in Quezon City which formed a counter-guerrilla militia, the Makabayang Pilipino or Makapili. The strength of the Makapili grew to about 5000; some were genuine Philippine patriots but many were misfits and outcasts, On November 15 Yamashita ordered the Kempeitai, assisted by the Makapili, to comb the city in 'a punitive campaign against armed guerrilla bands.'[92]

The Japanese and their allies systematically terrorized parts of Manila. The Makapili sealed off entire districts – '*zonas*.' Within the *zona* (the term was also used for the operation) the Kempeitai compelled all residents to file past the Makapili. These particular collaborators had concealed their identities by donning sinister-looking hoods with a narrow slit for the eyes. They resembled nothing so much as the nightmare figures in a Goya painting of the inquisition. Manileños knew them as 'the secret eyes.' A nod from a 'secret eye' and the Kempeitai would bundle a suspect out of line and off to Fort Santiago. Here Ohta's interrogation techniques – he had by now found a use for the old Spanish dungeons – would invariably produce more suspects. These had to be arrested in yet more raids. Ten-year-old Eduardo Lauchengco, who lived about three hundred yards from San Lazaro Racetrack in Santa Cruz, witnessed one *zona* in his street. Early one morning a truckload of Makapili roared up to a house opposite his own; the occupants were armed and exchanged shots with the Makapili until they ran out of ammunition and surrendered. To the Makapili there was no question as to their guilt – they had offered armed resistance. Eduardo remembered that 'all the men were ordered out into the street . . . Then there was shouting all around. The men in the street were beheaded one by one by another Makapili whose head was covered by a bag. Heads really rolled down the street.'[93]

Japanese and Makapili violence was not yet random, but it discouraged movement around the city. Food disappeared from markets, pushing Manileños to the edge of subsistence. Mayor Guinto ordered city officials to put up banners advising citizens to evacuate to the countryside. Many did but there was no mass semi-organized evacuation as there had been in December 1941. The *zonas* which had disrupted life in Manila since November 15 had been a hazard of life in the countryside for many months, where they were known as 'Penetration Operations.' Better to stay in the city, many thought, where even now life was more secure. But guerrilla attacks on the roads leading into Manila reduced ever further the supply of food, until even the black market began to dry up. Internees in Bilibid and Santo Tomás were particularly vulnerable;

by the end of December the first deaths from malnutrition were recorded.[94]

The situation on the outside was no better. Consuelo Hall's letters to her husband trace the decline. On November 8 she wrote to her husband by the official Japanese-monitored post: 'We are all very well tho I have lost some weight and now weigh what I did when we were first married 102 Lbs. Mother is thin but well . . .'[95] On December 15, with an air raid in progress, she typed out a much longer letter, folded it into the size of a postage stamp, and sent it into Santo Tomás inside a Band-Aid. Consuelo now painted a much grimmer picture: 'I always seem to be just one step away from the wolff [sic] . . . Every one in town is very low in rice. The grown-ups have lost weight including Rod . . . Every day we seem hungrier.' So desperate was the situation that she was now going to part with one of her most treasured possessions. 'I know if I had more money I would not feel so desperate, so, since jewelry is what brings the most, I am going to sell that little diamond broach you bought me from Dreyfus. Remember? I want to have 40,000 or 50,000 which isn't much these days right here with me. I want to buy two sacks of red beans.'[96]

By Christmas a sack of rice was selling for 5000 pesos, a fantastic sum even in 'Mickey Mouse money.' Consuelo's diamond broach was now worth about eight to ten sacks. City Hall had 200,000 people on its relief rolls, though in the absence of food and with the steady collapse of central authority, the maintenance of such lists was simply a bureaucratic formality.[97] The Japanese were in no better state. The official daily ration was reduced to 400gm in mid-November, though it was often impossible to provide more than 300. Troops were seen in the suburbs, gathering wild grasses, and malnutrition, dysentery and typhus became common.[98]

The decline in Japan's logistics paralleled a deterioration in her military situation. American carrier aircraft returned to the Leyte battle in mid-November; Yamashita now knew that the navy had suffered a catastrophic defeat and that Leyte was lost. And yet it took another month of table-thumping argument to have Terauchi's representatives (the field marshal had returned to Saigon on November 17) and Imperial Headquarters in Tokyo accept reality. And even when it was generally acknowledged that Japanese forces should concentrate for the defence of Luzon, there was violent disagreement between the army, air force and navy as to where they should deploy their forces.

Yamashita had some 270,000 troops on Luzon. His objective was to keep them in the field as long as possible, so that they could be used as bargaining chips in the peace negotiations which he now believed to be inevitable. Like MacArthur before him he knew that Lingayen Gulf was the only possible site for a large-scale landing on Luzon, with the exception of Manila Bay. But he had no intention of allowing his forces to be bottled up as MacArthur's had been in 1941, in a defence of the Bataan Peninsula or Manila. Rather he intended to demolish all installations in Manila which might be useful to the Americans and then abandon the city, relying on the garrison of the fortress island of Corregidor to deny the use of Manila Bay to the enemy. He would impose on the Americans the logistic burden of feeding a city of one million starving people. Meanwhile he intended to concentrate his forces well away from the coast and the devastating power of American naval gunfire. There were to be three large group. Shimbu Group, 80,000 strong, was to dig into the mountains directly east of Manila. Kembu Group, 30,000 strong, was to occupy hills 40 miles north of Manila to deny the Americans Clark Field. Shobu Group, 152,000 strong, and with virtually all the armor, was to be based in the rugged northeast of Luzon, from where they could harass any American advance from Lingayen to Manila.

Navy and air force commanders protested vigorously against the abandonment of Manila. Tominaga argued that Manila was the whole purpose of defending Luzon; without Manila it would be pointless. The navy agreed. Manila Bay contained numerous important naval installations – the Cavite naval base, dockyards, and warehouses filled with thousands of tons of stores. Yamashita went ahead with his plans; on December 26 he withdrew his headquarters northeast ward and took direct command of Shobu Group. Over the next ten days, with the support of Imperial Headquarters, he ensured that air and naval forces remaining in Manila were made subordinate to him, at least on paper. Tominaga and the air force finally obeyed orders and began pulling out of the city on January 1. Five days later Rear Admiral Sanji Iwabuchi, the commander of 31st Naval Special Base Force, the formation controlling most naval personnel in Manila, was informed that he too was under the operational control of the army in the person of Lieutenant General Shizuo

Yokoyama, the commander of Shimbu Group. Iwabuchi interpreted 'operational control' as meaning that he would cooperate with the army in certain operations. In the meantime he had a naval program to carry out which was different from that of the army.[99]

On January 9, when the Americans landed at Lingayen, there were still large Japanese forces in Manila. As the army left the city, Vice Admiral Okochi had sent in some 4000 additional naval personnel. This brought the total number of sailors in the city to about 12,500, who were now designated the Manila Naval Defence Force and placed under Iwabuchi's command. Okochi had given Iwabuchi clear instructions. He was to hold the Manila Bay area as long as possible and then carry out extensive demolitions. Iwabuchi organized the sailors – some survivors of naval battles, some belonging to shore establishments – into provisional battalions. Although these were called 'battalions' the emphasis should be on 'provisional' for many were little better than a confederation of armed gangs. They did not know their officers or NCOs and were plagued by indiscipline. In addition, there were still about 4500 army personnel, organized in two bodies – two provisional battalions and supporting troops under Colonel Katsuzo Noguchi stationed in the northern part of the city (Noguchi Force) and a reinforced provisional battalion under Captain Saburo Abe stationed in the south (Abe Force). Like the naval battalions, the army battalions had been cobbled together out of disparate elements but this did not mean they would not fight.

Iwabuchi's sailors had started building defenses in the city in the last week of December, and now the troops of Noguchi Force began helping them. They cut down the tall coconut palms on Dewey Boulevard so it could be used as a runway, and constructed barricades across the major streets. To oppose any American advance from Lingayen into the northern part of the city, Iwabuchi reinforced Noguchi with the First Independent Naval Battalion, which increased the strength of Noguchi Force to about 4500. The admiral now designated this grouping Northern Force and deployed it in a wide arc running west to east through the northern part of the city. Along with the rest of the naval high command, Iwabuchi believed that an American attack from Lingayen was unlikely. Much more likely was a landing to the south, followed by an American thrust to the north through Parañaque to Pasay and Nichols Field. To oppose this, Iwabuchi set up a Southern Force (which included Abe

Force) and placed it under the command of a naval officer, Captain Takusue Furuse. Southern Force was tasked with defending from Hagonoy Isthmus between Manila Bay and Laguna de Bay just south of Parañaque up to Nichols Field and Fort McKinley. It was here that the admiral deployed most of his best artillery, dual-purpose naval guns. Iwabuchi oganized the remainder of Japanese personnel into a Centre Force, which he deployed from Nielson Field back to the Ermita district.[100]

Japanese anxiety about guerrilla attacks increased with every passing day. Suspicion now fell on all European civilians and those Filipinos who had friends and relatives in prison and internment camps. These comprised a large number of people. On morning of December 28 the Kempeitai turned up at the Malate church to arrest three Irish priests, Fathers Kelly, Henaghan and Monaghan, men who had lived quite peacefully throughout the occupation. The Japanese took them to an old Spanish house on the junction of Vito Cruz and M. H. del Pilar, and tortured them until convinced they knew nothing. They then returned the badly injured men to the church.[101]

A few days later José Olbes made his last journey to his office on foot, public transport having stopped altogether. He had to pass through many barriers and at each one was searched and questioned. He remembered it was a very lonely walk. Manileños now tried to go out as little as possible, usually only to search for food. At 8.00 p.m. a few weeks later Olbes answered a knock at his front door. There stood an old friend he had not seen for years, Tony Chanko. Olbes remembered freezing with horror. Chanko was a Filipino but he was also a graduate of West Point and a colonel in the American army. He had infiltrated through Japanese lines in civilian clothes and now asked Olbes to put him up for the night. Olbes had just secreted Chanko in the garage when the Japanese arrived. Olbes recalled 'This was a terrifying moment. If you had pinched me, there would have been no blood.' That night the Olbeses were lucky; the Japanese took away a neighbouring Spanish family.[102]

The McMicking-Hall household was not so lucky. Like many other families they had a short-wave radio and had been listening to American broadcasts. Just before noon on January 20 the family was sitting on the porch when soldiers with fixed bayonets approached from both sides. Somebody may have reported them or it may simply have been a random sweep. The Japanese searched the house and discovered enough to incriminate everyone in it – some radios and some toy guns belonging to Rod and Ian. The Japanese forced Consuelo's mother, Angelina McMicking, to draw up a list of people in the house and then arrested every one named on it. They could not find Consuelo's two youngest children, who had gone to play at a neighbours. They tied the arms of the men, Consuelo's brother Alfred, and Carlos Perez-Rubio, the fiancé of Consuelo's sister Helen, behind their backs. They then marched the McMicking-Hall family – Angelina, Alfred, Helen, Consuelo, her two oldest boys Rod and Ian, along with Carlos Perez-Rubio and Marita Lopez Mena, a family friend staying with the Halls, up Taft Avenue to the Masonic Temple. As they went they were joined by other groups from the neighbourhood, also being shepherded at bayonet point to the Temple. Several hours later in the Temple a Japanese officer separated the children and servants from the adults and released them. It was the last time Rod and Ian saw their mother, grandmother, aunt and uncle. For about the next ten days the Hall children and the servants brought pots of hot food to the gates of the Temple and gave them to the guards to give to the prisoners. On or about January 30 the guards told Rod and Ian to stop coming – the food was no longer needed.[103]

# NOTES

1 Victor Buencamino, *Memoirs of Victor Buencamino* (Manila, 1977), p. 266.
2 Robin Prising, *Manila, Goodbye* (Boston, Mass., 1975), p. 6.
3 Author's interview with Roderick Hall, London, June 28, 1994;
4 Unpublished diary of Alaistair 'Shorty' Hall, entry for January 2, 1942.
5 A.V.H. Hartendorp, *The Japanese Occupation of the Philippines*, Vol. II (Manila, 1957).
6 Author's interview with Sr. José Olbes, Sotogrande, Spain, June 22, 1994.
7 Hall diary, entry for January 5, 1942.
8 Prising, *Manila, Goodbye*, p. 66.
9 Ibid., p. 68.
10 Ibid., p. 152.
11 Robert Coleman Allen, 'Philippine War Diary – A Prison Camp Saga' (Washington DC, 1991), p. 34.
12 Ibid., p. 35.
13 The Santo Tomás Prison Camp Papers
14 Allen, 'Philippine War Diary,' p. 68.
15 Carmen Guerrero Nakpil, *A Question of Identity. Selected Essays* (Manila, 1973), p. 197.
16 Pedro Picornell, 'The Remedios Hospital 1942–1945. A Saga of Malate' (Unpublished), p. 1.
17 Buencamino, *Memoirs of Victor Buencamino*, pp. 310–311.
18 Major General Charles A. *Willoughby, The Guerilla Resistance Movement in the Philippines 1941–1945* (New York, 1972), p. 358.
19 Ibid., p. 359.
20 Arthur Swinson, *Four Samurai: A Quartet of Japanese Commanders in the Second World War* (London, 1968), p. 193.

21 Motoe Terami-Wada, 'Strategy in Culture: Cultural Policy and Propaganda in the Philippines, 1941–45' in Gina V. Barte ed. *Studies on Philippine Art and Society, 1942–45* (Manila, 1992) pp. 23–24.
22 Ibid., p. 26.
23 Olbes interview, June 22, 1994.
24 Motoe Terami-Wada, 'Strategy in Culture' in Barte ed. *Studies on Philippine Art and Society*, p. 25.
25 *Manila Herald*, January 15, 1942.
26 Motoe Terami-Wada, 'Strategy in Culture' in Barte ed. *Studies on Philippine Art and Society*, p. 25.
27 Alfonso J. Aluit, *By Sword and Fire. The Destruction of Manila in World War II, 3 February - 3 March 1945*, (Manila, 1994), p. 154.
28 Motoe Terami-Wada, 'Strategy in Culture' in Barte ed. *Studies on Philippine Art and Society*, pp. 27–28.
29 Aluit, *By Sword and Fire*, p. 132.
30 Ibid., p. 133.
31 Ibid., p. 134.
32 Hall interview, June 28, 1994.
33 Aluit, *By Sword and Fire*, p. 135.
34 Ricardo T. José, *The Japanese Occupation of the Philippines – Sources and Directions* (Manila, 1988), p. 6.
35 Ibid., p. 8.
36 Ibid., p. 6.
37 Ibid., p. 6.
38 Ibid., p. 10.
39 Olbes interview, June 22, 1994.
40 Author's interview with Sr. Enrique Zobel, Sotogrande, Spain, June 22, 1994.
41 Hall correspondence: Consuelo Hall to Alaistair Hall, December 15, 1994.
42 Olbes interview, June 22, 1944.
43 Prising, *Manila, Goodbye*, p. 96.
44 Hall interview, June 28, 1994.
45 R. Constantino, *Under Japanese Rule* (Manila 1991), p. 87.
46 Ibid., p. 88; Zobel interview, June 22, 1994.
47 Olbes interview, June 22, 1944.
48 Constantino, *Under Japanese Rule*, p. 86.
49 Buencamino, *Memoirs*, p. 306.
50 Edgar Krohn and Walter Kühne, *The German Club 1906–1986. A History of the German Community in the Philippines* (Manila, 1986), p. 56.
51 Constantino, *Under Japanese Rule*, p. 223.
52 Ibid., p. 260.

53 Ibid., p. 259.
54 Ibid., p. 261.
55 Olbes interview, June 22, 1994.
56 Zobel interview, June 21, 1994.
57 Olbes interview, June 22, 1994.
58 Hall interview, June 28, 1994.
59 Prising, *Manila, Goodbye*, p. 92.
60 Agustin L. Soto, 'Var and the Aftermath in Philippine Cinema' in Barte ed. *Studies on Philippine Art and Society*, p. 72.
61 Olbes interview, June 22, 1994.
62 Constantino, *Under Japanese Rule*, p. 251.
63 Ibid., p. 251.
64 Hall interview, June 28, 1994.
65 Motoe Terami-Wada, 'Filipino Theatre under the Japanese Occupation' in Barte ed. *Studies on Philippine Art and Society*, p. 133.
66 Ibid., p. 134.
68 Constantino, *Under Japanese Rule*, p. 12; Zobel interview, June 21, 1994; Olbes interview, June 22, 1994.
69 Motoe Terami-Wada, 'Filipino Theatre,' p. 132.
70 Willoughby, *The Guerilla Resistance Movement in the Philippines 1941–1945* (New York, 1972), p. 210.
71 Ray C. Hunt and Bernard Norling, *Behind Japanese Lines* (Lexington, 1986), pp. 79–80.
72 Willoughby, *The Guerilla Resistance Movement in the Philippines 1941–1945*, p. 222.
73 Ibid., p. 226.
74 Swinson, *Four Samurai*, p. 193.
75 John Toland, *The Rising Sun* (New York, 1970), p. 665.
76 Ibid., p. 668.
77 Lieutenant General Akira Muto, 'Battle Report of General Muto,' (or 'Muto Memoirs') G-2 GHQ FEC, Translations of Japanese Documents, Vol. II, Item 20 (Washington DC, 1948) pp. 5–6.
78 Olbes interview, June 22, 1994.
79 Hall interview, June 28, 1994.
80 Olbes interview, June 22, 1994.
81 Willoughby, *The Guerilla Resistance Movement in the Philippines 1941–1945*, p. 427.
82 Prising, *Manila, Goodbye*, p. 149.
83 Peter C. Richards (ed.), *The Liberation Bulletin of Phillipine [sic] Internment Camp No. 1 At Santo Tomas University Manila 3 February 1945*
84 Ibid.
85 Constantino, *Under Japanese Rule*, p. 13; Zobel interview, June 21, 1941.

86 Willoughby, *The Guerilla Resistance Movement in the Philippines 1941–1945*, p. 429.
87 Hall correspondence: Mrs M.J. Hall to Alaistair Hall, May 13, 1944.
88 Olbes interview, June 22, 1944.
89 D. Clayton James, *The Years of MacArthur, 1941–1945*, Vol. II (Boston, Mass., 1975), p. 557.
90 Zobel interview, June 21, 1994.
91 Muto Memoirs, p. 21.
92 Aluit, *By Sword and Fire*, p. 137; Muto Memoirs, p. 21.
93 Constantino, *Under Japanese Rule*, p. 213.
94 A.V.H. Hartendorp, *The Santo Tomas Story* (New York, 1964), pp. 397–400.
95 Hall correspondence: Consuelo Hall to Alaistair Hall, November 8, 1944.
96 Ibid.: Consuelo Hall to Alaistair Hall, December 15, 1944.
97 Aluit, *By Sword and Fire*, p. 150.
98 Muto Memoirs, p. 14.
99 Robert Ross Smith, *United States Army in World War II. The War in the Pacific: Triumph in the Philippines* (Washington DC, 1963), pp. 241–242.
100 Ibid., p. 248.
101 Fr. Arthur Price, *Malate Martyers. The Columban Fathers in Manila before and during the Japanese Occupation 1942–45* (Unpublished paper) p. 6.
102 Olbes interview, June 22, 1994.
103 Hall interview, June 28, 1994.

# 3

# ENVELOPMENT

To the Japanese MacArthur's landing at Lingayen seemed the logical culmination of the twin American offensives from the Central and South West Pacific. In fact, as late as September 1944 the US Joint Chiefs of Staff had not yet decided on the ultimate objective; there was still a school of thought, very influential among the upper echelons of the US Navy, all of whom disliked MacArthur with varying degrees of intensity, that the Philippines should be bypassed altogether. They suggested as an alternative a landing on Formosa. Ever since he had left Corregidor MacArthur had fought for a return to the Philippines. In effect this meant a return to Manila. It was the scene of a defeat which had to be avenged but there were other motives. MacArthur knew of the terrible conditions in which the servicemen he had left behind, and the Allied civilians, were existing. He was supported in his desire to return by his 'Bataan Gang,' the men who had left Corregidor with him on the torpedo boats back in March 1942. Chief of Staff Sutherland and intelligence chief Willoughby were senior members of the gang, but it included in its more junior ranks Joe McMicking, now a lieutenant colonel and even Paul P. Rogers, now a master sergeant and personal assistant to Sutherland.

MacArthur had been a national figure since World War I. He was now a military 'mega-star,' as famous in Axis countries as he was in those of the Allies. In cities as far apart as Sacramento, Brisbane and Auckland parents christened their sons 'Douglas;' in Tokyo and Nagasaki mothers threatened their naughty children with a visit from the dreaded 'Maggada,' the harsh Japanese rendition of his name. Historians have condemned MacArthur's publicity-seeking as the product of a monstrous vanity. He was exceedingly vain, but he was also the first general to understand that the media was a multifaceted weapon which could be used for much more than producing and disseminating propaganda. He understood instinctively what are today called 'media operations.' He used his image not just against the Japanese but also against his superiors in Washington – this image frightened Roosevelt, Marshall and his other enemies into giving him his way. And this, ultimately, was why his armies landed at Lingayen and not on Formosa.

A media policy which focused attention on one individual prevented the Bataan Gang from ever emerging as autonomous personalities. This anonymity extended even to photographs, though occasionally they were caught in the background. There was one photograph, however, which captured the entire gang together. It was, of course, an accident. On October 20, 1944 the landing craft carrying MacArthur, President Osmena, and their staffs ashore at Leyte grounded in the shallows while still 100 yards from the beach. The commander of the craft could not bring it in any closer and so an irritated MacArthur, accompanied by Osmena and their respective staffs, had to wade ashore. An army photographer caught the moment. The picture was published all over the world and became one of the most famous images of World War II. In the picture MacArthur's irritation has become a look of grim determination. The public of the Allied nations saw a supreme commander leading his men ashore in what could well have been the first wave of the invasion. MacArthur was at the heart of the group. To his left were Sutherland and Willoughby, and to his right Osmena, while immediately behind Osmena came Lieutenant Colonel Joe McMicking.

Beyond the immediate Gang were two army commanders who had joined MacArthur in Australia. Lieutenant General Robert Eichelberger had been superintendent at West Point from 1940 to 1942, before flying to Brisbane in September 1942. He now commanded the US Eighth Army. In February 1943 German-born Lieutenant General Walter Krueger arrived in Brisbane to take command of the Sixth Army. Eichelberger and Krueger had developed uneasy relationships with MacArthur. Both were aware of MacArthur's obsession with being the focus of media attention though both were ambitious generals in their own right. They welcomed and craved publicity and recognition, but neither was prepared to cross MacArthur in search of it. When asked to provide his biographical details for use in a minor radio broadcast, Krueger replied: 'I should much prefer to have you drop the matter.' Similarly, Eichelberger once said: 'I would rather have you slip a rattlesnake in my pocket than to have you give me any publicity.'

While Eichelberger and Krueger had little option other than to concede primacy to MacArthur, both wanted to fill the second slot in the SWPA Command. They competed savagely with each other, and the competition festered into dislike (more so Eichelberger of Krueger than vice versa). MacArthur did, on very rare occasions, allow some publicity to percolate down, fully aware that he would bask in its reflected glory. On the occasion when Krueger appeared on the front cover of *Time*, Eichelberger's jealousy reached boiling point. In one of his daily letters to 'Miss Em,' his wife, he confided:

> If he is a great general or has any of the elements of greatness then I am no judge of my fellow man. Beyond a certain meanness, which scares those under him, and a willingness to work, he has little to offer. He doesn't even radiate courage, which is one thing we like to think a soldier has.

MacArthur recognized the competition and exploited it savagely. On one occasion while Eichelberger was visiting MacArthur's headquarters, they walked out on to the veranda. MacArthur, seeing Krueger below, sitting in his jeep, waiting his turn, ostentatiously put his arm over Eichelberger's shoulders. Eichelberger needed MacArthur's approval and obeyed him almost slavishly. Krueger was not so intensely committed to pleasing MacArthur, and on occasion would say no. In fact Krueger could irritate MacArthur so much so that Sutherland tried to persuade MacArthur to sack him; the chief of staff lived in hope of one day achieving command of the Sixth Army.

When the first of the Sixth Army's 200,000 troops landed at Lingayen on January 9, 1945 they met very little resistance. Since the beginning of the month Willoughby had been convinced that Yamashita now had only about 150,000 men left on Luzon. Shortly after the landing intelligence picked up signals that the Japanese were evacuating Manila. This was all MacArthur needed. On January 12 he urged Krueger to make an immediate dash for the city. Krueger's intelligence officers disagreed with Willoughby's assessment. They had concluded that the Japanese were very much stronger – at least 250,000. The ease of the Lingayen landing was deceptive. Krueger believed his own officers and reasoned that a mad dash to Manila was the very thing Yamashita wanted him to do. Once he had extended his comunications the 120 miles from Lingayen to Manila the wily Japanese general would strike. Krueger refused to move, insisting on waiting until his forces were fully established. After two weeks at loggerheads the tension between the supreme commander and the commander of the Sixth Army was palpable.

While the buildup continued Krueger's 43d and 25th divisions advanced rapidly to the northeast and were soon heavily engaged with part of Shobu Group. This only served to confirm Krueger's apprehension that if he were to advance on Manila, the Japanese to the northeast would advance across his line of communication and cut him off from Lingayen. And then, on January 23, 40th Division, advancing cautiously to the southwest, ran into Kembu Group just to the north of Clark Field. Krueger was now convinced that Manila was the bait in a trap.

At the end of January MacArthur's 65th birthday had come and gone. It had not been celebrated in Manila as intended. Still widely discussed, and the subject of detailed planning, was a massive media event in the style of a Champs-Elysées parade, when American forces, with MacArthur at their head, would make a triumphal entry into central Manila (see Appendix). There was the hope that General Yamashita would declare Manila an open city, just as MacArthur had done, but there was no hard evidence as to how the unknown quantity of the Japanese military in the city would react. There was therefore no detailed plan as to how Manila was to be taken. Supremely flexible, what passed as a plan consisted of an advance to contact, followed by suitable reactions according to the circumstances.

The 1st Cavalry Division had landed at San Fabian on Lingayen Gulf on January 27 and established their administrative base at Guimba some 42 miles inland and southeast of San Fabian. The division was assigned to Major General Oscar Griswold's XIV Corps. On January 31 MacArthur visited the 1st Cavalry and, during the course of his visit, said to the division's commander, Major General Vernon D. Mudge: 'Get to Manila! Go around the Japs, bounce off the Japs, save your men, but get to Manila! Free the internees at Santo Tomás. Take Malacañan Palace and the Legislative Building.'[1]

What MacArthur had asked of Mudge was a 100-mile operational dash through enemy-occupied territory, without so much as the benefit of 24-hour advance reconnaissance or flank protection. During daylight hours, Army spotter planes and Marine fighters would be available for tasking. General Mudge's plan, given to his commanders without the benefit of notes, involved the formation of what has been variously described as 'serials' or 'flying columns.' Three of these blacked-out, all-arms battle groups, with integral service support, crossed their start line: they began at one minute after midnight on February 1, leaving the remainder of the division to follow on behind at best speed.

The day before MacArthur's visit to the 1st Cavalry he had called on the 37th Infantry Division, which was ahead of the 1st Cavalry and advancing from Clark Field (where XIV Corps' other division, the 40th, was in occupation) southeast, toward Calumpit. Dissatisfied with progress and 'lack of drive,' MacArthur sent a note of protest to Krueger. This accounts for MacArthur's behavior the next day when he directly tasked one of Griswold's divisions.

It seems that Griswold was content for the two divisions on the road to fight it out as to who would be the first to enter Manila while staying on their separate lines of advance. Although the 1st Cavalry was a late entrant in the race, it was represented by three flying columns, smaller, lighter and more highly mechanized entities, led by Brigadier General William C. Chase. That much was recognized by the 37th Division's commander, Major General Robert S. Beightler, who wrote of the dash from the north: 'It was rather one sided. The First Cavalry had been provided with completely motorized equipment and it rode to Manila. The 37th Division slogged along on foot – the whole, weary, hot, dusty, fighting 150 miles from Lingayen to Manila.'[2]

But the race was not just between Griswold's two divisions, for a combined airborne and infantry force was approaching from the south. The second part of the pincer movement was put in place on January 31 with the landing on the beaches of Nasugbu, 30 miles southwest of Cavite, of Major General Joseph Swing's 11th

Airborne Division, less one regiment but including two battalions of the 24th Division. Of the tactical significance of this landing, MacArthur wrote:

> This operation places the Eighth Army on the south side of Manila which is now the centre of the converging columns of the Sixth and Eighth Armies. It largely seals off the possibility of the enemy troops south of Manila joining those to the north and definitely outflanks the enemy's defence lines in southern Luzon.[3]

At the time the communiqué was written, however, MacArthur had no intention of allowing Eichelberger to go on north to Manila. Intelligence advised of significant numbers of enemy troops on Tagaytay Ridge and it was only thus far that Eichelberger had the written authority to conduct a reconnaissance in force. Eichelberger's letters reveal he had no intention of stopping at Tagaytay Ridge. Just as General Clark had been drawn to Rome, Eichelberger was drawn to Manila, and he convinced himself that this was MacArthur's intention all along. His interpretation of MacArthur's oral instructions was creative: he assumed he would be allowed to press on beyond Tagaytay Ridge if circumstances permitted.

General Eichelberger was fortunate indeed to have in Major General Joe Swing's 11th Airborne Division one of the most professional divisions in the Philippines. It was certainly the smallest, half the size of the 37th. It was well led from top to bottom, had high morale and lots of élan. It was the instrument Eichelberger was personally backing to get the Eighth Army to Manila before the Sixth. Eichelberger's XI Corps, which had landed earlier, northwest of Subic Bay, 80 miles from Manila by road, on the southwestern coast of the province of Zambales, was virtually unsupervised by Eighth Army Headquarters. It was left in the capable hands of the corps' commander, Major General Charles Hall. If Swing's 11th Airborne Division was to succeed, it would depend upon surprise and speed of action to keep the Japanese off their guard. Other than a few jeeps and echelon vehicles, it had no transport of its own for, as a composite parachute and glider division, its role was to land on or near to its target. Realistically, the senior commanders must have known that if the momentum of the advance was allowed to slacken, or the division came up against well-prepared defenses, then it could not reach Manila. Eichelberger chaperoned Swing, although Swing was entirely convinced of Eichelberger's insistence on speed, even to the extent of setting aside time-consuming, indirect fire support.

Other than interference from Shinyo midget suicide boats which sank a USN patrol craft, the landing went ahead virtually unopposed and the division fanned out to the east. The vital Palico River bridge, five miles inland crossing a gorge over 250 feet wide and 85 feet deep, was seized from Japanese engineers preparing its demolition. With the bridge in their hands, the division now had access to the well-constructed, two-lane concrete road leading from Nasugbu to the strategically vital Tagaytay Ridge, and in their first day advanced 15 miles.

Route 17 climbed for 20 miles up to the dominating mountainous feature of the ridge. Once this had been passed, the road then ran downhill all the way into Manila. However, there were problems. The tanks and tracked artillery were almost out of fuel and would soon be unable to support the infantry. As Eichelberger told his wife in a letter dated February 3: 'I was informed that we only had one day's supply of 80 octane gasoline. This was partly due to the fact that we have had a terrific uphill pull for the motors since Tagaytay is 2000 feet above the ocean and there is a steady pull all the way.'

This logistic problem had further tactical significance, for the planned drop of the 511th Parachute Infantry Regiment behind enemy lines on Tagaytay Ridge could only go ahead if the juncture of the two groups could be assured within 24 hours. Meanwhile the ground attack, supported by P-38s and A-20s, made unexpectedly good progress against demoralized Japanese, who broke up into small groups which, in the months that followed, were sought out and killed. The parachute drop went ahead, but the second battalion to be dropped made no contribution to the tactical situation because the first battalion, which fought the battle, was dropped six miles off target. The pilots, seeing the parachutes on the ground, dropped the second battalion in the same place. (Therefore the second battalion was too late to influence events on the ground.) The Air Corps blamed the paras for their lack of jump discipline but:

The true reason was the refusal of the Air Force to cooperate in a combined training program for Airborne and Air Force troops, and it is sad indeed to note at the time of writing – over a year after the TAGAYTAY RIDGE jump – that the same losing battle to secure combined training is being once again fought by the division.[4]

Tagaytay Ridge had been secured in two days against weak opposition. By the time a juncture of the road and air-inserted forces had been achieved, sufficient additional transport had come over the beaches to transport an entire battalion and to operate a motor shuttle to resume an unauthorized advance on Manila with Eichelberger among the leading units.

From Tagaytay we could see Manila shining whitely in the bright Luzon sun. The curved forefinger of Cavite Peninsula hooked into Manila Bay. At first we were jubilant about getting to see Manila, the Pearl of the Orient, the first city we had seen since we left San Francisco almost a year before. But ominously fire began to break out all over the city.[5]

Swing's force was also supplemented by taking under command the 2000 guerrillas in the provinces of Batangas and Cavite.[6] Commanding one of Terry Hunter's ROTC divisions (the men were drawn from the under-aged members of the well-known colleges in Manila and reserve officers) was Lieutenant Colonel Emmanuel V. de Ocampo. (The guerrilla unit was formed in early 1942 by Miguel Ver. When Ver was captured, command was assumed by Eleuterio 'Terry' Adevoso, whose *nom de guerre* was 'Magtanggol' ('defender' or 'protector'). The guerrillas officially named themselves 'Hunter's ROTC Guerrillas.' Eventually they became known as 'The Hunters.') Ocampo fought all the way the 64 miles through Nasugbu to the General Post Office on the Pasig River. The Americans knew of the guerrillas before they landed and, for their part, the guerrillas, in direct radio communication with the Americans, knew exactly who and what was coming over the beaches. Therefore there were no suspicions harbored by the Americans or doubts as to the guerrillas' *bona fides*.

When the paras met opposition they bypassed it: when they came to the Parañaque River, they crossed it until, just south of Nichols Field on February 5, on the outskirts of Manila, they met fierce opposition.

Roads were heavily mined with 500 pound aerial bombs armed with low pressure detonators. Mutually supporting concrete pillboxes defended each block. A captured document identified the enemy defenses as the Japanese-styled Genko Line, designed to defend Manila against the originally expected American landing in southern Luzon.[7]

The pillboxes, some of them two or three storeys, extended to a depth of 6000 yards, stretching from Nichols Field (the site of today's international airport) to the high ground along Laguna de Bay with its rear on the high ground of Fort McKinley. Within the concrete emplacements were five and six-inch naval guns and 150mm mortars facing south, supported by 20mm, 40mm and 90mm cannon. A glider-infantry company commander radioed division headquarters saying: 'Tell Admiral Halsey to stop looking for the Jap Fleet. It's dug in here on Nichols Field.'[8] Communiqués from MacArthur's headquarters led the Japanese to believe a more substantial force was advancing from the south and, as a consequence, they reinforced the Genko Line. Clearly the nut was too big for one airborne division to crack, and heavy artillery was called forward from XIV Corps.[9]

One aspect of the Sixth Army's concern was the absence of a boundary between them and the Eighth, and the latter were not revealing a great deal to the former:

Furthermore, the only operational report covering the disposi- tions of the 11th Airborne Division was the daily Eighth Army operations report, which was quite general in nature. As a result neither force, as it advanced, was sure of the intents or current dispositions of the other.[10]

But Eichelberger felt similarly aggrieved. In a letter to his wife dated 6 February, he complained: 'The steady refusal of the Sixth Army to send me any information of our friendly troops indicates to me that they are not really in town or they would tell me.'

He then stretches a point by adding: 'As you know, Nichols Field is right in Manila.' Obviously the situation was unsatisfactory.

Here, against the Genko Line, the 11th Airborne's chances of being the first into Manila evaporated. The division lost 900 men killed, wounded or missing in this operation, two-thirds of whom were glider regiment men who landed in Nasugbu and became casualties caught out in the open on Nichols Field. An observation post in the airfield's water tower brought down effective fire upon the attackers. Their progress to this point, advancing 45 miles in 104 hours, had certainly been a source of concern for Krueger's headquarters. After visiting Sixth Army Headquarters, Major General William C. Dunkel wrote to Eichelberger:

> When you were pushing on Manila so rapidly, I visited Sixth Army Headquarters and found them greatly agitated over the fact that you would be in Manila before they were, and I believe to this day that we could have saved more of Manila if they had given you the means of coming in by way of Nasugbu.[11]

General Dunkel raises an interesting, strategic question here. Could more of Manila have been saved if Eichelberger had been given the 'means' of coming in by way of Nasugbu? It seems unlikely. The two-lane approach road climbing up through wooded, mountainous slopes from Nasugbu to Tagaytay Ridge would have become the focus of sterner and more effective Japanese resistance than it did. Even if an infantry division or corps had been preferred to 11th Airborne, the delivery of the significant amount of additional logistics over the shore would have imposed a substantial time penalty – something not experienced by General Swing's division. It is also reasonable to speculate that a stronger force seen to be approaching from the south would have triggered an even greater reciprocal reinforcement of the Genko Line. These troops would have been army men drawn from the Shimbu Group and not from Rear Admiral Iwabuchi's Naval Defense Force in Manila. The conclusion is that although it seems improbable, the 11th Airborne, through speed of action, amazing improvisation and surprise, achieved rather more in the available time than could have been achieved by a conventional formation.

On February 10, the 11th Airborne Division passed from the Eighth to the Sixth Army's control. The next day, their advance through the city was halted by XIV Corps, their new corps head-quarters. On 17 February, assisted by heavy napalm strikes, they seized Fort McKinley, and that concluded a phase of the division's operations in Luzon during which time they killed 5210 Japanese. Working in cooperation with the 1st Cavalry Division they had thereby cut the Manila Naval Defense Force's escape and reinforce-ment routes. They had destroyed the Third Naval Battalion, isolated the Abe Battalion prior to moving against it, and prepared to clear the Cavite region. And it is at this stage that we shall return to February 1 and operations to the north of the city.

The advance of the 1st Cavalry's serials was so designed that they would all make rendezvous at the village of Cabanatuan. There was a prisoner of war camp close to the town, where many of the survivors of the Bataan death march were incarcerated. By June 1943 over half of them had died.[12] It had been attacked the day before by a group from 6th Ranger Battalion and guerrillas who set the 500 Allied prisoners free. The Japanese garrison was therefore alert and prepared for the next American visitation. Their resistance was brushed aside and the important Valdefuente Bridge over the wide Pampanga River fell into Cavalry hands before the charges would be blown. It was one of a number of bridges prepared for demolition and captured intact. In daylight, the column averaged 15–20 miles an hour. A regimental history identified three important factors in the mission's favour: the hot, clear though dusty weather; the flat terrain; and 'General MacArthur's intuitive sense of how the Japanese planned to defend Luzon.'[13]

On February 1 the 1st Cavalry paused briefly in Cabanatuan. MacArthur's head of counterintelligence, Brigadier General Elliott Thorpe, sent two suitably disguised officers on ahead into Manila. Lieutenant Colonel John (Jack) N. Irwin II and the Sixth Army's counterintelligence chief, Major Blair Labatt, were to locate Japanese Headquarters and, once there, collect documents and talk to people about the enemy, particularly what they had done or were going to do. A subsidiary task was to build up a dossier on collaborators and propose what action should be taken against them. 'It was,' said Irwin, 'a difficult and unhappy task.'

In Cabanatuan Mudge designated the serials 'flying columns' and they departed that village at dawn on February 2. At a point just north of Manila at Plaridel, where Highway Three (along which 37th Division was moving) meets Highway Five (along which the 1st Cavalry were moving) the heavy infantry were forced to deploy to deal with a reinforced enemy infantry battalion lying astride their path. No sooner had the opposition been dealt with and the road re-opened than the Cavalry went streaming through and on toward Manila. The skirmishing and fighting through objectives continued into the next day until at 6.35 p.m. on February 3, the 1st Cavalry Division crossed the line of the city limits to claim the title 'First in Manila.' General Beightler ruefully recorded: 'We got to Manila a few hours after the First Cavalry.'[14]

The Cavalry fanned out to accomplish the missions given to them by MacArthur. The presidential Malacañan Palace proved a simple task since it was guarded by only a Filipino Presidential Guard battalion. They received the Americans with exchanges of salutes and a great deal of back-thumping all round. The Legislative Building was never reached. It is situated on the south side of the Pasig River, 190 yards southeast of Intramuros on Burgos Street and about 110 yards from City Hall. When the Cavalry arrived at the intersection of Azcarraga and Quezon Boulevard, about 440 yards from Santo Tomás, on their way to the Pasig to cross the Quezon Bridge, they met with fierce resistance from the well-entrenched defenders barricaded in the nearby Far Eastern University. The entire force beat a hasty retreat from the ambush site. Chase ordered the column to converge on Santo Tomás University, its mission unaccomplished. It had been one building too far. Why MacArthur included this building in his three objectives can perhaps be answered that, by occupying it, he could thereby announce that he had captured the seat of government. He had carefully planned his triumphant entry into the city, culminating precisely at the Legislative Building. He perhaps wished to ensure that the building was secure so the orders for his grand reception, prepared on February 2, 1945, could be implemented.

It is important to emphasize that the Cavalry had three missions. Historians have argued that the Santo Tomás operation was an American operation to save American lives. No nation could have been expected to have done otherwise, yet it bears repeating that the relief of Santo Tomás was but one of three goals, two of which were satisfactorily achieved.

The main body assigned to the university internment camp had the good fortune to be met on the outskirts of the city by two Filipino guerrillas who previously had served as scouts to the US Army. Sceptical at first, the Americans subjected the senior of the two, Captain Manuel Colayco, to intensive interrogation, until their doubts were allayed. Colayco had detailed knowledge of the Japanese defenses of northern Manila and was able to bypass the mined areas, bringing the lead column to the front gate of Santo Tomás. It was here that, sadly, Colayco was mortally wounded. Elsewhere in the city, starting with the port area on February 1, the Japanese, aided by the Makapili, set fire to their own stores and ammunition as a prelude to an intensification of wider, planned torching of the city. Rear Admiral Iwabuchi ordered his men: 'You must carry out effective suicide action as members of special attack units to turn the tide of battle by intercepting the attacking enemy at Manila.'[15] The sky that evening produced a remarkable and memorable red sunset which some saw as an omen of what was about to befall their city. The occupiers of Paris had been ordered to set fire to and destroy the city but disobeyed; as will be seen, the occupiers of Manila had been ordered not to set fire to and destroy the city but disobeyed.

Over the previous three years, one prisoner in Santo Tomás had become universally loathed – a Briton from the garden county of Worcestershire called Ernest Stanley. He arrived in Manila a few weeks before Pearl Harbor. Stanley spoke Japanese fluently and, because of this, became a rather obvious intermediary between the commandant and the internees. He lived apart from the prisoners in the Japanese commandanture, only having contact with the internees when it was necessary to pass instructions to their Executive Committee. Another man, Tobo, annoyed the internees considerably through his officiousness. Tobo, a longtime Japanese resident in the Philippines, was responsible for the camp's so-called 'package line,' the reception at the gate where servants and friends left food, laundry and messages for the internees. These two mysterious men, as we shall see, probably saved the lives of Santo Tomás' internees.[16]

The internees knew from the increased air sorties against Japanese facilities in the city and the sound of gunfire coming ever closer, that they would soon know whether they were to live or die. For some, it was no longer an issue. Even if some were spared the cruel attention of their Japanese guards, they were so far gone as to be beyond recovery. But the Japanese did realize that for them the writing was on the wall. The Commandant, Lieutenant Colonel Toshio Hayashi, attempted to pressurize Dr. Stevenson, the camp's senior medical officer, to delete the words 'starvation' and 'malnutrition' as causes of death on death certificates, insisting that the causes of death had been 'heart failure.' Ninety percent of the camp's deaths were starvation-related. The doctor's refusal to comply saw him placed on a 20-day starvation diet. But all this could not dispel the air of anticipation and excitement which ran throughout this camp of brutalized people, patiently awaiting their salvation. And then there came a positive sign. Just before dusk on February 3, a flight of P-38s seemingly flew deliberately low over the prison. Those below could see the pilots' reassuring smiles and a small object fell to the ground. It was a case for pilot's goggles, and inside was a message in code, taken from two popular contemporary songs: 'Roll out the barrel. There'll be a hot time in the old town tonight.' (There are within the literature at least three different versions of this message.) The Japanese might have had trouble deciphering the lyrics' meaning, but the American and British internees knew immediately what was going on.[17] The flying column was already at the city limits.

Unusually, at 6.30 p.m., the Japanese put out the camp lights. Prisoners jammed into the main lobby, unsettled and agitated like a herd of cattle before the storm, listening for what at first was a low, consistent sound interspersed by random explosions, until they could be certain. As if in a symphony of war, the heavy percussion had been joined by the continuous rumble of closing tanks. Then, at approximately 9 p.m., a burst of machine-gun fire was heard at the gate, followed by a huge explosion, after which a tank of the 44th Tank Battalion of the 1st Cavalry Division, its searchlight feeling out through the darkness, entered the front compound. Written on its turret, as though to confirm the wildest hopes of the internees that it was indeed American, were the words 'Battlin' Basic,' soon to be joined by 'Georgia Peach' and three others in quick succession.

There are various reports describing what happened next, but one of the more accurate has to be a composite prepared by the Civil Censorship Detachment, which checked all the internees' mail after their liberation:

A US Army nurse lifted her nose high in the air. 'That smells like GI gasoline,' she screamed. Immediately the cry resounded from all sides, 'The Americans are coming.' A shot was heard outside the door and the thud of a falling body – the Japanese guard. A heavy boot crashed the door open and a belligerent voice yelled, 'Are there any God damned Japs in there?' It was difficult for the prisoners to believe what they saw, in spite of this brawny, determined looking young United States soldier, carbine pointed menacingly in front of him. The uncertainty of them all was fully expressed by one elderly woman. Weak and feeble but with tears of happiness in her eyes, she touched his arm and said, 'Soldier, are you real?' She was met with the laconic reply, 'Yes, I reckon I am.' And thus was ended three years of illness, starvation and torture.[18]

A wave of excited screaming, clapping and cheering bodies flowed into the yard and over the tanks that stood in front of them. The crew found themselves submerged in a sea of instantaneously released emotions as hysterical, weeping and ecstatic people unashamedly poured out their feelings of relief and gratitude. As soon as they had recovered their composure and breath there was a spontaneous and emotional rendition of 'God Bless America,' followed by 'The Star-Spangled Banner.' But elsewhere throughout the campus the 200 soldiers who had arrived with the column were engaged in clearing through their objective. Theirs was a most precarious position, since it was highly vulnerable to counterattack until reinforced by the other Cavalry columns yet to arrive. The prisoners' main tormentor, a sadistic officer called Lieutenant Abiko, had rushed out in front of Battlin' Basic with sword and pistol drawn, but received a mortal wound in the stomach. He died slowly and painfully:

> Now groaning and writhing on the ground, he was seized by the legs and dragged to the main building clinic, internees kicking and spitting at him, one or two men even slashing him with knives, and some women burning him with cigarets (sic) as he was pulled past them.[19]

An American officer shouted out through his bullhorn: 'Where is Mr Stanley?' Quite naturally the assembled prisoners thought that, at last, the quisling in their midst would get his just deserts. They were not prepared for what happened next when Stanley emerged from the shadows. 'Mr Stanley, how glad we are to see you,' said the officer, who took from his jeep a helmet and a rifle which he handed to Stanley. It transpired that Stanley was operating an intelligence cell through the officious Tobo, who turned out to be a Nisei-American citizen planted as a hairdresser in the Quiapo market district area of Manila 16 years earlier. Tobo's job in the 'package line' was to act as linkman between Stanley and the guerrillas. It is reasonable to speculate that the flying column was dispatched so urgently to Santo Tomás as a result of some intelligence that had come into Stanley's hands. With the Japanese pulling out north of the Pasig comes a chilling reflection that the camp authority may have intended to massacre the internees.[20]

The bulk of the prison's military and civilian staff withdrew to the Education Building. They had offices on the ground floor while the prisoners had accommodation upstairs. The 63 Japanese now barricaded in the building held its 267 internees as hostages. When one of the prisoners, Walter Hoffman Diehl, told the Americans about the hostages, the exchange of fire ceased and preparations for negotiation began.

Just before first light, camp fires at the front and rear of the building lit up the darkness, followed by the tempting smell of ham and eggs percolating hypnotically through the building. This was a mouth-watering torment to the internees and, despite being low on both ammunition and rations, the cavalrymen generously shared their last remaining K rations with the men, women and children.

The standoff between the Cavalry and the Japanese in the Education Building continued through to the night of February 4, when Colonel Brady and the British interpreter, Ernest Stanley, met Hayashi face to face.

He demanded that his men be freed with all of their automatic weapons, grenades and individual arms. Lengthy talks followed (involving Brigadier-General Chase), after which it was finally agreed that if the internees were left unharmed, Colonel Hayashi and his men, carrying only individual arms, would be escorted through the front lines and released.[21]

At 7 a.m. on February 5 the prisoners, dressed in the best of what remained available, jeered Hayashi and his men when they came out of the Education Building accompanied by Ernest Stanley and an American escort. It was the wish of the Japanese that they be escorted to the Sampaloc Rotunda, from which Aviles Street leads to Malacañan Palace. Exchanging salutes at the Rotunda, the Americans returned to Santo Tomás and the Japanese, unaware of the tactical changes in the city, marched up Aviles Street towards the palace and into the gun-sights of the surprised American guards. Hayashi and a number behind him were killed, while the rest dispersed among the buildings. Meanwhile, at Santo Tomás, a large Stars and Stripes was unfurled over the balcony of the main building. The internees strove to overcome their emotions to sing

'God Bless America.' Perhaps it was reasonable for them to feel secure, but most of Manila was still in Japanese hands, and not one part of the city was beyond the range of their guns. Santo Tomás, with its tower surmounted by a cross, was a very easily identifiable target; the establishment of gun lines in the ground made it even more conspicuous. Japanese shells started to rain down, killing and maiming the hapless internees – a cruel end to the hopes of those who had suffered 37 months of imprisonment.

The killing of Filipino civilians by the Japanese military was already in an advanced state. Referring to a massacre conducted on Friday and Saturday, February 2–3, 37th Division's history records:

> The Japs in Tondo had told the Filipinos early in 1942: 'The Americans have gone. You will never see them again.' Now they intended to keep their part of the pledge, and if they could not prevent the Americans from returning they could and did drag men, women and children by the score into the Paco Lumber Yard along Moriones and Juan Luna Avenue, and beside the arms of the estuaries, bind them, bayonet them, shoot them and slash their throats and bellies. [More than 100 civilians died here.][22] Their bodies bearing the ghastly wounds, were left to rot in the sunshine, or were covered with gasoline and partly burned.[23]

Pushing on on February 4 toward the Pasig, American infantry came across the yellow wings of Bilibid prison. The prisoners had been given freedom of a kind by the commandant, Major Ebiko, who, with his men, had packed up and gone to a new assignment. The prisoners had been left food and medicine and warned of the dangers of venturing outside the prison. A sign in English erected by the prison gate read: 'Lawfully released Prisoners of War and Internees are quartered here. Please do not molest them unless they make positive resistance.' However, with much of the residential area north of the Pasig on fire and active snipers in the streets, the military and civilian prisoners needed no encouragement to stay put. When the Americans arrived they found 1275 internees – 447 civilian and 828 military.

When the prisoners of war gazed on their rescuers, they suddenly realized how much the world had changed during their three years in confinement:

What amazed us most about the 7th Cavalry [more likely infantry of 37th Infantry Division] contingent was their apparent youthfulness, their new helmets, which we had never seen before, and their combat uniforms that resembled the dungarees we wore before the war. The carbines they carried were an entirely new development. The number and variety of grenades, knives, pistols and other combat equipment they carried astounded us all.[24]

The setting fire to northern Manila by Colonel Noguchi's Northern Sector Unit of the Manila Naval Defense Force was a key component in the Japanese strategy of delaying the Americans so as to give them extra time to prepare their defenses south of the Pasig. The 37th Division's historian takes up the story:

Buildings which the enemy had charged with dynamite were blowing up as the fire reached them. The conflagration restricted the movement of our troops and added effectiveness to the Japanese machine gun and 20mm fire coming from the pillboxes emplaced at virtually every corner. However, these tactics of destruction backfired on the enemy when the Second Battalion killed more than two hundred Japanese flushed out from cover by the fire.[25]

An inferno raged around Bilibid prison. The 37th Division attempted to evacuate the internees through the bullet-swept streets – a mission which seemed destined to slaughter more than it saved. A fortuitous change of wind direction, however, meant that the 37th could return the prisoners to the relative security of their gaol.

MacArthur was by now itching to get into Manila. The 37th were tasked on the night of February 4–5 with conducting the route reconnaissance to bring the Commander in Chief along Route 5 and over the river into the 1st Cavalry's area. By this time the 1st Cavalry had been encircled and, somewhat embarrassingly, their entry point, the bridge at Novaliches, blown by the Japanese. MacArthur's motor column was forced to turn round; he had to wait for another opportunity. Meanwhile the 37th, 'upon request,' made contact with the 1st Cavalry, 'thus having the satisfaction of rescuing these forward elements who were "first in Manila."'[26]

It must have come as something of a surprise to those still knocking on Manila's door to hear MacArthur declare: 'At 6.30 this morning (Tuesday, February 6) Manila had fallen,' and further to read in *Time* magazine that Manila had fallen 'like a ripe plum.' An Associated Press report, dateline Luzon, February 5, declared:

> American troops reached the heart of Manila yesterday and raised the Stars and Stripes over the greatest Philippine capital for the first time in more than three years. Yanks of the hard-hitting 1st Cavalry Division, in a wide encircling movement by dark entered the city Saturday night against harassing sniper fire and quickly captured Malacañan Palace and the large Santo Tomás concentration camp where thousands of American and British civilians may be interned.[27]

In *Reminiscences* MacArthur qualifies his statement by saying that he meant Manila had fallen 'for all strategic purposes.'[28] He was not to enter Manila until the next day and, for a fallen city, tens of thousands, principally Filipinos, were still to die before the month was out. *Reminiscences* records in detail the congratulatory messages from the great and the good in response to the news which MacArthur had been perhaps a little overeager to release.

MacArthur's mask of command would allow no public display of emotion. However, he was clearly moved by the first visits he made to the prison camps. When he began his program he went first to Santo Tomás, still being targeted by Japanese guns. On that day alone, 22 people were killed and 39 wounded. MacArthur, who had witnessed a lifetime of emotional scenes, described this as the most moving of all:

> When I arrived, the pitiful, half-starved inmates broke out in excited yells. I entered the building and was immediately pressed back against the wall by thousands of emotionally charged people. In their ragged, filthy clothes, with tears streaming down their faces, they seemed to be using their last strength to fight their way close enough to grasp my hand . . . They wept and laughed hysterically, and all of them at once tried to tell me 'thank you.' I was grabbed by the jacket. I was kissed. I was hugged. It was a wonderful and never to be forgotten moment – to be a life-saver, not a life taker.[29]

Bilibid presented a set of different emotions. The visit to the civilian wing was less exuberant than that at Santo Tomás, no doubt reflecting the influence of a more formal regime. Natalie Crouter, her husband and 15-year-old daughter June were there at the time:

> When the General passed the bunk, he turned and looked into my face directly. He grabbed my hand and shook it, over and over, up and down. I could not say a word and just looked back at him speechless as we pumped our arms up and down, up and down. All of the last three years were in my mind and face and, at this actual moment of release, the biggest moment of my life, I felt no joy or relief, only deep sadness which could not come into words . . . He was sincerely comprehending of my strained face which showed what all of us had suffered . . . He was deeply shocked and sorry for all of us, and looked it without trying to say so. For this I was grateful.[30]

There is no information available to compare the lot of the civilians in Santo Tomás with that of those in Bilibid. There is a record of an officer, Captain William Montgomery, being transferred from Bilibid to Santo Tomás' hospital.

> One major characteristic that came to my attention almost as soon as I came in contact with the first interned person I met was the amount of tension that had generated within the confines of the institution, where no *esprit de corps* or pride of organization had been developed, where it was every man for himself and his children and wife . . . There were those who had enough, and those who were denied access to enough.[31]

The internees in Santo Tomás were bound to be divided economically and socially among themselves. Internment brought together the social extremes of the expatriate community. A managing director would be found bedded down in the same room as one of his junior employees. That these social divisions remained in place was sure to be irksome and divisive. Margaret Sams was to write after the war:

> Having just read Frederic Stevens' and A.V.H. Hartendorp's records of internment [in addition to the two massive volumes of *The Japanese Occupation of the Philippines*, Hartendorp wrote

*The Santo Tomás Story*] I now know for sure what I surmised was true. Those men had no idea in the world that there were many of us who were literally starving.[32]

The division within the camp was there but it seems not to have been recognized as such. Hartendorp was a conscientious practising journalist who took himself very seriously and would have been upset if he thought he had not taken a proper perspective. General Carlos P. Romulo said of the camp's historian, 'he was never trivial or mediocre.'

Of all the crosses MacArthur had to bear, none was heavier than his departure from Corregidor to safety while his men on the island and in Bataan were left to face certain death or long captivity as prisoners of the Japanese. It is true that MacArthur was ordered to escape by the President, and it is equally true it came good in the end when he fulfilled his promise to return. However, it is also true that among the abandoned, the number of the aggrieved far exceeded the number of the philosophical. The men whom MacArthur was about to meet in Bilibid were those very people he had been obliged to leave behind.

I looked down the lines of men, bearded and soiled, with hair that often reached below their shoulders, with ripped and soiled shirts and trousers, with toes sticking out of such shoes as remained, with suffering and torture written on their gaunt faces. Here was all that was left of my men of Bataan and Corregidor. The only sound was the occasional sniffle of a grown man who could not fight back the tears. As I passed slowly down the scrawny, suffering column, a murmur accompanied me as each man, barely speaking above a whisper, said 'you're back!' or 'you made it!' or 'God bless you.' I could only reply, 'I'm a little late, but we finally came.'[33]

Thus ended one part of the mission given originally to the 1st Cavalry on behalf of the Sixth Army to release the prisoners of war and internees on Luzon.

The 37th Infantry Division in capturing Bilibid prison released more than 800 prisoners of war and about 500 civilian internees including women and children. With the 3700 internees from Santo Tomás released by the 1st Cavalry Division, this brings the total rescued to approximately 5000. About 4000 were American and the rest British, Australian and other nationalities. Every facility of the armed forces is being devoted to the care and attention of those who have been rescued.[34]

February 4 was the first day of the Battle for Manila. The original XIV Corps plan was to assign Manila to the 37th Infantry Division while the 1st Cavalry Division was to turn toward the mountains northeast of the city. However, the growing indication that the Japanese intended to defend Manila in strength prompted the corps commander to modify that plan. The 37th Infantry Division were now to drive south through the city, with the 1st Cavalry Division making an enveloping movement from the east. The American advance through the northern suburbs had indeed been rapid. The fact that American lives were at risk had spurred on the advance: Colonel Noguchi's Northern Sector Defense Unit was thus caught off-guard and unable to complete the full schedule of demolition. The fight north of the Pasig was not as intense as that experienced once the river had been crossed, but here, close to the river's northern bank, the level of conflict intensified. The military aim was threefold: the destruction of Noguchi's screen; the absorption and defeat of Japanese counterattacks; and the preparation for an opposed river crossing.

The American entry into northern Manila was greeted by an overwhelming display of Filipino emotion, gratitude and hospitality. General Beightler wrote:

Flowers, fruit and even bottles of beer which I parried with my steel helmeted head were tossed into my jeep. A few Filipinos were still removing their hats and bowing low, just as they had to do when the Japanese soldiers passed by. Everything was wonderfully happy and funny. The grim business awaited us down town.[35]

One small interlude in the fighting did provide Beightler's men with an element of happiness and fun, principally because it was something not to be enjoyed by the 'dismounted horsemen' on their left flank. Within their boundary they came across the white, pristine, undamaged, Japanese-owned 'Balintawak Beer Brewery.' The advance slowed as men disappeared inside, to emerge with five-gallon water containers and helmets brimful with ice-cold BBB beer. In a matter of hours the brewery had run dry. General Beightler did not intercede; in fact he was highly amused to see 'the Division invading Manila gulping beer from steel helmets as it marched.'[36]

The 37th advanced with two regiments up, but their forward momentum was halted as buildings to their front, flank and rear were detonated in a calculated program of destruction. General Beightler surveyed the scene from the rooftop of his headquarters:

The sky was a copper-burnished dome of thick clouds. So great was the glare of the dying city that the streets, even back where we were, were alight as from the reflection of a reddish moon. Great sheets of flame swept across the roof-tops, sometimes spanning several city blocks in their consuming flight. The roar, even at that distance, was like a Bessemer converter, and the earth shook frequently as yet more of the powerful demolition charges exploded, sending fountains of flame and debris in a hot, swirling eruption to meet the dense clouds overhead. We saw the awful pyrotechnics of destruction, spreading ever faster to encompass and destroy the most beautiful city in the Far East.[37]

The fires that followed killed many Filipinos and the Americans were forced to withdraw until the conflagration subsided. Throughout February 5 and 6 (during which the evacuation of Bilibid occurred and MacArthur was frustrated in his attempt to enter Manila) the battle for the north of the city continued in much the same manner. Japanese demolition teams were supplemented by enemy mortar and artillery fire, while crossroads and street junctions, pillboxes and houses were manned by enemy machine-gunners intent upon being killed in position. Snipers were posted in tall buildings, the streets had been mined, and the Japanese capitalized on the Westerners' general inability to distinguish Filipinos from Japanese by infiltrating the attackers' lines disguised as guerrillas.

The 37th Infantry Division, the 'Buckeye' division, was a federalized Ohio State National Guard division. General Beightler, who commanded the division throughout the war in the Pacific, had been the state's transport director. The members of the division, drawn from such cities as Cincinatti, Cleveland and Columbus, had no difficulty in adapting from jungle warfare to the different tactical requirements of fighting in built-up areas. 'The adjustment was made rapidly and completely at the sound of the first shot fired from a building within the city.'[38] American doctrine was well advanced and only two alterations were made to the principles contained in the field manuals. First, artillery support was only permitted against a precise, observed target (this restriction changed as the battle developed). The second amendment, which did not change, was that air support within the city was denied. In fact, prior to the advance on Manila, the division apparently underwent training in fighting in built-up areas. As the 37th moved on towards the Pasig their companies, battalions and regiments were significantly understrength. The daily attrition they were about to face meant that by the time the division emerged at the other end of Manila, it had lost almost all its veterans.

Utilities such as electricity and water are as much weapons of war as rifles, artillery pieces or fighter aircraft. There is no hard-and-fast rule governing the relationship between attack and defense and the preservation or destruction of utilities. In the case of Manila, where there was a noncombatant, civilian population of one million in place, it was the attacker's aim to capture the utilities which the defender planned to destroy. Thus the utilities featured prominently in early phases of the American operational plan.

Because much of Manila is at sea level, the water table lies close to the surface and therefore artesian wells were able to supply the city's need for an estimated two weeks. It was a useful though inadequate resource. Among XIV Corps' first-phase utility objectives were the Novaliches Dam, the Balara Water Filters five miles to the northeast of Manila's city limits, the San Juan Reservoir some three miles closer to the city, and the essential pipelines which delivered the water into the city. Some of the power supply was linked to the water system but the major resource was located far to the south, in Laguna province, deep inside Japanese-held territory. The only power plant of substance within reach of the Americans was a steam-driven plant located on Provisor Island in the Pasig. The 1st Cavalry Division successfully wrested the water supply out of Japanese hands early in the operation, leaving the power resources to be captured in association with later moves across the river.

The Americans secured the northern bank of the Pasig on February 6 yet there still remained hotspots of resistance, infiltrations over the river as well as attacks along the lines of supply. These continuing mopping-up operations, and a major effort against strong, Japanese resistance in the Tondo and Malabon districts, went on until February 9. A significant proportion of the infantry division's resources was tied down in containment operations and guard duties. On February 8, while guarding a command post, Private Pahr observed a grubby-looking, armed Filipino walking towards him. To someone from a 'right to bear arms' society this apparition presented no obvious hazard. After all, the Japanese were firing as much at the Filipinos as at the Americans.

> Pahr casually turned away from the approaching civilian and then hit the ground as a bullet whizzed past his head and a second one thudded into human flesh. He spun around and saw the Filipino ten yards away, lying flat on his face, and dead. A more careful examination indicated that the 'Filipino' was a Japanese soldier, and an alert comrade had saved Pahr's life by 'being from Missouri' [Missouri is the 'show me state' – they claim to take nothing for granted].[39]

Even while these minor, irritating actions flared up here and in the northern suburbs, General Griswold, the Corps Commander, had at 10.15 a.m. on February 7, ordered the commanding generals of the 1st Cavalry and 37th Infantry to cross the Pasig as soon as possible. The principal objective was the Provisor Island generating plant.

When the Japanese presence was eventually removed from the north of the Pasig they had lost approximately 1500 men killed. American casualties, 50 men killed and 150 wounded, were small by comparison. This is because the vast majority of the Japanese casualties were attributed to artillery, mortar and tank fire.[40] The number of civilian casualties is not known. The operation north of the river proved to be a heaven-sent opportunity to rehearse street-fighting procedures in a relatively low-intensity environment. As soon as the Americans crossed the 150-yard ribbon of water that was the Pasig, they found their resources of military skills, courage and determination severely tested. Revealed now was the stage upon which one of the grimmest battles in the annals of military history would be fought.

# NOTES

1  D. Clayton James, *The Years of MacArthur, 1941–1945*, Vol. II (Boston, Mass., 1975), p. 512.
2  Major General Robert S. Beightler, *Report on the Activities of the 37th Infantry Division 1940–1945* (1945).
3  GHQ SWPA Communiqué No. 1031, February 2, 1945.
4  *Report After Action with the Enemy. 11th Airborne Division. Operation Mike VI, Luzon Campaign, January 1946*, pp. 3–6.
5  Edward M. Flanagan, *The Angels. A History of the 11th Airborne Division 1943–1946* (Washington DC, 1948), p. 77.
6  *Report After Action with the Enemy. 11th Airborne Division*, pp. 3–6.
7  Ibid.
8  Author's interview with Colonel Emmanuel V. de Ocampo, Manila, July 21, 1994.
9  *Report After Action. XIV Corps. M-1 Operation 29 July 1945*, pp. 91–94.
10  *Sixth United States Army Report of the Luzon Campaign 9 January 1945–20 June 1945*, Vol. I, p. 38.
11  John F. Shortal, *Forged by Fire. General Robert L. Eichelberger and the Pacific War* (Columbia, 1987), p. 112.
12  GHQ SWPA Military Intelligence Section, 'Report on Conditions in the Philippine Islands' (June 1943), p. 2.
13  Lieutenant General Arthur G. Trudeau, *The First Team* (Dallas, 1984), p. 86.
14  Beightler, *Report on the Activities of the 37th Infantry Division*.
15  'Philippine Area Naval Operations, Part IV, January 1945–August 1945', *Japanese Monograph No 114* (Military History Section HQ Army Forces Far East, 1952), p. 12.
16  Based on the evidence of Peter Richards, a prewar representative of Gestetner and postwar correspondent for Reuters.

17  Trudeau, *The First Team*, p. 88.
18  Civil Censorship Detachment, Manila's PH/USAFFE, dated February 24, 1945.
19  A.V.H. Hartendorp, *The Japanese Occupation of the Philippines*, Vol. II (Manila, 1957), p. 525.
20  Richards' evidence.
21  Bertram C. Wright, *The First Cavalry Division in World War II* (Tokyo, 1947), p. 132.
22  Yamashita Trial, Bill of Particulars No. 93.
23  Stanley A. Frankel, *The 37th Infantry Division in World War II* (Washington DC, 1948), p. 252.
24  William H. Montgomery, 'I Hired Out to Fight. The Military History of William H. Montgomery. November 1927-November 1947,' US Army Military History Research Collection (Unpublished), p. 154.
25  Ibid.
26  Ibid.
27  Associated Press report, General MacArthur's headquarters, Luzon, Monday, February 5, 1945.
28  General Douglas MacArthur, *Reminiscences* (New York, 1964), pp. 246–247.
29  Ibid.
30  Alfonso J. Aluit, *By Sword and Fire. The Destruction of Manila in World War II, 3 February-3 March 1945* (Manila, 1994), p. 195.
31  Montgomery, 'I Hired Out to Fight,' p. 161.
32  Margaret Sams, *Forbidden Family. A Wartime Memoir of the Philippines 1941–1945* (Wisconsin, 1989), pp. 72–73.
33  MacArthur, *Reminiscences*, p. 248.
34  GHQ SWPA Communiqué No. 1035, February 6, 1945.
35  Beightler, *Report on the Activities of the 37th Infantry Division.*
36  Ibid.
37  Ibid.
38  Robert Ross Smith, *United States Army in World War II. The War in the Pacific: Triumph in the Philippines* (Washington DC, 1963), p. 250.
39  Frankel, *The 37th Infantry Division in World War II*, p. 262.
40  Smith, *Triumph in the Philippines*, p. 258.

# 4

# OVER THE PASIG

A jeep sped through smoking streets under a white flag. In it were three men. Behind the driver sat a Japanese colonel, coming to 37th Infantry Division's HQ to discuss the surrender terms of his component, and an American interpreter. All around were excited Filipinos shouting: 'Victory Joe! Victory Joe!' The Japanese colonel chuckled. The interpreter asked him what he found amusing. 'It's just like it was when we came in,' he said laughing, 'only they used to shout "Banzai!" for us and now it's "Veectoreee Joe."'[1]

Much had changed since those heady days. As the American envelopment of the city became more effective, so the civilian relationship with the Japanese deteriorated further. The Japanese attitude put quite simply was: 'If you are not for us, you are against us.' They thus declared that all Filipinos, including women and children, found inside the battle area were to be considered guerrillas and exterminated. This was a cruel and heartless order, for a combination of Japanese military activities and other social considerations meant that Manila's noncombatant civilian population would find themselves involuntarily transfixed inside the battle area. The Japanese issued orders for the mass murders to begin. One such read:

The Americans who have penetrated into Manila have about 1000 troops, and there are several thousand Filipino guerrillas. Even women and children have become guerrillas. All people on the battlefield with the exception of Japanese military personnel,

107

Japanese civilians, Special Construction Units, will be put to death. House . . . [the order breaks off at this point].[2]

One obvious question is whether Manila might have been bypassed by the Americans and, had they done so, whether the inhabitants would have been spared. Colonel Emmanuel V. de Ocampo, the guerrilla leader, was quite categorical:

If the Americans had bypassed the city an even higher proportion of civilians would have been massacred. The process had already begun. The Japs were too well armed for us to fight them on equal terms. We needed American guns. Had there been any order to bypass Manila, the guerrillas would have acted against it and would have gone in without the Americans.[3]

By February 3, the majority of the bridges over the Pasig had been destroyed. There were a number of reserve demolitions over which Colonel Noguchi withdrew his force and these were brought down into the river, probably on that day. The American approach from the north caught the Japanese off-balance. They anticipated an attack either from the south or from Manila Bay. The Japanese order which restructured the defense of Manila was dated January 23, 1945. The roadblocks and street barricades in such districts as Paco, Ermita, Port and Malate were hurriedly strengthened as part of a defensive plan centered on the inner stronghold of the ancient walled city of Intramuros. Beyond the walls was a semicircle of public buildings prepared for defense to the last man. Streets and structures were mined, and each building was adequately victualled to be self-sufficient. Intermixed with and beyond the public buildings was a cat's cradle of mutually supporting antitank, machine-gun and rifle fire covering existing obstacles. Such a defense was effective only as long as its overall integrity was retained. Once inroads were made into it, it would be a matter of divide and fall as groups became isolated and virtually marooned in their own designated public building.

Intramuros held the attention of the American operational planners. They were uncertain whether the Japanese would position the bulk of their 14,000 men outside the walls and garrison the city only thinly or, conversely, hold the Walled City in strength. The choice of positions where the assault river crossing could be made was limited by the existence of sea walls which precluded the operation of amphibious tractors and scaling by infantry from assault boats. An area just to the east of Malacañan Palace was selected because none of those restrictions applied and intelligence suggested the core of the Japanese defense lay to the west. General Beightler ordered the 148th Regiment (three battalions) to cross the river first on February 7, clear the Paco and Pandacan districts, then wheel in a westerly direction toward Intramuros. Once they were over the river, they were to be followed on February 8 by the 129th Regiment, whose rather more limited objective was to move west along the river to capture the power plant on Provisor Island. Only one battalion of the 145th Regiment was to cross as the battalion reserve. The remainder of that regiment and the available supporting arms and services formed a special force dedicated to rear-area security.

The division had at its disposal as the means of crossing the river an Amphibian Tractor battalion and 30 engineer assault boats. At 3.15 p.m. the first wave set off from four widely separated and hidden launch-points behind a barrage of artillery fire and smoke. Their passage had been uncontested and the fortunate soldiers deployed to take up defensive positions in the Malacañan botanical gardens. Now forewarned, the Japanese hit subsequent waves with heavy mortar and machine-gun fire. Major Chuck Henne watched in amazement:

Hollywood could not have staged the smoke, flash and bang more dramatically. Leaving the river bank, the Company I boats were making good progress, moving in a ragged crescent when the Jap fire stormed through them. The worst damage came from automatic weapons; machine guns and automatic cannon. These fires coming from the west, from down river, ripped through the formation, scattering the boats, turning the move into a mad dash for the cover of the bank. It was spellbinding to watch pieces of paddles and splintered chunks of boat plywood fly through the air while men paddled with shattered oars and rifles to work their boats to the far bank, seemingly oblivious to what was happening to them.

The opposition had come from the 1st Naval Battalion of the Central Force. The battalion had a strength of approximately 800 riflemen and was supported by machine- and heavier-calibre guns. They were deployed south of Provisor Island and down the length of the Estero de Paco for about a mile. By last light two American battalions had crossed the Pasig, having lost 15 men killed and approximately 100 wounded. They had already experienced a new phenomenon, coming under fire from 200mm and 447mm rockets. 'The big projectiles, so huge that they could be seen in flight, gushed through the air.'[4] Their bark was worse than their bite since they were concussion rather than fragment ordnance. They caused little physical damage, although, had they not been dealt with expeditiously, they could well have become a serious psychological weapon.

On the morning of the 8th, the 148th Regiment picked itself up and advanced against heavy enemy opposition toward Paco railroad station. That afternoon the 129th crossed the river, passing civilians escaping from the south over the river toward Malacañan Palace. Meanwhile in Intramuros the Japanese took all the men of the walled city into Fort Santiago. There the Spaniards were separated from the Filipinos, whose numbers were variously estimated at between 1000 and 3000. The actual figure is closer to 3000. One who was there at the time, Dr. Antonio Gisbert, tells of having been 'separated from my father and brother and I never saw them again.' They were murdered where the Palacio del Gobernador now stands. The Filipinos:

> were surrounded and drenched with gasoline. A few survived and escaped. I am one of those few survivors, not more than 50 in all out of more than 3000 men herded into Fort Santiago and, two days later, massacred. They were bombarded by a cannon placed at a distance of a hundred metres from their prison building.[5] The Japanese had begun clearing the decks of potential opponents during what seemed to be the inevitable battle for the Walled City.

As far as the Spanish clergy caught in the net were concerned, the Japanese took away their possessions under the pretext of making an investigation. The investigation was never held yet the confiscated items, among them wristwatches and personal papers, were never returned. The clerics would remain in prison for a further three days. The Japanese jailers intercepted the food sent to them from the Church of San Agustín and consumed it themselves. Only once would they be fed during their incarceration and they had so little to drink that they were in danger of dying of thirst. They passed a most uncomfortable time in a cell so small that they could not all lie down together to sleep. Some had to remain standing. The Japanese refused them permission to leave the cell and they were therefore obliged to use their earth-floor bed as a lavatory. For their amusement, the Japanese tossed grenades in front of the cell from the top of the wall along the riverfront. No one was killed but some of the clerics were injured by grenade fragments. On the third day they were released but warned that if they related to anyone what had happened they would suffer the consequences. And so they returned to their church, to discover that the Japanese had set it on fire. Because it was made essentially of stone, it did not burn down and is the only original building in Intramuros to have survived the battle.

During the morning of February 9, reconnaissance parties of the 129th Regiment sought out suitable launch pads from which to cross the 25 yards from the south bank of the Pasig on to Provisor Island. The island, 400 yards long and 125 yards wide, close to the mouths of the Estero de Tonque and the Estero de Paco, was stoutly defended from hastily constructed defenses, as was discovered by a probing mission of one officer and 16 men in two assault boats. Both boats sank in a hail of fire. Eight of the party were killed instantly. The nine survivors, all of whom had been wounded, reached the island but efforts to reinforce them were frustrated by the weight of fire. The Japanese, aware of the beleaguered group's predicament, closed in for the kill. Two of the Americans on the island tried to get back across to the south bank but were shot down in the water. Finally Staff Sergeant George Keil got across under cover of smoke and immediately directed mortar fire to keep the Japanese away from his comrades. At 5 p.m. a company commander swam across to the island, towing an assault boat with a rope behind him. He supervised the loading of the wounded and stayed on the island while the six men were towed back across the water. When the boat was within a few yards of beaching, the Japanese opened up on it. It sank, and three of the original survivors were killed.[6]

The first major nut to be cracked by the 148th Regiment was the Paco railroad station. It had been fortified in great depth.

111

> The enemy had an elaborate system of machine gun emplacements surrounding the station, with riflemen in foxholes protecting the pillboxes. Inside the station were sandbagged fortifications at each corner, containing 20mm guns, and one large concrete pillbox housed a clip-fed 37mm gun.[7]

Three hundred of the 800 Japanese in the Paco sector defended the station. As is so often the case in conflict, the cracking of a nut can be achieved by a few brave and resolute men. In this case two GIs, heavily burdened with ammunition, took up a position 60 yards from the station. They engaged the 300 Japanese in the station building for two and a half hours, firing 1600 rounds. In that time they killed at least 82 of the enemy, and wounded many more. They accounted for a heavy machine-gun and a 20mm antiaircraft gun. So determined had been their attack that they unhinged the station's defenses, which capitulated soon after. But not before Privates Reese and Cleto, out of ammunition and withdrawing back to their own lines, were killed by the Japanese. For their bravery, both men were posthumously awarded the Medal of Honor. By now, elements of the 1st Cavalry Division were across the Pasig. Contact between the two divisions was made on the east bank of the Estero de Paco.

Even before the station fell on February 10, the supporting outstations at the Paco cemetery, church, market and school began to tumble like dominoes. But it had not been without a price. Casualties in the 37th Division on February 9 were 19 dead and 216 wounded – more than any other single day in the entire Luzon campaign. That statistic, once digested over the next 24 hours, would change the American approach to the liberation of Manila. Greater latitude was given to the use of artillery in order to save American lives.

With the combined forces of the 1st Cavalry and 37th Infantry approaching from the north and the 11th Airborne from the south, the envelopment process was not complete and the door to the east still remained open if the Japanese wished to withdraw from Manila. Rear Admiral Iwabuchi and some of his staff did withdraw to Fort McKinley on February 9 and, at the same time, the admiral sent a liaison officer to Shimbu Group headquarters 'to report on the unfavorable situation existing in Manila and to submit a recommendation for withdrawing his force to the east.'[8] When the liaison officer arrived at Shimbu Group headquarters the next day, the report he presented to Lieutenant General Yokoyama, while bad, was not rated as critical. The Shimbu Group's plans to attack the Americans were accordingly expanded to incorporate raids to be conducted by the Japanese naval forces in Manila. Iwabuchi did not hear of Yokoyama's intentions, for he had left Fort McKinley to return to Manila. (Before his departure to Shimbu Group headquarters, Iwabuchi placed the former Northern Force commander, Colonel Noguchi, in overall command in Manila. Noguchi found the predominantly naval element within his command irresponsive and requested that a senior naval officer be appointed. Since it now seemed to Iwabuchi that Fort McKinley might fall before Manila, and having been appraised of the command difficulties in the city, he decided to return.) As Iwabuchi passed into the city, the door that had been open to the mountains to the east closed behind him when contact was made between the 1st Cavalry Division driving southwest to Manila Bay and the 11th Airborne Division.

What this aspect of XIV Corps' plan achieved was to bypass a hard core of enemy opposition in the Makati area. The enemy accordingly attacked both divisions to their north and south and continued for a number of days with their grisly business of the unrestrained murder of Manila's residents. The lesson here is that when bypassing action is taken, the centres of continuing resistance have to be neutralized immediately by reserves. If sufficient reserves are not immediately available, the attack must not be permitted to roll on but should be controlled by phase lines until the bypassed strongpoints are eliminated.[9]

It was also at this time that the scale of Japanese atrocities increased and continued virtually unabated for a fortnight. Squads of Japanese rampaged through the residential areas, picking out for particular attention institutions and houses swollen with refugees. Either they entered the buildings shooting and bayoneting those inside, or they set fire to the buildings and shot those attempting to escape. They wantonly destroyed many civic buildings and seemed to derive pleasure from attacking civilians in air-raid shelters with hand grenades. Massacres continued throughout the city, often in schools, hospitals and convents, among which were San Juan de Dios Hospital, Santa Rosa College, Santo Domingo Church, Manila Cathedral, Paco Church, St Paul's Convent and St Vincent de Paul Church on Marcelino Street. A witness recalled how:

violence spread throughout the city. Several hundred innocents were beheaded, bayonetted, or shot only because they angered or displeased the Japanese. On one street in Pasay, all the inhabitants, including the women and children were murdered. The men were wired together, drenched with gasoline, and set afire with grenades.[10]

By February 9 the American shelling of Manila had begun to set houses on fire in a number of districts. One such was the Ermita district. During the afternoon and evening, Japanese patrols combed the district telling the people in the private houses and businesses that it was no longer safe for them to remain where they were. The Japanese recommended that they should come with them to an assembly area at the Plaza Ferguson so that they might then be moved into a safe area. So plausible was the Japanese proposal that most people went along willingly.

Two thousand men, women and children of all nationalities had assembled in the plaza by 5 p.m. A Japanese officer then appeared, to set in train one of the foulest of organized incidents in modern warfare. First he separated the men and the teenage boys from the women and children and ordered them to be taken to the Manila Hotel. Then the females aged 15 to 22 were further separated from the older women and children. Of these, approximately 25 were taken to the Coffee Pot Café to the rear of the Bay View Hotel. Later, similar groups, mostly of Filipino extraction, were taken to the Miramar Apartments, Boulevard Apartments and Alhambra Apartments. What the Japanese had done was to establish *joro* houses, or brothels, close to the combat areas so that marines coming off duty might gratify themselves and satisfy their fantasies before dying in battle.

Later in the evening, all the girls in the Coffee Pot were taken under armed escort into the Bay View Hotel and put into a small, dingy room. There was no electricity. Marines came in in dribs and drabs – they were positively identified as Japanese marines – holding torches or even candles, moving the hair of the terrified girls away from their faces. They came, they went, and all they did at first was ogle their prey.

Among the 25 were the three García sisters: Esther, 24; Priscilla, 15; and Evangeline, 14. In evidence to the Yamashita Trial hearing in Manila, Esther García gave evidence of the first girls to be taken from the room by the marines:

> They grabbed my two sisters. They were in back of me. And we didn't know what they were going to do. So my two sisters started fighting them, but they couldn't do anything. So they grabbed my two sisters by the arm and took them out of the room. And we waited and waited and waited and finally my youngest sister came back and she was crying. And I asked her, 'Where is Pris? Where is Pris?' And she said, 'Oh! They are doing things to her, Esther! They are doing things to her, Esther!' So everybody in the room knew what was going to happen to us. They didn't touch my youngest sister because she was menstruating.

When another Japanese came to take Evangeline away he did not believe her, so he took a piece of cotton on the end of his finger and put it inside so as to verify her claim. He left her alone and she fled to find her mother being detained somewhere above her.

Approximately 20 minutes later, Priscilla came back. 'She was perspiring,' stated Esther.

> Her hair was all messed up, her dress was torn around and she was bleeding all over. And she said 'Esther, they did something to me. I want to die. I want to die!' A marine had stripped her to her knickers, told her to lie down on the floor and undressed himself.[11] On either side of her he placed his gun and bayonet. 'And he wanted to – oh my God. He – then he started to do something to me but he couldn't do anything. So he took his knife and cut me open and then he finally succeeded. He had – he had sexual intercourse.'

Then, three Japanese came in to drag Esther away.

> I tried to resist, but I couldn't do anything about it. They were just dragging me out. And they took me to a room and all three of them were there and they started slapping me when I started to resist. I couldn't do anything. They tore my pants off and they pushed me down on the floor, and I laid there while one of them stood guard. One of them had a bayonet fixed in his rifle and the other two had a bayonet here [indicating]. When the first one was

doing things to me two of them were just looking and laughing all the time. It took him about ten minutes to have his intercourse with me, and after he finished, the other one jumped on top of me, and after the other finished the other jumped on top of me.

During the night she was raped 12 to 15 times. On the night of the 12th, the hotel caught fire and the girls took the opportunity to escape into the street.

A number of the Filipino women were released on February 10.[12] When one woman asked why this was, a Japanese officer, believing her to be white, replied: 'We hate white women . . . There are orders that we are to kill all of you, but we are waiting because we may decide to use all of the white women as our front line to keep the Americans from coming in on us.'

The truth was that the Japanese placed much store on white complexions and it appealed to their sense of superiority to abuse white and mestizo women. A 14-year-old British girl was taken with her sister, pushed and kicked along the corridor to another room and raped at least four times. She was allowed finally to return to her room, bleeding and torn.[13]

There is one important point to make: during the course of research it became apparent that there were isolated occasions where individual Japanese did behave in a compassionate manner towards Manila's population. The case of Isabel Caro is indicative of that fact.[14] She was a 14-year-old girl and among those confined to the Bay View Hotel. Her story began on February 4, 1945. At 8 a.m. a guarded telephone call from her father to their home on the corner of Padre Faura and M.H. del Pilar Streets in Ermita urged those in the house to cross over the river to their other home near Malacañan Palace. After giving Mr Caro assurances that they would move immediately, Isabel, her spinster aunt, male cousin and houseboy set off for the north, to cross over the Pasig. To their despair, they discovered that all the bridges across the Pasig had been blown by the retreating Japanese and the telephone lines were dead. Cut off as they were, the Caro party was obliged to return to their house in Ermita.

Isabel's father's company, Ramcar, was one of the best auto-repair shops in Manila. It had been taken over by the Japanese Navy as soon as they occupied Manila in 1942. A Japanese captain was put in charge of the factory's production. At 6 p.m. on February 4 the captain entered the Ermita house accompanied by other military. He claimed that Isabel's father and, by extension, those in the house as well, had been assisting the guerrillas. To corroborate his statement, the Japanese pointed to the short-wave radio and the large batteries used to provide light when the black-out curtains were drawn. Isabel, her cousin and the houseboy, despite the tearful entreaties of her aunt, were blindfolded, had their hands tied behind their backs and were driven away. They were taken a short distance to the Ortigas compound on M.H. del Pilar. Before handing the party over, the captain spoke gently to Isabel: 'Cooperate and do not be frightened. I will be around and will take care of you.'

At 7 a.m. the next morning a Japanese interrogated Isabel as to her father's 'guerrilla activities.' 'The other prisoners are looters,' he declared, 'and they will be shot.' In all honesty, the young girl claimed her innocence. Unable to get what he wanted, the Japanese left her in disgust. Isabel tells in her own words how, at sunset, the Japanese captain:

> kneels beside me and explains he is going to take me home. I ask about my cousin and houseboy – he says not to worry, they will soon be released. A 14-year-old girl, frightened and lost, is not heroic and I did not press the issue. The captain leads me to his car, puts me inside the trunk and drives off. Presently he is leading me inside my house to the hysterical relief of my aunt. We again ask about the two men who have been left behind and he again reassures us of their safety. My cousin and houseboy are never heard from again. The captain strongly suggests we move in with him so that he can give us protection. My aunt placates him and assures him we would be safe with relatives. He leaves, promising to come back soon.

As soon as he had left, Isabel picked up her fox terrier and together with her aunt left their house for the Ateneo College, a Jesuit school on Padre Faura. Inside, they found many of their friends and neighbors, who, like them, felt there to be safety in numbers.

A week later the Jesuits advised their group of refugees that they should leave, for the building was to be blasted by the retreating Japanese. The people did not need persuading, for they had heard the continuous sounds of bombardment, incessant blasts and the sight of fires on the horizon. Exhilarated as they were by the nearness of the fighting, they were completely lost and ignorant of their fate. On leaving the building, the groups dispersed. Isabel and her aunt joined a group of neighbors heading toward Dewey Boulevard. *En route* a woman stepped on one of the mined barbed-wire barricades. Immediately, the group fell flat on their faces. The woman was killed. They picked themselves up and shortly, more than a little lost and bewildered, they gathered under an acacia tree on the boulevard. It was here that they were intercepted by the Japanese and divided into male and female groups. A Japanese refused Isabel's pleas to take her frightened little fox terrier with her into the Bay View Hotel. He thrust his bayonet through the dog before shoving the females into the hotel.

At dusk Isabel found herself huddled by the window among a roomful of women. Then a sentry came in, peering through the darkness, looking at each woman in turn. He stopped at Isabel, lit a match which he held up to her face, grunted 'okeh, okeh' and dragged her off amid the protests of her aunt and the others in the room. He took her out into the street and into another building behind the hotel, the Peralta Apartments. After climbing the stairs, she entered a room and stood in front of a man. Judging from her escort's obsequious manner in addressing the man, she decided he must have been an officer. He eyed her. Although 14 years old, Isabel had very long hair and looked older than she was. The man grabbed her, pawing her in the dark. He grunted and stabbed out questions at her, and she guessed that he was asking her if she was a married woman. She replied in the affirmative, at which point he screamed out that he wanted '*daraga, daraga*' (*dalaga* is a Tagalog word for a single female). A subordinate hurriedly appeared and took Isabel away, making her wait at the foot of the stairs. The sentry on duty there made a grab for her. Fortunately she was rescued by her escort, who gave her some biscuits. 'I can only think that he sees how young I truly am and has an innate sense of decency and compassion.' Taking the dazed girl's hand, the Japanese led her back to the Bay View Hotel in pitch-darkness, where he took her from room to room until she was reunited with her aunt.

As soon as the man had left, the women in the room gathered around her to ask what had happened. She explained every detail, whereupon they exclaimed, 'They will abuse the girl.' The word 'abuse' was not in the young girl's vocabulary and this would cause her difficulties later. However, for the time being, all the young girls were sent to the corners of the room, surrounded by worried and concerned older women. It soon transpired that their concern was justified. Shortly, a Japanese came in, muttered 'okeh, okeh,' and took away the first woman to offer herself. The woman – the first of many – stood up to go with the soldiers in order to protect the young ones. 'They were raped,' said Isabel, 'to preserve our innocence.'

The women remained in their cramped hotel room, subjected to all kinds of indignities. The one bathroom stank, as obviously did they, but the Japanese still called periodically throughout the day and night to take selected women away. By now they were in a bad way, with cracked lips, itching hair, and sleep coming only spasmodically because of uncertainty and fear. They spent a week in these dreadful conditions. All the while, rumors abounded. It was said that the Japanese were going to blow up the hotel with them in it. These fears proved groundless, for eventually they were released into the thick of the battle going on all around them. Aunt and niece found their Ermita home flattened and persuaded some Americans to take them north, over the Pasig, where Isabel was reunited with her father, a captain in the Army Transport Corporation. The relief proved overwhelming for the young girl, now feverish, with a headful of lice and totally disoriented. Her grandmother scrutinized her and probed as to whether she had been 'abused.' There was that word again, which she still did not comprehend, and no one seemed prepared to explain to her what it meant. Not knowing what 'abuse' meant, she told her grandmother that it was possible she had been abused, to which her grandmother replied that she should thank God for keeping her alive. When, some time later, Isabel discovered what to 'abuse girls' meant, she thanked God for her blessings.

Many of the expatriates in Manila belonged to their own national clubs. The Germans were no exception. Their club on San Luis Street, Ermita, established in 1906, was one of the oldest in the Far East. Unlike the combustible buildings which surrounded it, the German Club was stoutly constructed of concrete. As the houses around the club became progressively untenable, the residents took refuge in the space at ground level below the first floor and upper rooms. Not only did they draw comfort from the building's strength but they were also aware that Germany was Japan's principal Axis ally. On February 9 there were almost 1500 people crammed into the club.

On the morning of the 10th the Japanese, placing a guard around the club, blocked the exits with chairs, tables and other combustibles which they doused in gasoline and set afire. The *de facto* German manager, Herr Martin Ohaus, went into the street to intercede with the Japanese on behalf of the refugees now choking inside the club from the great volume of smoke generated by the fires. They pushed him away unceremoniously. He was followed shortly by a delegation of mothers with babes in arms. The unbelieving refugees watched in horror as the babies were bayoneted in their mothers' arms and the military then picked out women to ravish. Francisco Lopez, Metro-Goldwyn-Mayer's representative in the Philippines, described the atrocity:

> The women volunteered to go out and explain that they were civilians. They went and knelt before them and begged for mercy, but the Japs ripped babies from mothers' arms and then started tearing off women's and young girls' clothes and raping them. I saw at least twenty Japs abuse one thirteen year old girl. I saw at least three girls lying on the ground after being repeatedly raped.

Lopez, giving evidence before the Tokyo War Crimes Trial, described how the breasts of some of the women had been cut off by the Japanese. Further, he told how his houseboy, Bernardino Calub, had been tied to a pillar, where his genitals were cut off and his severed penis forced into his mouth.[15] Soon the fire had taken hold and a number in the club decided to make a dash for safety, but none was to get very far, being shot down in their attempt to escape. The serious situation in which the refugees found themselves became critical when the Japanese began to roll hand grenades into the cellar. In a move of last resort to capitalize on the Japanese fondness for children, five small boys were escorted by their parents to the entrance to indicate to the Japanese that there were but harmless noncombatants in the club. The Japanese killed them in the doorway.

By midday, the club was well alight. The Japanese machine-gunned those who emerged from the building in terror and often on fire. For the military it was a game. They laughed at the plight of their victims, whom they killed whenever the opportunity presented itself. One family alone, the Rocha Beech family, lost 12 members and a nursemaid at the club, burned alive or bayoneted. One of Antonio V. Rocha's cousins, aged 15, was raped by a Japanese in the street. While the man was performing, people rushed around him, shouting, shooting, dying. When he had finished, he took out his bayonet, stuck it into the girl's groin and opened her up.

In the afternoon, the second floor of the building collapsed into the first. Five hundred people were roasted alive in the pyre that had been the German Club. Among those killed were five Germans. A further 13 Germans were killed elsewhere in separate incidents through shelling or being killed by the Japanese. There were also the 12 German Christian Brothers murdered in the chapel at La Salle College. The Japanese paid scant regard to the notion of the inviolability of allies or neutrals. The Vichy French Consul, M. Louis Lerocque, transferred to Manila from Saigon, was found dead in New Manila Quezon City on February 8. A sabre cut in the forehead and another behind the ear, inflicted by Japanese soldiers, had almost decapitated him. It is estimated that over 235 Spanish nationals died.[16] One consular official wrapped himself in a Spanish flag to emphasize his neutrality. He was shot dead in the street. On February 13, in Malate, the 60-year-old Venezuelan honorary consul was killed by the Japanese. So intense had their xenophobia become that any Caucasian or anyone resembling a Caucasian represented an irresistible case for extermination.

On February 10 military attention turned to Provisor Island, described as follows by Smith:[17] 'Five large buildings and many smaller, shed-like structures covered almost every foot of the island's surface.' More significantly, since it was an island mutual support could be provided by those Japanese forces to the west, south and southwest. The next attempt to secure the island began at 2.30 a.m., when, covered by artillery fire, 90 US infantrymen in six boats moved across the Estero de Tonque. The moon had been hidden by clouds but just as the first two boats reached the island it came out, bathing the scene in light. Japanese mortars and machine-guns sank three of the boats and set afire a small fuel tank, the flames further illuminating the scene. The Americans were effectively tied down behind a large pile of coal until 5 a.m., when the fire went out and the moon was once again hidden by cloud. Taking that as their cue, they dashed into the Municipal Light and Power building.

A macabre game of hide and seek went on around the machinery

inside until dawn, by which time Company E had gained possession of the eastern half of the building. The Japanese still held
the western half.[18]

Eventually the Japanese inside the building were overwhelmed, but
now the Americans found themselves trapped inside their prize,
unable to venture out because of effective Japanese fire. While they
held on to what they had won, the division's artillery and mortars,
supplemented by fire from tanks and tank destroyers, blasted the
western half of the island in preparation for a further attack on the
morning of the 11th.
Until now the American artillery fire had been confined to
observed fire upon recognized targets.

> Every effort had been made to spare the civilian population known
> to be held in captivity somewhere in the area, but as the tactical
> need for heavy fire power increased, permission was sought and
> obtained to place area artillery fire in front of our advancing
> lines without regard to pinpointed targets. Literal destruction
> of a building in advance of the area of friendly troops became
> essential and the Division had yet to determine upon a method of
> reducing the public buildings near Intramuros which were known
> to be veritable fortifications so heavy was their construction in
> earthquake subjected Manila.[19]

The Americans had discovered that 4.2-inch mortars could not penetrate reinforced concrete. That could only be achieved by massed
artillery fire, which had the collateral benefit of reducing casualties
in costly hand-to-hand fighting. The attack on Provisor Island cost
the 129th Regiment 35 killed, 240 wounded and 10 missing. They
had had no battle-casualty replacements since January 9. The 148th
Regiment had had only five.[20]

> The losses had manifestly been too heavy for the gains achieved. If
> the city were to be secured without the destruction of the 37th and
> the 1st Cavalry Divisions, no further effort could be made to save
> buildings, everything holding up progress would be pounded.

The problem was a matter of control, for the license to use heavy
firepower flowed over into residential areas despite assertions that:

. . . artillery fire was still kept out of installations known to contain civilians, such as hospitals, churches and the like. The Japanese soon became aware of this attitude and not only were such areas reinforced, but civilians were often used as a screen.[21]

Thus it came about that Manila's residents were being killed from two sources. Tentative estimates suggest that for every six Filipinos murdered by the Japanese, four were killed in the attempt to liberate Manila.[22] 'Those who had survived Japanese hate did not survive American love,' wrote Carmen Guerrero Cruz. 'Both were equally deadly, the latter more so because sought and longed for.'[23]

On Saturday afternoon, February 10, a group of four Japanese marines entered the cramped Philippine Red Cross building at the corner of General Luna and Isaac Peral Streets, Ermita, next to the University of the Philippines' campus, and began to shoot and bayonet everybody they found in the building. The Red Cross headquarters was overflowing at the time with approximately 100 refugees from the surrounding area whose own houses had been burned or otherwise destroyed. It was the only building still intact in the entire neighborhood.

'The fact that only three shells out of hundreds of thousands fired into that part of the city for an entire week every minute of the day and night had hit the Red Cross building, testified to the accuracy of American fire,' said the acting manager, Modesto Farolan, in a sworn deposition.[24] 'Thus it was the only safe place for refuge.'

The real Red Cross saga began on February 4, when the staff heard that US forces had liberated the Santo Tomás internment camp. They had a duty to provide relief. It was a contingency for which they had been preparing for weeks, but only surreptitiously, for the Japanese authorities had specifically warned them not to become involved either with the camp or 'enemy aliens.' Up to this date, three members of staff had been removed by the Kempeitai, allegedly for ignoring this order. They were not seen again. The Red Cross men and women, together with a group of dedicated volunteers, worked without rest right through to February 10. Their freedom of movement was stopped on February 6, when the Japanese barricaded the whole area. Even civilians escaping fire or collapsing buildings were shot down in the streets.

On Friday, February 9 a squad of marines entered the building to ask the authorities why they were admitting so many refugees.

They were told it was the staff's moral duty. Apparently satisfied, the marines said that no more were to be taken in, particularly if they were not Filipino or German, and that no one should be permitted to go upstairs. In the afternoon an artillery decoy detachment arrived and set up its machines around the Red Cross building. The machines made noises similar to artillery volleys and were intended to confuse the American artillery observers with regard to the quantity of Japanese guns and the accuracy of American fire. The marines came and went, finding nothing untoward until the morning of February 10.

The two Red Cross flags which signified the building's neutrality had blown down in the artillery barrage that night. The building was therefore unidentified. Modesto Farolan was heard telling a boy to go out and replace them. The Japanese became agitated and intervened, saying in broken English, 'No good, Americans very bad, no like Red Cross. Japanese OK.' They also took grave exception to a cardboard sign which Farolan had been writing in his office. It said: 'Philippine Red Cross Emergency Hospital – Operations Going On – Refugee House – Women and Children.' A marine removed the notice from his desk with a bayonet, saying he was not to hang it. Farolan's evidence continues:

> When they came back at six in the evening, what had been back of all their interest became clear: they did not like the Red Cross; they did not want us there, hence the cold-blooded murder, without any warning of any kind and without asking my explanations or as to who was who.[25]

In the late afternoon the volunteer surgeon, Dr. German de Venecia, assisted by an attendant, was preparing two patients for emergency surgery. Out in the corridor a volunteer nurse, Miss Rosario Andaya, was trying to keep order among the throng of refugees. Suddenly, and without warning, the shooting and bayoneting began. A marine with bayonet drawn burst into the office which served also as the operating theatre and ward. Dr. de Venecia was shot twice and died instantly where he sat. Two patients were bayoneted to death while the nurses in the room sought refuge under a pile of mattresses. The one on the top of the pile suffered a bayonet wound. The soldier spied the acting manager crouching under his desk and loosed off two shots at him. Both bullets went between his feet, scraping the bottom rim of his Red Cross steel helmet. The marine then turned on Mrs Juan P. Juan, her daughter and ten-day-old granddaughter, shooting all three. Believing he had accounted for everyone in the room, the marine made his exit.

This procedure had been repeated throughout the building.

'From where we were we could hear victims in their death agony, the shrill cries of children and the sobs of dying mothers and girls. We did not dare move,' testified Farolan.[26]

Below them they heard the marines ransacking the pharmacies and eating the meager meal they had prepared but had not had time to eat. Ten, mostly elderly, expatriate German Jews had set themselves up in the downstairs women's lavatory. The Japanese found them and, believing them to be Americans, got among them with their bayonets. Only a Filipino girl and one of the Jews survived the attack. Up to 60 percent of the refugees in the Red Cross building that afternoon died there.

On the morning of the 11th the American assault force on Provisor Island found that their opponents had either absconded or been killed. American counter-battery fire had been most effective in attacking Japanese fire positions in the south and west which had been interfering with the Provisor operation. The plant which had been fought over at such great cost to both sides was a wreck – destroyed by artillery and mortar fire. There was no prospect of the plant producing any electricity at all for Manila in the medium-to-long term.

February 12 was a day of consolidation against hard going. The Japanese artillery and mortar concentrations had been sought out by Cub spotter aircraft and rendered virtually ineffective. In reality their guns had been poorly fought. On occasion they were used to cover key points with defensive fire, but hardly ever were they used in a counter-battery role and when they were it was in a piecemeal manner. The Americans had considerably more artillery at their disposal and this day was a typical one on which to observe their employment. Once the infantry had forced the Japanese into small sectors, they were ravaged by massive artillery fire.

During February 12 this pounding fired a fuel dump near City Hall and destroyed a large-caliber weapon near the Manila Hotel as well as a 75mm gun and an ammunition dump near the General Post Office. Another fuel dump was ignited on Dewey Boulevard and four direct hits were scored on a sunken ship in Manila Harbor from which enemy guns were sniping at the artillery's Cub planes.[27]

One of the 129th Regiment's battalions had bogged down in front of a defended complex comprising the Manila Club (the British club), Santa Teresa College and the New Police Station. Another had extended to the north to Ayala Bridge. In the 148th Regiment's sector the weight of fire around Pennsylvania Street, Ermita, prompted the infantry to put their heads down after calling in comprehensive artillery support. The signs were there that the infantry were in for a hard slog. Formations of the 1st Cavalry Division attacked Fort McKinley and swept through Nichols Field to reach Manila Bay. With the encirclement of the Japanese complete, the noose had now to be tightened.

Yamashita's decision not to defend Manila was understandably a decision he had not confided in advance with any other than his closest staff. From November 1944 through January 1945, the clearest evidence from the preparations within the city was that the military anticipated defending Manila. Miguel Perez-Rubio recalled a Japanese Air Force colonel coming to the family home as early as August 1944 in anticipation of requisitioning the building for his own use. Since they had already taken 40 of the family's apartments his father, Carlos, 58, successfully argued that they had had enough. The colonel, a boisterous, boastful man, nevertheless remained to talk – mostly about himself and his exploits as a combat pilot in New Guinea. Naturally he had shot down many US aircraft. Before he left, however, he made a chilling statement to his audience, to whom, with a sweep of a pointing finger he said: 'The Americans will come, but you will not see them.'

Miguel had set aside his father's protestations and joined the guerrillas operating in Manila and its suburbs. His original role had been to gather details of Japanese dispositions within the city. Later he moved north to Baguio and, at the time of Manila's liberation, was in the hands of the Kempeitai. The last time he saw his father was in December 1944. During a return visit to Manila he recognized with a deep sense of foreboding the changes and strengthening of defenses which were so apparent. The son advised his father to evacuate the family immediately from their home at 150–160 Vito Cruz and to go and stay with friends at Nasugbu, or move into the family house at Baguio. 'What guarantee can you give me that nothing will happen there?' asked his father. He had a point. Nasugbu, for example, would be scheduled for heavy naval and air bombardment as a preliminary to the 11th Airborne Division's beach landing. The bombardment did not proceed. It was called off by an American liaison officer attached to the guerrillas who could see that the Japanese had abandoned the town. It was so often the case that bad luck found so many of the future victims in the wrong place at the wrong time.

In reality it was extremely difficult for the Filipinos to evacuate Manila. The majority, many living in rented accommodation, had nowhere to go. Very often there were extended families living under the same roof, ranging from infant to geriatric – not so easy to pick them all up and go. From the Japanese restrictions placed on the use of motor transport (January 17, 1942) to those approved by the Department of Administration of the Japanese Army, movement in and out of the city became progressively more difficult. By January 1945 some bridges had been blown, streets mined and wired off and, in some circumstances, people were being shot in the streets. By now contradictory evidence confused the Filipinos. Manila's defenses had been strengthened while at the same time the roads leading out of the city were congested with Japanese Army units moving in the direction of Baguio. For the Japanese Army it was a humiliating episode. Shortages of gasoline and vehicles left them with no option but to press into service whatever means of transport was available. Bringing up the rear of their convoys would be horses and carts and even soldiers, stripped down to their loincloths, pushing or pulling handcarts. So those in Manila were confused by the mixed messages but, ultimately, there was the overwhelming hope that the Japanese, like the Americans before them, would at the appropriate time declare Manila to be an open city.

The front of the Perez-Rubio house overlooked the wide expanse of Harrison Park, at the northeastern end of which stood the Rizal Stadium. The days leading up to February 12 had been ones of careful vigilance.[28] Carlos, 25, one of the sons of the house and engaged to be married to Helen McMicking, had been arrested at the McMicking-Halls' house on January 20. Another brother, Javier, 23, with José, a houseboy, stood on the upstairs terrace watching for signs of movement, good or bad. Just before noon, they saw soldiers in the distance, across the park. At first they were confused because the helmets worn by the soldiers were not Japanese; nor were they the flying-saucer-type, British helmet worn by the Americans in the Philippines. The only conclusion they could draw was that the soldiers were indeed American. The men they had seen were almost certainly members of the 5th Cavalry Regiment.

Javier rushed downstairs to tell his father that he had seen soldiers and that they were American. The news caused great excitement among the 30 or so people gathered at the house. Believing that they would soon be evacuated, Carlos senior said: 'That means we are about to be liberated so we ought to have lunch.' So the family, together with the refugees they had taken in, and the house staff, had an early meal. Before they had finished, soldiers moved through the back of the house and into the basement. Someone in the group shouted 'The Americans are here! The Americans are here!' They were not. They were Japanese marines. Everyone was ordered out. 'Line up at the back of the house,' barked their officer in fluent English. As soon as the assorted people had obeyed, the officer said: 'Do not talk!' and led his men inside the house. One of the house staff spoke anxiously to another standing next to him. Suddenly the officer was there. 'I said' – he drew his pistol – 'do not talk.' He put the muzzle to the Filipino's forehead and squeezed the trigger.

Once all the Japanese had come back out of the house, the civilians were ordered to go up to the first floor. All around them the Japanese busied themselves moving furniture, stacking it high from the wooden floors to the tops of the doors. The combustible piles were doused with kerosene. And then came the smoke. The cook peered out through the iron security grille across the window. A shot rang out. He fell back dead.

With much composure, the father assembled his family and the others in the house. Summarizing the all-too-obvious truth, he said to the group: 'If we do not escape, we shall be burnt alive. Split up, don't bunch up. Go in different directions. Think of yourself. Run and save yourself.' With hurried, tearful farewells some chose to chance their luck, to leave the house on what they must have realized was very much a forlorn hope. The Japanese cordon had its machine-guns prepared for such a contingency. As soon as they observed the metal grilles being wrenched inwards, away from the windows, weapons were cocked and they waited.

The daughter, Guadaloupe (Loupe), 17, went out through the

front of the house and was bayoneted in the thigh. She did not die immediately but lay on the ground throughout the night, moaning in pain and anguish. There was evidence that the soldiers abused her. There were by now other bodies scattered around the front of the house. The father had chanced his luck by going out at the back but was killed by a shot in the head. Hubert Thornton Fox and Nattie Perez-Rubio Fox, an uncle and aunt, both British nationals of advanced years, were among those who chose to stay where they were. They knelt down with their rosaries and were burned to death. When found among the ashes in the basement, parts of their rosaries were still in their hands.

Javier Perez-Rubio and the houseboy, Dionisio, both chose the back garden wall as their point of escape. Dionisio was to recount to Miguel how one of the Japanese was occupied at the time, running around with one of the servants' babies impaled on the end of his bayonet. As Javier jumped up at the wall, a bayonet went through his back, killing him. Dionisio was lucky. He managed to scramble over the wall and hide in the long grass until the morning of the 13th, when the nearby sound of English being spoken prompted him to reveal himself to the Americans.

The mother, Milagros, 48, and Aunt Rosa (Rosy), 52, were among six or seven who somehow had got out of the house and sought sanctuary under the external staircase. Hearing the sound of the moaning of the wounded, a Japanese marine detected the group huddled there and got to work with his bayonet. In one of its passes the blade tore through José's scalp. Although there was much blood, the head wound was relatively superficial. By now the house and servants' quarters to the rear were well alight. Neighbors found themselves powerless to intervene. Mrs Justine Abadilla never forgot the sound of people screaming inside the house as they were burnt alive.

What the Perez-Rubio killings reveal is a pattern, a routine, even a system of clinical killing, as though there existed a manual on how to exterminate civilians. Among the recurring similarities were the manner of torching houses to burn the occupants alive, the bayoneting of babies after throwing them up into the air (of which there are at least six recorded instances), and the lining up of victims for execution by sword or bullet. There is a fragment of an instruction contained in a Japanese battalion order dated February 13, 1945:

> When Filipinos are to be killed, they must be gathered into one place and disposed of with the consideration that ammunition and manpower must not be used to excess. Because the disposal of dead bodies is a troublesome task, they should be gathered into houses which are scheduled to be burned or demolished. They should also be thrown into the river.[29]

Of all the massacres, few were more notorious than that conducted at La Salle College.

When the Japanese requisitioned his house and church in Baclaran, Father Francis Cosgrave accepted the invitation of Brother Xavier, Director of La Salle College, Taft Avenue, to live there and to assume the post of chaplain. Over the period of Christmas 1944, four families moved into La Salle because their homes had been requisitioned by the Japanese. These were the Vasquez-Pradas, Judge Carlos, Dr Cojuanco, and the family of his brother-in-law. Brother Xavier called on José Olbes, a former student at La Salle, and suggested that he too might like to bring his household into the protection of the college. Olbes' luck held. He was tempted but decided to remain where he was. The total occupying the college's southern wing was approximately 70 people comprising 30 women and children, 15 Brothers, a priest, the adult males of the four families and perhaps a dozen servants.

The first episode in the unfolding atrocity was the appearance on Wednesday, February 7, 1945 of a group of Japanese military accompanied by a well-dressed Filipino, presumably a Makapili, who appeared to be giving them directions. Brother Xavier and Judge Carlos were called for and taken away to the adjacent Japanese Club, which subsequently burnt down. Neither Brother Xavier nor the judge was ever seen again. Those remaining were ordered by the Japanese not to leave the building even to go into the garden, nor to look out of the windows.

On Monday, February 12 the occupants of La Salle's southern wing had taken lunch and most had gathered at the foot of the staircase for protection from the shelling. So intense had this been that Mass was not celebrated that morning because Father Cosgrave would not risk gathering so many people in one spot. A Japanese officer accompanied by 20 soldiers entered the college and took away three servants and two priests, supposedly for interrogation. It is believed that the Japanese suspected La Salle had been used as a refuge for snipers. When they were returned, those who had been taken away showed signs of the most intense form of torture. One of the Brothers carried his intestines in his hands. Those who witnessed the spectacle were gripped by fear. Then the Japanese officer barked an order. Fernando Vasquez-Prada records:

> Brother Leo, who knew how to speak Japanese, realized that the order was 'kill everyone!' Brother Leo knew that the order was to be carried out. He shouted, 'Please kneel and say the Act of Contrition. Father Cosgrave, give us Absolution!' As the prayers commenced, and as Father Cosgrave raised his hand to administer absolution, the shooting and bayoneting started. Fifty-eight people died that moment.

Father Cosgrave takes up the story:

> Some of the brothers managed to escape up the stairs. These were pursued by the soldiers, some being bayoneted at the entrance to the chapel, others within the chapel itself. If anyone resisted, the officer would fire at them with his pistol or cut at them with his sword. As a result, several, in addition to bayonet wounds, were otherwise badly wounded. Some of the children were only two or three years old, a few were even younger. These were given the same treatment as their elders. When the Japanese had finished bayoneting us they pulled and dragged the bodies and threw them in a heap at the foot of the stairs, the dead being thrown upon the living. Not many were killed outright by the bayoneting, a few died within one or two hours, the rest slowly bled to death.

Among the Brothers killed, 12 were German nationals.

Unable at first to comprehend what was happening around him was five-year-old Fernando Vasquez-Prada, but the explicit details of that event were left indelibly printed on his mind. Not until 1994 did he discuss the subject in public because:

> I've always avoided going into this part of my life simply because the mere thought of what happened opens up wounds that took so many years to heal. Wounds that are so fragile that it took my Catholic upbringing to forgive. To forget is not required of a

Christian. I cannot and I will not forget the atrocities committed to my family during the Japanese occupation.

What Manila was witnessing in February 1945 was a system extensively rehearsed in China: *Senko-Seisaku*, a three-part paradigm of 'kill all, burn all, destroy all.' Among the victims of the massacre in the chapel at La Salle College had been Fernando's family. His father, very ill with pleurisy, was 59 year old – 18 years older than his mother. In the initial Japanese onslaught his two brother, Enrique, 22 and Herman, 21 were the first to fall, hit in the throat by Japanese bayonets and killed instantly. Behind the two brothers, uncomprehending and unconscious of the dangers lurking, stood little Fernando and his mother, who was about to make a supreme, heroic sacrifice.

The Japanese attacked the boy, bayoneting him twice in the chest. His horrified mother, seeing the Japanese soldier preparing for a third lunge, sprang forward, scooping her son from the floor. Like an enraged tigress she attacked the soldiers, kicking, biting and swinging her fists. Perplexed, the Japanese stepped back momentarily, but could not allow such a humiliation to pass. They turned on Mrs Vasquez-Prada. Bayonets flashed, rising and falling. They cut into her shoulder and a large piece of flesh was hacked out of one thigh. In agony, she raised her hands to fend off further blows. The fingers of both hands were sliced away. A bayonet thrust into the abdomen caused her to fall to the floor, never to rise again. She heard the Japanese officer say: 'Let her not die now, let her take time to die.' Then a number of Japanese soldiers began a gruesome game of cutting up her body until she lapsed into unconsciousness.[30] The Japanese soldiers left her to die in that manner, slowly, as her life blood ebbed away.

The soldiers went after my third brother, Alfonso, 14 years old, and killed him; after that, my sick father, stabbing him twice in the chest. He survived this attack. As the hours passed, my poor mother lay agonizing, her entire body mutilated, the cadavers of my brothers surrounding her. I gave her water and tried to clean her wounds. My poor father took me to the second floor seeking food. We found a tin of *adobo* [stew] and my father fed me. It was while feeding me that a team of Japanese soldiers reentered the room and attacked my father, who was killed in front of my eyes. I crept back to my mother's side, perhaps to seek warmth. She knew my father had died.

At 10 p.m. Father Cosgrave was able to free himself from the tangle of bodies and set about anointing some of the victims. What he found edifying was the patience and the resignation with which the people there met their death, 'some of them actually praying to God to forgive those who had put them to death.' He took refuge for the night behind the high altar and in the morning was joined by eight or ten survivors. The sickness of the atrocity had not yet run its full course: 'Sometimes the Japanese soldiers came in and tried to violate the young girls who were actually dying.' Looters moved through the chapel stealing personal possessions and sacred vessels. From Monday through to Thursday, 15 February the college remained under shell fire and, at the same time, the Japanese were blasting different parts of the house, especially under the chapel. On Wednesday this place of worship was deliberately set alight but, as it was principally of concrete, only books and furniture caught fire. The smoke proved to be suffocating and, drawing on his last reserves of energy, the dying Brother Hubert extinguished the fire at the entrance to the chapel. Helen Vasquez-Prada had survived three agonizing days, screaming day and night from the pain of her wounds until, on Thursday, February 15, Japanese soldiers came and put an end to her life. At about 4.30 the same afternoon, the Americans captured the college and took away the survivors.

The Quirinos had their family home in the Ermita district at 506 Colorado Street, close to its junction with Oregon Street.[31] Ermita was a quiet, genteel district bounded by Dewey (now Roxas) Boulevard to the west, San Luis (now T. Kalaw) Street to the north, Taft Avenue to the east and Herran Street (now Pedro Gil) to the south. Elpidio Quirino, the head of the family, had been trained as a lawyer before entering politics. Before the war he had been a cabinet minister in President Quezon's Commonwealth Government but now, in February 1945, he was a Senator-in-limbo, for the Senate to which he had been elected in 1941 had not, for obvious reasons, been convened. (Despite the tragic massacre of almost all his family, when Elpidio Quirino was elected President of the Philippines in 1949, one of his first official acts was to issue a Presidental proclamation pardoning all Japanese war criminals who had been tried, convicted and incarcerated in the Philippines. They were repatriated to Japan. In pardoning them, President Quirino's noble words were: 'I canot live the rest of my life harboring hatred toward our former enemies.'

Living in the Quirino residence were Elpidio's vivacious wife, Alicia Syquia, and their children: Tomás (Tommy), 21; Armando (Dody), 20; Norma, 18; Victoria (Vicky), 13; and two-year-old Fe Angela. As was usual for a family of this status, they had a live-in household staff.

After the war, Elpidio became President Manuel Roxas' Vice President. Physically, he could be described as chubby and, on April 14, 1948, he was in fact on a ship returning from Cebu after a recuperative rest following a heart attack. The next morning he was awoken in his cabin with the news that while visiting Clark Field, President Roxas had suffered a fatal heart attack. Elpidio had therefore become President of the Philippines. In December 1949 he won a term as President in his own right. As the following story will explain, his wife and others in his immediate family were killed in the war and, for that reason, the duties of the First Lady of the Philippines fell upon his teenage daughter Vicky.

The Quirino episode began on the morning of February 9, which found the Ermita district engulfed in flames and smoke due to intensive American shelling. The Japanese had interposed their positions between the residential blocks of houses but, seemingly, the ploy offered them no greater protection; it merely increased the hazard to the civilians in residence as the ranging of American artillery and heavy mortars continued apace. At about 11 a.m. the Quirino house took a direct hit, but no one was hurt. It seemed obvious to Elpidio that to remain would be foolhardy since the next salvo might well kill them all. He sent his wife, with baby Fe in her arms, to lead Tommy, Norma and Vicky down Colorado Street toward her mother's house, situated close to the junction with California Street. Elpidio remained with Armando to gather up some groceries, with the intention of following on behind.

Concepción Jiménez de Syquia lived in a comfortable house with her unmarried daughter, Margarita, and her son, Hector, whose wife was in the USA. Concepción's married daughter, Petronila, and her lawyer husband, Vicente Mendoza, also lived with her. The couple had six children: Gregorio, 18; Luis, 16; Raul, 13; Milagros (Milly), 11; Enrique, 8; and Renato, 5. There was a Japanese strongpoint at the former home and headquarters of General Masaharu Homma, just up the road from the Syquias' house, at the junction of Colorado and California Streets. A machine-gun nest between Pennsylvania and California, manned by four marines, covered the intersection of Colorado and California. The Japanese had narrowed the passage at this junction by putting in place a mined roadblock. It was while they were negotiating this chicane that the machine-gun opened up on the Quirinos' advance party. The bullets passed in front of, and behind, Vicky. Tommy, who was slightly in the lead, leapt into his grandmother's garden, followed by Vicky. The bullets had, however, killed Norma and mortally wounded her mother. When baby Fe fell from her mother's arms she was uninjured but, striking her head on the pavement, she became unconscious.

The American artillery barrage continued relentlessly. Those in the relative shelter of the Syquia home were unable to assist their kith and kin on the far side of the obstacle. Vicky heard her mother scream in anguish something that still haunts her, 'mother, my daughter.' And then she was silent. By this time, Fe had come to, her mother and sister dead beside her, and all the time the incessant noise of the artillery and mortars. The impact of all this upon a two-year-old child can be imagined. She screamed out in panic and desperation. Two hands reached down for her and, in one movement, hurled her skywards. When she descended, she became impaled on the bayonet thrust up at her by a Japanese marine. She died instantly.

As Elpidio surveyed the situation outside before finally abandoning his wrecked house, the artillery fire continued unabated and machine-gun fire raked the streets. Putting aside the food, he set out to reach California Street over the intervening garden walls. He lost contact with Armando. The young man, dazed, desperate and disoriented by the crescendo of explosions and the smoke, ended up in a neighbor's house, from where the men were later rounded up by the Japanese. When he tried to escape, he was shot in the face. The bullet which killed him struck him on the bridge of his nose, making its exit by his right ear.

It was dark by the time Elpidio reached his mother-in-law's house. He quickly surveyed the horror of the scene of his dead wife and daughter but, under the impression that Fe was still alive, he scooped her up as he sprinted into the Syquia garden. Once inside, they discovered the fatal wound right through her body. They buried her in the garden. The shelling had intensified and the family decided to seek sanctuary in the Rodriguez house at the junction of Colorado and Herran. This they reached by way of garden fences. Three of the females, Concepción, Margarita and Vicky, went into the bathroom to clean up. From somewhere unknown, there rose the enticing aroma of food cooking. Keen to discover the source of this temptation, Vicky vacated the bathroom seconds before an American shell exploded in the room. Concepción was killed and Margarita had a good part of her posterior torn away. With the Rodriguez house now on fire, the Quirinos were forced to move on once again. Although Margarita was obviously dying, she was laid carefully in a rattan sofa as the family headed off in the direction of the shoe-box-like building of the Philippine Women's University and the angular, art deco building of the Scottish Rites Masonic Temple on Taft Avenue. In between, not one building was left standing.

Eventually the group came to a halt in the ruins of a house where the stair-well remained virtually intact. Here Elpidio left the family to take shelter from the effects of the sun under groundsheets rigged above them while he sought a better place. They were now quite close to the Masonic Temple, which seemed to be the focus of the American gunners' attention. It had long been thought to be the headquarters of the Kempeitai. Suddenly one of the shells fell short, and close by. One of the splinters opened up an unstoppable flow of blood from Gregorio Mendoza's lower limbs. The same piece of shrapnel went through Tommy's left leg. Young Raul Mendoza had his arm shattered so that the bones were exposed, while his father was hit in the stomach. Hector had been fatally wounded when a piece of shrapnel tore through his lung. Unaware of the damage around her, Vicky, who, like Milly Mendoza, had her head against the lap of the Mendoza's cook, turned to look up at the servant to ask her where she thought the shell had exploded. She saw to her horror that the woman, who had not flinched a muscle, had half her face blown away and much of the debris had showered down on Vicky.

By now they were beginning to suffer the effects of not having had food or water. The wounded were desperate for the latter. Vicky then set out in search of her father. Impossible as it was, she thought she saw him standing atop an air-raid shelter, and when she went inside, to her astonishment she found him there. She gave him the news and confirmed where the family could be found.

In the shelter, she found a *palayok*, a small, clay cooking pot and, while her father left to locate the family, Vicky went in search of water. After finding some in a well surrounded by blood, she made rendezvous with the family and tore up a spare shirt to apply tourniquets to the limbs of the injured. Following a lull in the shelling, Elpidio said they had to move on. He realized that if Tommy was to be saved, he needed immediate and appropriate medical attention. Supporting one another, they limped toward the American lines. Vicente Mendoza, however, was too far gone. He struggled gamely on, holding his stomach wound, but only his shirt and his hands prevented his intestines from spewing out. He died in an air-raid shelter. And then, within minutes, to the west of the Estero de Paco, they stumbled into the Americans. They were encouraged forward, passed through the American lines, and over the creek to safety.

Behind them they had left baby Fe and her mother and her daughter Norma, both of whom were to lie out on the street where they had fallen for a further six days. No one had found time to bury them – there were hundreds of scattered corpses – but someone had found time to loot their bodies. Also left behind were those killed on February 12, the very day of rescue: Concepción Syquia, her son Hector, her daughter Margarita, Vicente Mendoza and his son Gregorio. The bright spot lay in the saving of Tommy's leg and life, and Raul's arm. The first American doctor encountered by the group said Tommy's leg had to come off, but Elpidio held out for the second opinion of a relative who was also a doctor. Once over the Estero de Paco, they slept under groundsheets – the sleep of the dead. When they awoke, they found they had indeed bedded down in a collecting point for the dead. Death had followed them every foot of the way.

Elpidio decided to move on to Malacañan Palace, and persuaded an American jeep driver to take them there. When he inquired what was being carried in the vehicle's trailer, the matter-of-fact reply was 'stiffs.'

The attention of an American patrol moving up Isaac Peral Street became transfixed by the manner in which three civilians came toward them. They stumbled and staggered for the best part of 200 yards before falling down. On examination, they were found to be dead. They were Chinese. Their throats had been so completely cut through by a sword that they had almost been beheaded. What was so eerie was the realization that this barbarity had occurred so recently and so close to where the soldiers had encountered the Chinese. The same group pressed on until they came to a gas station. They found inside a huddle of bodies of men, women and children of all ages. A soldier saw the body of a child tremble. Stepping over the corpses, the man touched the body, that of an eight-year-old girl, and found her still alive, her small fists clutching tightly to her mother's blouse. The child's body was slashed and pierced by thrusts of a bayonet. Then it was noticed that the mother, who bore similar wounds, also showed signs of life. These were the only survivors. After receiving first aid, they were taken to the rear and to hospital.[32]

With the Americans had come the Filipino guerrilla units. The unending atrocities committed against their own people horrified them. Colonel de Ocampo arrived at Pennsylvania Avenue, where his family lived. He discovered that all four had been murdered by the Japanese. He heard that Norma Quirino, whom he knew, had also been killed. His reaction was one common to all returning guerrillas: an intense feeling of self-blame and guilt. Totally unrealistic mental arguments surfaced. If they had been there, they might have been able to achieve something; they might have been able to infiltrate the Japanese lines. The shock which the initial experience of Manila had upon the guerrillas affected their whole attitude and way of fighting. They fought as only angry men do.

# NOTES

1 Major General Robert S. Beightler, *Report on the Activities of the 37th Infantry Division 1940–1945* (1945).

2 Kobayashi Group (*Heidan*) Order dated February 13, 1945, quoted in 'Japanese Defense of Cities as exemplified by The Battle for Manila,' *A Report by XIV Corps* (HQ Sixth Army, July 1, 1945).

3 Author's interview with Colonel Emmanuel V. de Ocampo, Manila, July 21, 1994.

4 Stanley A. Frankel, *The 37th Infantry Division in World War II* (Washington DC, 1948), p. 271.

5 Nick Joaquín, *Manila my Manila* (Manila, 1990), p. 198.

6 Frankel, *The 37th Infantry Division in World War II*, p. 273.

7 Ibid.

8 *Reports of General MacArthur*, Vol. II, Part II, 'Japanese Operations in the South West Pacific Area' (Washington DC, 1966), p. 497.

9 'Japanese Defense of Cities,' p. 20.

10 Andrew Gonzales and Alejandro T. Reyes, *These Hallowed Halls* (Manila, 1982), p. 3.

11 Alfonso J. Aluit, *By Sword and Fire. The Destruction of Manila in World War II, 3 February-3 March 1945* (Manila, 1994), p. 231.

12 *The Tokyo War Crimes Trial*, Vol. 6, p. 12/522.

13 Ibid.

14 What follows is based upon Ambassador Isabel Caro Wilson's 'Chronology of Events – Last Days of the Liberation of Manila, 3–27 February 1945.'

15 *Tokyo War Crimes Trial*, Vol. 6, Prosecution Exhibit No. 1366, p. 12/424.

16 El Secretario de Kebajada, *Encargado de la redacción del Inventario de pérdidas españolas en Pilipinas durante la ocupación japonesa* (Manila, June 19, 1946).

17   Robert Ross Smith, *United States Army in World War II. The War in the Pacific: Triumph in the Philippines* (Washington DC, 1963), p. 261.
18   Ibid, p. 263.
19   *Report After Action. Operations of the 37th Infantry Division Luzon P.I., 1 November 1944–30 June 1945*, p. 53.
20   Smith, *Triumph in the Philippines*, p. 264.
21   *Operations of the 37th Infantry Division*, p. 53.
22   Based on research conducted during the preparation of this book.
23   Carmen Guerrero Nakpil, *A Question of Identity. Selected Essays* (Manila, 1973), 'Benevolence,' p. 206.
24   Major General Charles A. Willoughby, *The Guerilla Resistance Movement in the Philippines 1941–1945* (New York, 1972), deposition signed in Manila by Modesto Farolan, February 14, 1945.
25   Ibid.
26   Ibid.
27   Frankel, *The 37th Infantry Division in World War II*, p. 277.
28   What follows is an account based on an interview conducted by the author in Manila on July 20, 1994 with Ambassador Miguel Perez-Rubio, which, in turn, is based on his own, meticulous, reconstruction of events.
29   *Sack of Manila*, US Senate Committee on Military Affairs (1945), pp. 14–15.
30   Gonzalez and Reyes, *These Hallowed Halls*, p. 22.
31   The Quirino account that follows is based on interviews conducted by the author in Manila in July 1994 with Victoria Quirino Delgado.
32   Frankel, *The 37th Infantry Division in World War II*, p. 276.

# 5

# THE BATTLE JOINED

Lieutenant General Yokoyama's Shimbu Group's difficulty in formulating a strategy for the Manila area was as much due to poor information and poor communications as their failure to get Rear Admiral Iwabuchi's naval force to conform to their wishes. Iwabuchi was boxed in. By February 12 his northern front was the Pasig River, his eastern front ran through General Luna, Paco market and the Estero de Paco, while the southern front ran to the east and west of the Manila Polo Club.

On or about February 13 the parlous situation in Manila eventually became clear to Yokoyama in his headquarters at Montalban, 21 miles northeast of Manila. He directed the Manila Naval Defense Force headquarters to withdraw to Fort McKinley as a preliminary toward evacuating the city and not to concern themselves with an imminent Shimbu Group counterattack. General Yamashita, the Fourteenth Area Army commander, 125 miles to the north at Baguio, was unaware that Iwabuchi had reentered the city. Yamashita oversaw the fighting which continued in the mountains in the north and which was bypassed by the US XIV Corps. When, on February 13, Yamashita was advised that Iwabuchi was already in Manila, he demanded to know from Yokoyama why the move had taken place and ordered the Shimbu Group commander to get all troops out of the city without further delay. Iwabuchi received his orders on February 15 and replied: 'The headquarters will not move.'[1] He covered his position by making a signal to the Japanese Commander-in-Chief Southwest Area Fleet:

I am overwhelmed with shame for the many casualties among my subordinates and for being unable to discharge my duty because of my incompetence. The men have exerted their utmost efforts in the fighting. We are very glad and grateful for the opportunity of being able to serve our country in this epoch [epic?] battle. Now, with what strength remains, we will daringly engage the enemy. 'Banzai to the Emperor!' We are determined to fight to the last man.

To the Shimbu Group headquarters, he sent a less explicit signal:

In view of the general situation, I consider it very important to hold the strategic positions within the city. The transfer of the headquarters will hinder the execution of operations. We have tried to make ground contact with Fort McKinley but failed. Escape is believed impossible. Will you please understand this situation?[2]

Unimpressed, Yokoyama ordered Iwabuchi to break out during the night of February 17–18 in conjunction with two planned Shimbu Group counterattacks, one toward the Novaliches Dam and the other toward Grace Park. The Army had sought to persuade Iwabuchi that, from their experience during the Lingayen operations, it was not difficult to penetrate the American lines during the night. The diversionary attacks foundered in the face of strong American opposition. The remnants of the Third and Fourth Naval Battalions which were already at Fort McKinley, 1900 troops, moved to join the Shimbu Group near Antipolo.[3] Iwabuchi and what were by now little more than 6000 men in Manila had not budged. He advised the Shimbu Group that he had planned to break out but said, with some truth, that it was difficult to do so in one night. He did not say in so many words that he was resolutely determined to stay put, but pointed out the strength of fixed positions from where severe losses could be inflicted on the Americans.

The closure of the Japanese escape route to the east was *the* strategic blunder of the Philippines campaign. Given the perceived continuing importance of Manila in the fight against Japan, the presence of a large, captive, civilian population and an enemy with an established reputation of fighting to the last bullet, the failure to leave open a withdrawal route for the Japanese was a fundamental mistake. The negotiated withdrawal of Colonel Hayashi from Santo Tomás demonstrated, albeit on a smaller scale, how a standoff could be defused and the enemy accounted for in the fullness of time. Rear Admiral Iwabuchi's encirclement provided him with an excuse to ignore the orders of Generals Yamashita and Yokoyama. The implications were the destruction of Manila, a quarter of a million civilian casualties and, ironically, in a vengeful example of victor's justice, the execution of General Yamashita. It may be uncharitable to postulate that the closing of all the doors in and out of Manila was not an error but part of the calculated campaign of a man whose personal determination to reach the city with the minimum of delay and to settle outstanding scores, had become a dangerous and fatal obsession.

Iwabuchi had in his order of battle the remnants of his Central Force (First and Second Naval Battalions), the Fifth Naval Battalion, Colonel Noguchi's much depleted Second Provisional Infantry Battalion, and the Northern Force's Third Provisional Infantry Battalion. There is in Manila a well-established myth that the atrocities committed against the residents of the city were the work of Formosans and Koreans. The small number of Formosans and Koreans who were in Manila were labor troops, part of the Imperial Work Force who were employed on menial duties, treated like dirt, had no love for the Japanese and who surrendered to the Americans at the first opportunity. There was one division formed in Korea that went to the Philippines in 1944 but it did not stay in Manila. Similarly, there was a Formosan regiment in Bataan, but it was reassigned to Java. It was not uncommon for the taller, bigger and bearded Japanese who came from Kyushu to be mistaken for Koreans.[4] This case of misinformation, which has slighted the people of Taiwan and Korea for 50 years, can now be safely laid to rest.

All three of Japan's armed forces were inculcated with the same offensive spirit that, when forced upon the defensive, they not only fought to the death but demonstrated a determination to wreak maximum attrition on their enemy. This aspect of their military doctrine was seen not only in Manila but also out on Pacific islands, in the way they fought their ships and in the activities of their *kamikaze* suicide pilots. The concept of no surrender was embodied in their *Military Field Code*: 'Rather than live and bear the shame of imprisonment by the enemy, he should die and avoid leaving a dishonorable name.'[5]

By February 12 the Battle for Manila had lost most of its fluidity. It was now gradually becoming a grinding slog around and within buildings. All of Iwabuchi's artillery and heavy mortars had been located and destroyed. There were a number of 50mm grenade dischargers employed by the Japanese inside buildings as direct-fire weapons. The weapons which remained – machine-guns, rifles and mines – suited their enforced new environment. As the defensive perimeter shrank, these indoctrinated men, including the sick and wounded, were assigned to strongpoints, in the full knowledge that there was no plan for withdrawal or regrouping. Each man had his meager supply of rations, barely sufficient arms and ammunition, and a building in which his life would end in a last stand to preserve 'the honor of his homeland and live up to what is expected of him.'[6]

When the two regiments of the 1st Cavalry Division reached Manila Bay on February 12, in the vicinity of Manila Yacht Club, on the boundary of Pasay and Manila, they turned north to face an area defended in strength by the Second Naval Battalion. To the southeast of the old Fort Antonio Abad lay Harrison Park, an open area bounded by avenues. In its southeastern corner was a baseball stadium. The key structure in the defended area was undoubtedly the Olympic-standard Rizal Stadium, two blocks square, built of concrete and consisting of four large stands. The drainage ditch which ran to the east of the stadium, 15 feet wide and 10 feet deep, proved to be an effective tank trap. In addition, this approach was protected by a wall 15 feet high and two feet thick. The western approach across Harrison Park was open, as was the southern approach down the wide avenue of Vito Cruz, where the Perez-Rubios had their home. The northern extremity of the defended area included La Salle College on Taft Avenue, site of the earlier massacre of priests and civilians. Rizal Stadium was strongly contested as it was an important Japanese supply dump. It would take the Cavalry two days to capture it, after which long columns of locals were to be seen carrying away their prizes down Vito Cruz.

In the Malate district, the Remedios Hospital, with its distinctive red crosses on the roof, came under sustained artillery fire commencing on February 13. There were at the time some 800–1000 refugees and patients in the building. When, above the din of incoming shells, the distinctive sound of a Piper Cub spotter plane could be heard, some brave souls rushed out of the building, risking sniper fire, to show the artillery aerial observer that they were civilians. The plane waggled its wings and shortly a barrage of artillery swept toward and over the hospital, and back again. There were a few isolated Japanese in the area but, for the most part, there had been a general withdrawal toward the Bay View and Manila Hotels, the public buildings and inside Intramuros. It was apparent that the military commanders at the tactical level took the view that war was hell and casualties were inevitable. If they found it necessary to employ batteries of artillery against area targets in which there were snipers capable of taking American lives, then this they did. Four hundred civilians were killed in and around Remedios Hospital. 'And most of them were killed by American artillery bombardments.'[7]

Meanwhile the Japanese had again visited the Malate Church. They arrested Fathers Kelly, Henaghan, Monaghan and Fallon, together with nine or ten parishioners. They marched them to the Syquia Apartments, a large block close to the church. 'Neighbors assured us that no shots were heard from the building and it is surmised that they were taken away at night time and killed by the Japanese and buried in a common grave.'[8]

The Malate Church had now but one priest, Father John Lalor, whose work had taken him away to the Remedios Hospital. On Sunday, February 11, the Feast of Our Lady of Lourdes, Father Lalor said Mass in the hospital's courtyard. Soon after, the area around the hospital began to burn. Fearful of his church, Father Lalor left the hospital: '. . . and we saw Fr. Lalor with tears in his eyes, crouched behind one of the ashes of the lower corridor, [as he] watched it burn.'[9] The Father returned to his duties at the hospital, to tend to the dead and wounded resulting from the American shelling which had begun on February 12. The shelling continued into Tuesday, February 13. 'We wondered what they were trying to hit as there were no Japanese to be seen and at most, there were only a few snipers hiding in the ruins.'[10] Father Lalor pressed on with his duties among the patients until late afternoon when, close to exhaustion, he and Dr. Tony Lahorra flopped down with their backs against a wall. 'We had gone a few paces,' wrote Pedro Picornell,

> when I heard the whistle of a shell and threw myself on the ground. Shell after shell followed, hitting the Hospital and the

crowded courtyard for unending minutes as shrapnel and bits of bodies flew all over the place . . . I do not know how long the barrage lasted but it stopped as suddenly as it had started . . . I saw the bodies of Fr. John Lalor and Dr. Tony Lahorra sitting on the ground with their backs against the wall. They were not mangled – a shell hit the wall a meter or two above them and they had been killed by the concussion.

Despite all this, when the Americans came to Malate they were generally well received. People sang 'God Bless America,' children shouted 'Hello Joe' and 'Victory Joe.' Joe handed over candy and Hershey bars. The people here had suffered greatly.

Here in Malate lived 23 members of the Rocha family group, relatives of the Rocha Beech family which had suffered such devastation at the German Club. The Japanese had already burned all the houses in their block on February 11 and 12. The shelling from the American forces had intensified during the 13th. Taking advantage of a lull in the shelling, Antonio V. Rocha's wife, Josefina, together with her maid Milar and the houseboy Pedro Palileo, left their cement stairway refuge at the Hilario residence, two houses away from their own. Josefina intended to check the family belongings inside their house. When the shelling suddenly recommenced, Pedro made Josefina squat against the corner of the back wall of the house next door, then had the maid lie on top of her, before he himself lay on top of both of them. Unfortunately a shell exploded on the other side of the wall against which they were sheltering. A large piece of shrapnel cut through the adobe stone, went through Josefina's forehead and almost severed Milar's right arm, which had been cradling Josefina's head. Pedro, unscathed, ran back to the refuge to convey the bad news. He stood there looking bewildered as he told the family what had happened, his face covered with blood and brain matter. 'Why not me,' he asked, 'when I offered my body to protect my mistress?'

On the morning of February 15, the Rochas were told that the Americans were at the San Andrés market (200 meters from their refuge on Carolina Street). Antonio V. Rocha, the head of the family, decided that rather than wait it would be better to reach the American lines as the shelling, which had been continuous since the 13th, had become unbearable. On reaching the American forces, Antonio observed the mortars set just forward of the vertical. He told an officer that there were only civilians in front of them. In a patronizing 'let us get on with the war' attitude, the officer replied, 'You're safe now, just follow the lines,' meaning the telegraph wires. Later the Rochas heard that the Americans, who had been in position there since February 13, did not move forward until the 16th.

Only a small minority showed visible anger and hostility to the tired, dirty and often scared-looking American soldiers whose eyes probed the ruins. What came as a surprise was only whispered among the recently liberated: 'They're all yellow' – one of the side-effects of their Atabrine anti-malaria tablets. The fact was that the civilian population's anger and hatred of the Japanese defied dilution. There was little room or capacity for them to vent their spleen on the Americans. Besides, it was the Japanese who were the belligerent occupants; the Americans their saving grace. The people had lived in an environment of

> fear of such an intensity that people were afraid to talk to their closest friends except about vague generalities . . . The great phrase of hope at the time was 'Pagdating ni Cano' (when the Americans come back, things will be better).[11]

And the joy of liberation took away the sting of heartache for lost relatives and friends. Obviously that was not always the case. Some had cause for grievance.

Carmen Guerrero, walking through Malate that day, pregnant and with a child in her arms, had not eaten or slept for over a week. Her husband, Ismael Cruz Jr., had been tortured in front of her before being taken away and shot. He, and his brother and father, Don Ismael Cruz, a nephew of the Philippine hero José Rizal, had fallen victim to the bands of marauding Japanese who barged into houses in the residential districts of Ermita and Paco. Once inside, they collected together adolescent and grown males, often dispatching them with bayonet and sword. Carmen Guerrero had seen the family home ransacked, set afire and shelled consistently.

> I had seen the head of the aunt who had taught me to read and write roll under the kitchen stove, the face of a friend who had been crawling next to me on the pavement as we tried to reach shelter under the Ermita Church obliterated by a bullet, a legless

147

cousin dragging himself out of a shallow trench in the churchyard and a young mother carrying a baby, plucking at my father's sleeve – 'Doctor, can you help me? I think I'm wounded' – and the shreds of her ribs and her lungs could be seen as she turned around.

An American soldier crouching behind a tree shouted out to her: 'Hey you! Wanna get killed?' She crossed over from the middle of the street and spat on him.[12]

International law relating to armed conflict, the *jus in bello*, affords protection to hospitals. That same law forbids the use of hospitals or their surrounds for warlike purposes. The two-storey Philippine General Hospital on Taft Avenue suffered the same artillery bombardment as the Remedios. Apart from the wall of sandbags around the door, the main part of the hospital is the same today as it was in 1945. On February 13 the number of refugees who had sought refuge in what should have been a protected building stood at some 7000. In any siege situation, it is a reasonable assumption that the inhabitants will seek refuge in hospitals because of the theoretical protection which they attract. The Americans claimed that they were unaware there were civilians in the hospital. Civilians stood packed together in rooms and corridors, shuddering as each shell hit the roof followed by the tinkling of tiles breaking on the floor above them.

The next day the 140th Field Artillery Battalion fired 2091 high-explosive rounds, and the 82nd Chemical Mortar Battalion's 4.2-inch mortars pumped 1101 high-explosive and 263 rounds of inflammable white-phosphorus shells into the complex of the hospital and the adjoining University of the Philippines. Japanese forces around these buildings were effectively holding up the advance of the 148th Regiment across Taft Avenue, yet the artillery and mortars were unable to stem the Japanese fire emanating from in front of the hospital's administration building.[13] Dr Antonio G. Sison, the hospital's director, testified at the Yamashita trial that the Japanese never entered the main hospital.[14] They may not have conducted offensive military operations from within the building, yet there is evidence that some risked being caught out of bounds.

Mr Edgar Krohn, and his wife and son, Edgar junior, were among the refugees. They were a German family. For them and the other German survivors of the Battle for Manila, 'liberation' meant internment in Bilibid prison. One night, standing in the dark

– there was no electricity – two Japanese came into their corridor and, by the light of candles, inspected the faces of the young women. Finding one to their liking, they pulled her toward them, but she, a Russian, feigned a deep cough. 'You don't want me,' she croaked, 'I have TB.' The Japanese recoiled in horror and resumed their search. They found another victim and took her away screaming. The next morning, her dead body was found outside the hospital. There was evidence of multiple rape. The Krohn's son, only 16 at the time, looks back on that incident today with anguish.

> You know, they took that poor woman away, and not one of the many in the room that night interceded on her behalf. I have often thought to myself – why? Obviously everyone was fearful of the consequences, but I believe it was because there was no community or corporate identity. We were all strangers to one another, brought together by circumstances for a brief, painful interlude.[15]

There was no food or running water in the hospital. In respect of food, the refugees were more often than not better placed than the hospital's patients. Many of the family groups arrived with small supplies of canned food which they eked out among themselves. Water was a major problem. Although February is one of the cooler months in the Philippines, the temperature was nevertheless over 85°F, with humidity ranging between 80 and 90 percent.[16] Smoke from fires, fumes from shelling and the perpetual dust merely exacerbated the situation by making dry throats drier. Providentially there was an artesian well in the grounds behind the hospital, but to reach it involved putting lives at risk due to the attention of snipers and the artillery fire. Luis Estebán, then 13 years old, recounts how members of each group took it in turn to collect water. Since there were 7000 refugees in the hospital and only one well, waiting in line was inevitable. While he was waiting patiently for his turn, there was an artillery attack. The man in front of him was killed by a piece of shrapnel entering his back, and one or two others were also killed or injured. When eventually he filled his glass jar for the group (three spoonfuls of water each, three times a day), he returned, yet was acutely tormented by the experience *en route*. The patients he passed lying in beds in wards and corridors were infrequently tended.

> They would feebly stretch out an arm and beg for water as I passed them with my precious cargo. Unable to speak from weakness, their hollow cheeks and sunken eyes pleaded more eloquently than words for succor and a life giving drink.

His loyalty was to his family, for whom he had risked his life to secure a simple jar of water. Shutting out their pleas from his mind he ran past the beds, 'unwillingly ignoring the unfortunate occupants.'

A volunteer came forward to leave the hospital to tell the Americans that there were only civilians in the hospital buildings. Inching the main door open he squeezed through, then shut the door behind him. Shortly after, there was the sound of shots. No one was prepared to risk his life to see what had happened, so it was never known whether the man had succeeded in his mission.

The infantry attack on the hospital continued to make slow progress through to February 16, which is the first time the Americans became aware of the presence of the refugees. Estebán tells of two air force P-51 Mustang fighters coming in and strafing the hospital, 'but stopped when they saw we were civilians.' Perhaps that was how the truth was discovered. Fire was accordingly moderated to the foundation defenses 'in so far as practicable.' On the 17th, 2000 civilians had come out of the building,[17], followed by a further 5000 at night. For these people who had been endangered in the American artillery's firing line, there was no evidence of animosity. The contrary was true:

> We couldn't contain ourselves. The poor soldiers realized that there were still snipers about and they were trying to quiet us down. It was hopeless. The snipers didn't worry us. We were with the Americans! We were safe! We were liberated![18]

Slowly the people in the hospital had been ushered out through the main door to stare unbelievingly at the death and destruction around them. Sprawled in front of the door, in the driveway, lay a dead Japanese. Estebán, the boy, went up to the body and spat on it. His father, who had seen what he did, came to him saying gently: 'Don't do that. He was a human being.'[19] The next day the 148th consolidated its position at the hospital, cleared the Japanese out of the University, and partially cleared Assumption College before handing over the sector to the Cavalry on February.[19]

A brigade of the 1st Cavalry, comprising the 5th and 12th Cavalry Regiments, came under command of the 37th Infantry Division at Rizal Stadium on February 16. With the Japanese-defended perimeter shrinking, such a reorganization was a sensible command and control expedient. The fight for the Rizal Stadium complex had been severe. The breakthrough occurred when three tanks burst through the eastern wall of the baseball ground to support the cavalrymen pinned down by fire from strong bunkers inside the stadium. After that, on February 18, the coliseum, Rizal Stadium and the ruins of Fort Antonio Abad were declared clear of the enemy. The Americans had destroyed the Second Naval Battalion, who had lost 750 men killed. The remainder infiltrated north to join up with their comrades still fighting. The American Cavalry lost 40 men killed and 315 wounded.[20] By this action the attackers were able to leapfrog up to Taft Avenue and also to open a line of advance northward along the shore. Thus the erosion of the Japanese position in Manila carried on relentlessly, the Japanese falling back under pressure from the north (where the attack was temporarily stalled up against the General Post Office and Manila City Hall), and the south and east toward an obvious showdown at Intramuros. The nature of the fighting was typically one of attrition. For every American killed, they killed 17 Japanese. They were able to maintain their high score rate not by taking unnecessary risks with their infantry but by pummeling even the most lightly held Japanese positions with great barrages of artillery and mortar fire, often supported by armor. The residents were caught in between. For every American soldier who died, so did 100 civilians.

On February 16 the McMicking-Hall residence's population had grown to 100 people, many the survivors from the St Paul's Convent massacre. It was a house surrounded by a cauldron of fire. Many of the homes around Dakota Street were built of wood. At night the sky was painted red from the crackling fires whose crashing timbers released spirals of golden sparks upward through the clouds of smoke. The next-door house was on fire and, as a precaution, those in the McMicking-Halls' house had their most precious possessions laid out in family piles in the garden. It was here where the refugees routinely passed their time, sitting out among the fires late into the night. They had become somewhat *blasé* about the shelling, listening for and recognizing the sound of the incomings, waiting until the last moment before deciding to dive for cover. When a more substantial barrage was evident, the people took shelter in sandbagged rooms inside, or under the house, but always someone was detailed to remain in the garden to safeguard the family belongings.

It was on the afternoon of the 16th that one of the group in the garden met a man who should not have been there, and asked: 'What are you doing here, you should be in North Manila?'

'I came in with the American soldiers, who are about a block away, to locate my family,' came the reply.

This caused a commotion, for no one there had known quite how close the Americans were. To prove the point, the visitor took two men and Rod Hall, aged 12, half a block to meet the soldier.

'Should we cross over to the American lines?' the American was asked.

He replied in the affirmative. Rod returned to the house, collected up his two younger brothers, Ian, 11, and Alaistair, 9, his sister Consuelo, 7, and the house staff, and, with most of the people there, abandoned their home. Inside the garage, on blocks, sat a 1941 Studebaker. It survived the war undamaged, only to be appropriated by the Americans.

The motley group of refugees followed the Americans closely, fully aware that sheltering in the ruins there were Japanese snipers. A shot rang out and a boy next to Rod fell to the ground, screaming. Rod stood transfixed, looking down at the body, only to be shaken out of his trance by an American shouting: 'For God's sake move! Get out of here!' On Taft Avenue they were held up by machine-gun fire. Their adopted American said: 'Wait here, I'll get some help.' Taking another GI with him, he dashed across the avenue, diving for cover safely on the other side. Half an hour later he returned, accompanied by a tank. While the tank fired bursts to keep the enemy's heads down, the children got behind the tank, crouching and walking along its safe side, then dashed the remaining distance across the avenue. By now they were all physically and emotionally exhausted. They spent the remainder of the night in the open on California Street, to be awoken by some friendly Americans who had in their trailer the many components of the traditional American breakfast. Having eaten their fill, they set about the construction of a shelter until, quite by chance, they were spotted by a distant relative, Arturo Ortigas. 'Your father's frantic with worry,' the man said. 'I'll take you to him.' They skirted the fighting in the city center, taking a circuitous route to the east to Santo Tomás, where they had an emotional reunion with their father.[21] The obvious question was: 'Where is mother?' The answer is supplied by Rod Hall's uncle, J.R. McMicking. (Joseph McMicking was the only Philippine-born member of MacArthur's party which left Corregidor in 1942. He returned as a lieutenant colonel and was the guiding light in the development of Makati, the new center of Manila.)

> At the retaking of Manila in February 1945 by the US Forces, of which I was a part, my sisters Consuelo [Rod Hall's mother] and Helen, my brother Alfred and my mother, all of whom had been arrested, were assassinated by the remnants of the Japanese Forces. I was asked to identify the bodies but it was not possible to do so as two weeks had elapsed since they were killed by machine-gun and grenades. They were four out of about 200 corpses piled up in the basement of the Masonic Temple of Manila on Taft Avenue.[22]

The Moreta residence was another that became a haven. On the night of February 14 a group of up to 60 people, of both sexes, varying ages and different nationalities, their homes destroyed, took refuge in the only remaining house in the neighborhood, that of Dr. Rafael Moreta.[23] It was located at 417 Isaac Peral Street, on the corner of Florida Street, in Ermita. Attempts to escape from the incessant shelling and fires by moving out of the area and into a safer location were frustrated by armed Japanese who, on occasion, machine-gunned the refugees, killing and wounding them. Those who had found themselves in the Moreta house therefore had no option for the time being but to stay put.[24]

At approximately midday on February 17 a group of about 20–25 Imperial Japanese Marines, armed with bayoneted rifles and pistols and led by an officer, entered the shattered building. The officer was described as a short, stocky man with slanting eyes, and short hair visible under his steel helmet. He had a big, thick mustache and a permanent, devilish, sarcastic smile. He ordered the men to be separated from the women and children. The Japanese took the 20 men into the dining room, where they were searched for arms and then forced to hand over their remaining valuables. Once that process had been completed, the men were forced into the bathroom. They had been there for less than five minutes when an elderly Spanish man was called out. There was a shot, and the thud of a body hitting the ground. Another man was called out and the process repeated. The next to be summoned was Mr Prudencio Chicote, but the soldiers had dragged him only a few steps when the officer intervened, directing Chicote to return to the bathroom. Flight from the room was impossible because two armed men stood guard at the door. Then, in Chicote's words: 'At the same time that we heard our women screaming and our children weeping out in the living room, the Japs opened the bathroom door cautiously and threw a hand grenade into the crowded bathroom.'

Men fell dead and wounded, and then came another grenade, taking a further toll. When the third was tossed in, José Maldonado instinctively kicked it. He lost the toes of his right foot and both he and Chicote fell, wounded. Chicote lost consciousness. When he came to, he was aware of the soft groans of the terrified wounded. A number of dead lay on the tiled floor. His wife, his child, his two sisters and their children had been left in the dining room. Despite a broken and shattered leg, he hurried out of the bathroom.

> And there I saw the most horrible picture I've ever seen. Sprawled on the floor, full of blood, one over the other, lay some 30 or 35 women and children. I sought for my wife. I found her, face downward, arms tightly embracing my child, stiff, cold and dead. She had five big bayonet wounds on the back, pierced to the chest. The child had three. And all around, the dead and the dying and the wounded showed the same bayonet wounds.

Three mutilated bodies showed plainly that they had been brutally raped before being murdered.

On February 18 a fragmentation grenade and then an incendiary grenade were lobbed among the survivors. The ensuing fire forced them to abandon the house, and straight into the gunfire of the Japanese. Just when it seemed that all the witnesses to the atrocity would be dispatched, American artillery fire forced the Japanese to take cover. During that interval the survivors of the Moreta massacre crawled off into the surrounding ruins. Chicote found refuge in his father's house on the corner of San Luis and San Carlos Streets. He remained there for five days, wounded, with very little water, practically no food, and with the anguish of what he had seen. Meanwhile the fight to liberate Manila had moved on.

The advance of the cavalry on the left flank up the shoreline of

Manila Bay was confronted by four potential problem areas before reaching the South Port adjoining Intramuros on the west. The first was the office and residence of the US High Commissioner to the Philippines on Dewey Boulevard, at the western end of Padre Faura Street. The second comprised two clubs, the Army and Navy and the Elks, both of which had served as headquarters for the defending Japanese. The third problem area was the wide open spaces of New Luneta, Burnham Green and Old Luneta. To the north of this green area sat the Manila Hotel. The penthouse of this five-storey building was the palatial family home of the MacArthurs, a gift to the great man by the Commonwealth government. In addition to the provision of a palatial residence, MacArthur was also given a gift of US$500,000 in cash.

The northward, armored approach into this sector began at 11 a.m. on February 19. The Japanese had arranged their defenses so that the Commissioner's residence and the two clubs were mutually supportive. The tanks were unable to break through on the first day and withdrew until a close artillery support fire plan could be drawn up, with a view to resuming the attack at 8.15 a.m. the next day. When launched, the resistance in and around the residence crumbled, and the clubs offered no further resistance. The Japanese had withdrawn toward Intramuros during the night. The cavalry stopped along San Luis Street, short of the open area, to contemplate the hotel. It was here that the menfolk of the unfortunate women of the Bay View Hotel had been taken. The Americans knew that the hotel and its surrounding area were defended in strength. Just to concentrate their minds, their Commander-in-Chief, Douglas MacArthur, arrived on the scene.

MacArthur was particularly anxious to rescue the possessions he had left behind. By all accounts the penthouse was still intact, due, he surmised, to the presence at the entrance of two vases given to his father by the Emperor of Japan. The General's optimism was supported by an account[25] that his furnishings and personal belongings had remained largely intact throughout the three and a half years the penthouse had been in Japanese use. There was a belief that some of the Japanese military chiefs, including General Yamashita, had removed some items as souvenirs to decorate their own homes in Japan. This belief was corroborated by the finding in a warehouse of a barrel marked 'Japanese Medical Supplies.' 'Carried to the General's headquarters (MacArthur's), the barrel yielded, in all, one complete silver tea service, a silver cocktail shaker with matching cups, a silver candelabra and a silver pitcher.' The villain was suspected to have been General Yamashita.[26]

The attack, supported by artillery, including two 105mm self-propelled guns and a platoon of tanks, began on February 21.[27] The point of entry was the old eastern wing, which was found to be defended in the usual way, centered on interior strongpoints, most of which were in the cellar and in interconnecting tunnels. The eastern wing fell, intact, by mid-afternoon, but the new or west wing, which included MacArthur's penthouse, proved to be a tougher nut to crack during the course of the fighting. Fortunately the civilians inside the hotel were able to make their escape. On the 22nd, MacArthur watched the battle from the New Luneta, despite being under machine-gun fire from the hotel itself. Then, to his horror, MacArthur saw that his home had been set afire. 'I watched with indescribable feelings, the destruction of my fine military library, my souvenirs, my personal belongings of a lifetime. It was not a pleasant moment.'[28] Not one to fear for his personal safety, the general entered the hotel and climbed the stairs, escorted by machine-gunners.

> Every landing was a fight. Of the penthouse, nothing was left but ashes. It had evidently been the command post of a rearguard action. We left its colonel dead on the smouldering threshold, the remains of the broken bases of the Emperor at his head and feet – a grim shroud for his bloody bier.[29]

However, the fall of the Manila Hotel had cleared the left approach towards Intramuros.

Over on the right flank, the advance on Intramuros had been delayed for eight days by Japanese holding a complex centered on the New Police Station on Isaac Peral Street and the St Vincent de Paul Church (San Marcelino), San Pablo Church and the Manila Club, both on San Marcelino Street. The division did not have the option to contain and bypass the area, for to have done so would have left a dangerous salient within the divisional area.[30] The battle for the buildings swung to and fro. The Americans would gain a foothold only to have to release it again. Unusually, the Japanese held the upper floors and had destroyed the stairways. Unable to employ their usual 'top-down' tactics, the Americans were forced to adopt a 'bottom-up' approach, suffering the effects of Japanese dropping grenades on them through holes in the upper floors. Eventually the tried-and-true tactics of massive artillery and superimposed direct fire from tanks won the day as each strongpoint succumbed until, on February 20, the complex was in American hands. All that now remained on the outer periphery of Intramuros were the General Post Office and the City Hall.

The City Hall was manned by 200 Japanese, who fought with their customary fanaticism to the last man. After eight days, the defence had been reduced to 20 men located on the second floor. Called upon to surrender they, like the Old Guard before them at Waterloo, refused. They were incinerated by flames from flamethrowers pouring their fiery liquid through holes in the ceiling above them. The attack on the General Post Office occurred concurrently with that on the City Hall. Strategically, the Post Office was the more important of the two, for it controlled the north-south approach to the northerly access into Intramuros as well as being connected to the walled city by trenches and tunnels. Robert Ross Smith, author of *Triumph in the Philippines*, expressed surprise that, in view of these factors, 'why the Japanese made no greater effort to hold the structure is a mystery'.[31] The Corps and Divisional artillery blasted the General Post Office for three days, during which the infantry made multiple attempts to secure a foothold. That was not achieved until February 22 and it was not until the 23rd that all became still inside the ruined building. That night the last Japanese survivors of the battle for Rizal Hall, on the northern side of Padre Faura Street, on the University of the Philippines campus, faced the inevitable and took their lives. The fighting which had begun in this central sector ten days earlier with the Philippine General Hospital had cost the Americans 600 casualties, of which over 100 infantry casualties were not battle-related.

Sickness and the strain of combat were now taking a toll that could not be ignored. February 23 had wider significance in so far as the ending of resistance in the Rizal Hall coincided with the planned attack at 8.30 a.m. on Intramuros. Three public buildings to the southeast of Intramuros – the Legislative Building, the Finance Building and the Agricultural Building – were still in Japanese hands. Other than these, there were no other Japanese defenses remaining in Manila except for Intramuros and the adjoining South Port district. Intramuros was in the hands of the Japanese

Manila Naval Defense Force. They had the benefit of some very minor reinforcements from the Central Force and the Fifth Naval Battalion, which otherwise, to all intents and purposes, had been destroyed where they had stood.

# NOTES

1 'Philippine Area Naval Operations, Part IV, January 1945–August 1945,' *Japanese Monograph No. 114* (Military History Section HQ Army Forces Far East, 1952).

2 Ibid.

3 *Reports of General MacArthur*, Vol II., Part II 'Japanese Operations in the South West Pacific Area' (Washington DC, 1966), p. 499.

4 Based on information supplied by Ricardo T. José, Tokyo.

5 *Japanese Military Field Code.*

6 For details of Japanese defenses, see 'Japanese Defense of Cities as exemplified by The Battle for Manila,' *A Report by XIV Corps* (HQ Sixth Army, July 1 1945); also Chapter 7, below.

7 Pedro Picornell, 'The Remedios Hospital 1942–1945. A Saga of Malate' (Unpublished), p. 69.

8 Fr. Arthur Price, 'Malate Martyrs. The Columban Fathers in Manila before and during the Japanese Occupation 1942–1945' (Unpublished), p. 6.

9 Picornell, 'The Remedios Hospital,' p. 52.

10 Ibid., p. 55.

11 Price, 'Malate Martyrs,' p. 3.

12 Carmen Guerrero Nakpil, *A Question of Identity. Selected Essays* (Manila, 1973), 'Benevolence', pp. 204–205.

13 Robert Ross Smith, *United States Army in World War II. The War in the Pacific: Triumph in the Philippines* (Washington DC, 1963), p. 286.

14 A point corroborated by Luis R. Estebán, 'My War. A Personal Narrative' (Unpublished), p. 29: 'As it happened there were no troops in the hospital itself; the buildings of the University of the Philippines, next door, and other buildings behind the hospital, were being used by soldiers as defensive posts.'

15  Interview with the author, Manila, July 26, 1994.
16  This account is based on Estebán, 'My War.'
17  Smith, *Triumph in the Philippines*, p. 287.
18  Estebán, 'My War,' p. 33.
19  Ibid.
20  Smith, *Triumph in the Philippines*, pp. 278–279.
21  The foregoing is based on interviews conducted in London between the author and Roderick Hall.
22  Taken from a dictation of J.R. ('Joe') McMicking and supplied by Consuelo H. McHugh, Tiburon, California.
23  The account of the massacre at the Moreta residence is based on the report of Prudencio Chicote before the War Crimes Commission dated October 31, 1945, and the testimonies of Maria Elena and José Manuel Maldonado, *USA v. Tomoyuki Yamashita*, Vol. VII, pp. 738–756.
24  See also testimony given by José Manuel Maldonado, ibid., p. 741.
25  Beth Day Romulo, *The Manila Hotel* (Manila, 1987), p. 135.
26  Ibid.
27  Smith, *Triumph in the Philippines*, p. 280.
28  General Douglas MacArthur, *Reminiscences* (New York, 1964), p. 247.
29  Ibid.
30  Smith, *Triumph in the Philippines*, p. 282.
31  Ibid, p. 285.

# 6

# WITHIN WALLS

The comprehensive American observation of Intramuros began as soon as they crossed the Pasig. It was self-evident that the final Battle for Manila would be fought here. The investment of a moated fortress such as Intramuros, with two-thirds of its two-and-a-half mile circumference, 20-feet-high, stone-block walls still intact, was unique. But the outcome was never in doubt. What should have been a principal complication was the presence of the community of civilian noncombatants within the Walled City. These were essentially the women and children of the men whose burnt and rotting bodies lay stacked five deep within the fortress's dungeons.

The Japanese had built their defense inside and around the wall, which was 40 feet thick at its base, tapering to 20 feet at the top. The wall had been honeycombed in parts by a series of tunnels which gave the Japanese freedom of movement both to redeploy men and weapons within the fort and also to engage attackers from embrasures and apertures cut in the stone. The dungeons and tunnels had been strengthened to form strongpoints, and gun emplacements were to be found along the length of the wall. These external positions had, for the most part, been registered by the Americans, to be taken out before or during the fire plan designed to open up paths through which the infantry would attack.

The attack on Intramuros can be conveniently divided into three phases: planning and preparation, the main bombardment, and fighting through the objective. An essential prerequisite, however,

was to give to the Japanese a final request from the XIV Corps commander to release the internees and for the Japanese to surrender.
The message was broadcast in Japanese from the northern shore
of the Pasig at 1.30 p.m. on February 16, and repeated on enemy
radio frequencies:

> Your situation is hopeless – your defeat inevitable. I offer you an
> honorable surrender. If you decide to accept, raise a large Filipino
> flag over the Red Cross flag now flying and send an unarmed
> emissary with a white flag to our lines. This must be done within
> four hours or I am coming in. In the event you do not accept my
> offer, I exhort you that, true to the spirit of BUSHIDO and the
> code of the SAMURAI, you permit all civilians to evacuate the
> Intramuros by the Victoria Gate without delay in order that no
> innocent blood be shed.[1]

There was no reaction from the Japanese, although escapees
reported that a number of the sailors and marines who heard
the American broadcast wanted to surrender. They were prevented
from doing so by their officers. The planning and preparations to
take Intramuros went ahead with renewed vigor.

Before the Americans could adopt their plan of action they had
to consider all the factors relating to the attack, finessing these into
a series of courses of action before selecting one preferred course as
which the plan was built. They knew, from their own observation and
through the debriefing of escapees, that the Japanese defenses were
strongest in the east and south – that is, along the obvious approach
routes. Moreover the enemy, who still held in their possession the
Legislative, Finance and Agricultural Buildings, could bring fire to
bear against any attacks from the southerly and easterly sectors.
Obviously these buildings could have been taken out in advance of
the attack on Intramuros, but there was a preference to leave them
until last. It was always possible that the Japanese forces could be
screened out by smoke and contained by troops on the ground – and
this was done. It would transpire that this, the final clutch of public
buildings, would prove to be more difficult a task than the Walled
City. There were problems associated with an attack from the west,
not least the securing of start lines within the maze that was the South
Port area. In addition, infantry prefer fire support to be behind
them or to the flanks. Since the best fire positions were to the east

and northeast of Intramuros, this would have meant the infantry advancing into friendly gunfire. Given the Americans' sensitivity about their own casualties and the real risks of inflicting casualties on their own people, such a course of action was a nonstarter.

Whereas the approach from the north – the north bank of the Pasig – had the advantage of being home territory, the south bank had suffered the effects of the attention of heavy artillery fire. In consequence, the approach up into the fort on the south bank was strewn with a scree of rubble, stretching down to the low-water mark. Attacking infantry would be slowed considerably at this, the most vulnerable point in an assault river crossing.[2] The hazard could be largely overcome by attacking when the tidal Pasig was at its high-water mark. Such factors as these lead planners toward determining when and where, or rather the time and place of the attack. Providentially, the great wall ended at the Intendencia building, or Government Mint, so that a gap like an open door led through into the enclosed city. Surprisingly the gap appeared to be only lightly defended; the weight of the defense on this, the northern wall, being centered around the northeast corner.[3] To succeed, the assault river crossing would require dedicated and accurate close support from artillery, armor and mortars. Better still, the allocation of a number of sorties of fighter-ground attack aircraft would be a useful bonus.

General Beightler's argument for the use of aircraft not only to support the infantry but also to help reduce the obstacle was convincingly put to General Griswold, the XIV Corps' commander. Central to Beightler's argument was his forecast of likely high casualties if he were to be denied the use of all means at the corps' disposal. All the generals at the tactical and operational levels were so imbued with the fear of being identified with high casualties that they were prepared to call into being any measure likely to reduce the threat to their own men.[4] Griswold did, admittedly reluctantly, concede to Beightler's request and passed it along the chain of command to be rubber-stamped by General Krueger, Commander Sixth Army.

The corps commander asked Krueger for all the dive bomber squadrons of Marine Air Groups 24 and 32 (from Mangaldan Field at Lingayen Gulf) and for a squadron of Fifth Air Force P-38s equipped to conduct air strikes.[5]

163

With the exception of a number of air-strikes within Manila city and Intramuros which had slipped through the net, air power had been contained to the city's periphery and beyond. Krueger, aware of MacArthur's specific orders denying the use of air attacks within the city, requested MacArthur's opinion of the XIV Corps proposal, for otherwise he intended to give it his approval. MacArthur vetoed the plan in the following terms:

> The use of air on a part of a city occupied by a friendly and allied population is unthinkable. The inaccuracy of this type of bombardment would result beyond question in the death of thousands of innocent civilians. It is not believed moreover that this would appreciably lower our own casualty rate although it would unquestionably hasten the conclusion of operations. For these reasons I do not approve the use of our bombardment on the Intramuros district.[6]

Frustrated in their endeavors here, the corps and divisional commanders earmarked a hefty package of firepower from their own combined resources totalling nine battalions of 105–240mm howitzers, a battalion of tanks, and a battalion of tank destroyers. When 24 4.2-inch mortars of the 82nd Chemical Mortar Battalion and the self-propelled guns of the regimental Cannon Companies were included, the total number of artillery pieces used in support of the assault on Intramuros exceeded 140.

Although the planners were impressed with the possibility of attacking over the Pasig, they feared that the Japanese, through the device of their many tunnels, would reinforce at the point of attack and thereby throw their infantry back over the river. The obvious deduction was that there had to be multiple points of attack, which, when taken further, meant that the wall would have to be breached in one or more places. In order to accommodate this aim, on February 19 two breaches were made in the eastern wall. One was between Quezon and Parian Gates. One hundred and fifty rounds of 8-inch howitzer shells fired indirectly[7] made a clean breach in the wall. The second breach was made between Parian and Victoria Gates, utilizing 150 rounds of 155mm howitzer shells fired directly,[7] followed by 29 rounds of 8-inch howitzer shells to blast away the rubble. Concurrently, the 129th Infantry Regiment assembled at Caloocan, north of the Pasig.

It was definitely decided that the assault upon Intramuros would initiate with an amphibious crossing over the Pasig River by the 129th Infantry, while the 145th Infantry moved overland west and through the breaches made by the artillery.[8]

The role of the 145th Infantry Regiment seemed on the face of it to be an unenviable one. History is replete with examples of bloody stormings of breaches, yet the planners had thought the situation through well and were reasonably optimistic of success.

Although the breaching of the walls by the heavy artillery caused rubble to slide into the breaches and block them for movement of vehicles, it was expected that, with close co-ordination between the preliminary artillery and mortar bombardment and the infantry assault, the infantry would be able to negotiate the rubble blocking the breaches and enter the city with a minimum of casualties.[9]

Having therefore decided on the place of the attacks, the next question related to timings: whether by day or night, and the precise time. Attacking a warren of blitzed streets that were mined and covered by interlocking and enfilade machine-gun fire calls for absolute control, a level of control which cannot be achieved at night. Surprise was not a consideration in deciding between a day or a night attack, for the Americans had spelled out their intentions to the Japanese. In daylight, the infantry could move effectively, and assuredly come in behind the preparatory fire. Moreover, when elements got into difficulty, observed supporting fire could more easily be brought down. If troops are to be used *en masse* in an urban environment, daylight is preferable to night. 'To have sent small raiding parties into the area in the face of known enemy defenses would have resulted in heavy loss of life.'[10]

So it was to be a daylight attack. The Pasig reached its high-water point in the early afternoon but, since it was more important on Day 1 to have the maximum number of available daylight hours, the tidal Pasig did not become the controlling factor.

Gun positions were carefully reconnoitered in daylight two to three days before the attacks began. Headquarters 37th Infantry Division's Field Order Number 30, issued at 6 p.m. on February

22, announced that the assault would be made at 8.30 a.m. on the 23rd. Ammunition was prepared and, under cover of darkness, the guns fanned out to their predetermined positions and there took place the

> assigning (of) definite sectors of the wall as targets to each howitzer and gun section, preparation and erection of parapets in front of each howitzer and gun, laying wire, checking radio communications and digging holes for the trail spades of each piece.[11]

Observation posts in high buildings were occupied and machine-guns placed in position both to superimpose fire upon the artillery targets and to cover the withdrawal of the guns. In the small estuary across from the Government Mint, the Estero de Binondo, the engineer boats which would take the 129th Regiment over the river were slipped into the water. In the buildings to the east and west of the estuary, 26 guns awaited orders to fire on prelocated enemy positions and opportunity targets which would arise during the course of the attack. One key strongpoint close to the Government Mint had already been taken out. The bulk of the artillery was positioned to the east of Intramuros, the large-caliber weapons being situated opposite the two gaps in the wall. Also in support, and interspersed among the big guns, were 105mm self-propelled howitzers, tank destroyers and medium tanks, some as close to the wall as 60 yards.

At 7.30 a.m. on February 23 the order 'Fire!' was given. The corps and divisional artillery, tanks, tank destroyers, mortars and machine-guns, some of which 'had been nettling the Japs inter-mittently throughout the night, belched out volley after volley'[12] in what has been described as the most highly coordinated and devastating preparation of the entire Luzon operation.[13] Few areas within Intramuros were spared the detailed attention of the guns as they proceeded for one hour to go through the divisional fire plan. The missions of the direct-fire weapons were oriented around the Government Mint and the Quezon-Parian Gate area to the east. Then finally, at exactly 8.30 a.m., the guns fired a round of red smoke, signifying to the infantry that it was over to them.

The assault troops of the 145th Regiment waiting nervously behind the General Post Office raced off across the open area between the

Post Office and the wall. At the same time, the 129th Regiment's 3rd Battalion, in engineer assault boats, sped across the short expanse of water for the gap in the north wall close to the Government Mint. The preliminary bombardment had accounted for the mines, barricades and other obstructions at the entry points. Moreover its sheer intensity had served to shock and neutralize most of the defenders it had not killed. The inter-regimental boundary was Beaterio Street, running northeast to southwest. At 8.40 a.m. the artillery resumed, putting down a 100-yard barrier of high explosive, smoke and white phosphorus between the east and west walls in order to isolate the southern sector. The boats of the 129th went ashore unopposed between 8.35 and 8.40 a.m.[14]

> And the doughboys went over the rubble and into the city. We were firing into the city with 155[mm] howitzers, and when we made the amphibious assault, the first people to come out of there were two nuns, each one bearing a Filipino child. How they ever lived through that, I'll never know.[15].

Within a further ten minutes the 129th had made contact with the 145th coming in from the east. Their leading troops had not suffered casualties as they went through the breach south of Quezon Gate. Their comrades who followed walked through Quezon and Parian Gates unopposed. It was only as they cleared through to the center and Fort Santiago that they came under fire of any consequence. Just as the attack was beginning to lose its momentum, the Japanese shrewdly released 3000 hostages, mostly women and children, from San Agustín Church and the Del Monico Hotel. The Americans were then forced into a hurried plan to escort the internees out of the battle area.

Japanese paranoia of guerrillas in their midst within the Walled City accounted for the continuing pogrom against males. On February 17 Japanese marines ejected medical staff of the San Juan de Dios Hospital from the ruins of the Santa Rosa College where they had been sheltering. Lined up in front of the Santo Domingo Church, each one was bayoneted to death. Not satisfied with these killings, the Japanese entered the church and proceeded to kill the priests and some of the nuns found in the building. On February 18 it was the turn of San Agustín Church to suffer the attention of the Japanese.

The Spanish priests[16] who, after the original mass killings, had been allowed to return to San Agustín, had been relatively well treated, although there was little point in pretending that they were not under some form of open arrest. On February 18 all men were ordered to assemble in the church. There were a number of Filipinos among them, but they were self-confessed Japanese spies. One way – perhaps the only way – Filipinos imprisoned in Fort Santiago could secure their release was to agree to spy for the Japanese. For most of them, it was not an activity they relished or one they conducted with any sense of pride. The priests knew the score and, according to Father Belarmino: 'We tried to hide our feelings, even though there was always somebody who, on account of his temperament or of pain, could not contain himself any longer and would break into a tirade against the Japanese.'

The Japanese officer in charge assured the Filipino women in the convent that they were only taking the men of religion away for two or three days and that they should remain calm – the priests would not be harmed.

Without being permitted an evening meal, the clergy were taken off to a *bodega* in front of Santa Clara Convent. Once there, the officer in charge repeated his earlier promise to his anxious charges that nothing would happen and they would be released in two or three days. They stayed at the *bodega* for a further day without food or water. On the evening of February 19, between 8 and 9 p.m., an officer and several soldiers arrived. The priests and others were told to assemble in the street. 'Only the Spaniards,' said the Japanese officer, and repeated, it a number of times. He told the Spaniards that the building in which they had been was unsafe; they were being moved to one which was safer. They then formed ranks and, unusually for priests, were marched to General Luna Street. Suddenly, without warning, the Japanese encircled the priests. Reinforcements arrived in an obviously planned operation to give assistance in shepherding the Spaniards into shelters in front of the Cathedral, on the corner of General Luna and Aduana. There were about 125 men, of whom 37 were priests. Eighty men were crammed into Father Belarmino's stoutly constructed shelter. 'I remained near the door,' he wrote.

In about half an hour the Japanese began to throw hand grenades in through the air-holes. We were all very badly wounded. We ran to the door in order to go out and a group of soldiers received us with a volley, and what is worse, they laughed while they were doing it. Quite a number of us remained dead at the door. Then the Japanese covered the entrance with large stones, gasoline barrels full of earth. They covered the entrance as best they could so that we were being suffocated.

Father Belarmino had fared better than his colleagues and, working at the mound of earth blocking the doorway, he opened up an air-hole. Unfortunately, on February 20, a Japanese marine spotted the hole, fired several shots through it and then resealed the door with more earth. After a while, Father Belarmino repeated the earlier exercise, which was achieved without any further reaction. The conditions within the tomb became unbearable. He lay on top of the corpses of his companions while shells falling nearby shook earth and stones from the ceiling of the shelter, slowly but surely burying them. 'The groans of the dying could still be heard,' he continued. 'The dead bodies were already decomposing – there were already worms in them – and a swarm of flies covered everything.' Father Belarmino's side had been shattered by a grenade, but he was strong enough to assist a man more severely injured than him to escape in moonlight, just before midnight on February 22.

Both were weakened, having had nothing to eat or drink for four days. Father Belarmino left his friend to rest in the Bureau of Justice while he went off to the Santa Clara Convent for food and drink. The nuns, being assembled to move to San Agustín, had nothing to offer. Father Belarmino returned to the Bureau of Justice and scoured the building for food and drink. One of the toilet cisterns was found to be full of water and, once he had drunk his share, he took a canful back to his wounded colleague. Dawn on February 23 broke with the preparatory American barrage of artillery and machine-gun fire, 'so much so that it seemed a very inferno.' At 9 a.m. Father Belarmino heard a voice saying, 'Come on, come out.' 'I knew by the voice that it was truly an American – and my joy knew no bounds.' No one else had managed to escape from the particular shelter in which the two fortunate escapees had spent 70 hours. In all there were only six survivors.

In the course of one day, the representative units of the two American regiments had almost cleared Intramuros. The 129th had some difficulty in the American prewar headquarters of Fort

Santiago, where the Japanese had gone underground. White phosphorus, hand grenades and fuel oil poured through holes and then ignited reduced resistance to a token but, by nightfall, a few pockets of resistance remained. The two battalions of the 145th Regiment had similarly not completed their task of reaching the West Gate on Real Street and the South Gate of Gral Luna, 'but the Gates were covered by 145th fire to deny their use to the Japs, now being relentlessly compressed into the southwest corner of Intramuros.'[17] In addition to its containment role in and around the Legislative, Finance and Agricultural Buildings, the 1st Cavalry Brigade was responsible for clearing through the South Port district. By nightfall they had reached 16th Street and made contact with the infantry inside the Walled City. The taking of Intramuros was almost complete as the sun sank into Manila Bay. The success was beyond the planners' wildest dreams. The day's fighting had cost the 37th Infantry Division five dead and 62 wounded.[18]

One of the most bizarre events during the course of the first day's fighting had been the appearance of Japanese, impeccably dressed in American uniforms and equipped with Garand M-1 rifles, who sought by ruse to deploy into more beneficial positions. They were all killed. In addition: 'At one time, the white flag appeared accompanied by rifle fire.'[19] But that also did not work. The American success had been achieved through the impeccable timing and coordination of the very different roles performed by all arms throughout the battle. The infantry's sound platform had been provided by accurate and devastating, often superimposed, fire of artillery, armor, mortars and machine-guns. The gunners had fired 7896 rounds of artillery ammunition during the assault on Intramuros. But, as Smith wrote: 'The artillery alone could not win the fight; as usual, the last battle belonged to the infantry.'[20]

The 129th Regiment continued the mopping up in Fort Santiago throughout the night of February 23–24, but the all-clear was not finally declared until 12 noon on the 25th. In the southern sector, on the 24th, the rubble had been cleared sufficiently to allow tanks, flamethrowers and self-propelled cannon to come into the Walled City in support of the 145th Regiment. At 10.20 a.m. the all-arms group had secured the Santa Lucia Gate and by 12.15 San Agustín Church was in American hands. At 2.30 p.m. the final bastion of the Aquarium in the southwest corner fell and by 6 p.m. the whole of Intramuros was in American hands. The cavalry on the west flank drove through the Port district, seizing the Customs House by 12.30 and, at 4.55 p.m. declared the port area south of the Pasig River, including Engineer Island, free of Japanese. The Japanese defenders, presumed to have been in the region of 2000, had been annihilated. The infantry claimed to have killed half the garrison. Almost all the 25 prisoners were Formosan members of the Imperial Japanese Labor Force. At dawn on February 26 Rear Admiral Iwabuchi and the other officers with him committed suicide.[21]

The fort of Intramuros, built in 1571, had been destroyed. Smith's attitude to this sensitive matter was summarized as follows:

That the artillery had almost razed the ancient Walled City could not be helped. To the XIV Corps and the 37th Division at this stage of the battle for Manila, American lives were understandably far more valuable than historic landmarks. The destruction had stemmed from the American decision to save lives in a battle against Japanese troops who had decided to sacrifice their lives as dearly as possible.[22]

Smith does not make the point that inside the city walls the Japanese had already systematically burnt and destroyed most of the buildings. This is a point fairly made by General Krueger, Commander Sixth Army:

Most of the devastation was produced by the demolition work of the Japanese and by the fires they set. That this devastation was deliberate was evidenced by the Japanese commander's order to that effect which fell into our hands during the battle.

He went on:

Much of the destruction caused by our own artillery fire could have been avoided if the Japanese, where further resistance on their part was clearly futile, had heeded several radio broadcasts urging them to surrender.[23]

There were no reasonable options facing the Americans in their investment of Intramuros. If they had laid siege to the city, Japanese infiltration in and out of the fort would have represented an undesirable, festering wound. Moreover the many civilian internees might well have been progressively put to the sword or died of starvation during the course of a drawn-out siege. If the military commanders are to be criticized for their conduct of the battle, it was not at Intramuros but elsewhere in the city that reasonable objections can be levelled.

Other than pockets of resistance inadvertently bypassed on Burnham Green, the last remaining Japanese resistance in Manila was centered around three buildings in the triangular area bounded by Gral Luna, Burgos and Taft Avenue. The Legislative, Finance and Agricultural Buildings were much like Washington DC architecture yet built of reinforced concrete to the strongest, anti-earthquake specifications. Moreover, they sat out in parkland, thus presenting intending attackers with approaches across great expanses of open space.

> The buildings had been laboriously converted by the Japanese into individual fortresses of the most formidable type, with sandbagged gun emplacements and barricades in the doors and windows covering all approaches to each building as well as adjacent ones. Machine guns within the buildings themselves were sited to fire down corridors, stairways, and even inside rooms.[24]

The plan was simple. Mass artillery and other firepower means would soften up the three buildings with massive and intensive barrages from the morning of the 24th until the morning of the 26th. The 148th Regiment was assigned two of the buildings. Their mission was to attack and secure the Legislative Building before similarly addressing the Finance Building. Concurrent with the 148th's move against the Legislative Building was the 5th Cavalry Regiment's assault on the Agricultural Building. At 9 a.m. on February 26 the infantry and cavalry crossed the open ground to get to grips with their respective buildings. The procedure of clearing these buildings was much the same as had been experienced before, but the level of ferocity with which the Japanese defended their positions was more intense. The fight ebbed and flowed inside. Sometimes the Americans would withdraw for more artillery fire or flamethrower tanks to take over before the men on foot resumed their struggle. Not until midday on the 28th had the 148th secured the total wreck of what had been the Legislative Building.

The 5th Cavalry Regiment's initial assault was disrupted by flank fire coming from neighboring buildings and this delayed the assault proper on the Agricultural Building until February 28. By this time, the ongoing preparatory fire had been so devastating that most of the building had collapsed, like cards, leaving only one storey standing. 'The destruction appeared so complete,' records Smith, 'that as the cavalrymen moved in from the south they felt that not a single Japanese could be alive amid the mass of twisted steel and concrete rubble'.[25] They were wrong. It took the Cavalry the whole day to clear the remaining floor and by nightfall there were still Japanese fighting on in the basements. After an appeal to the Japanese to surrender had been ignored, gasoline and oil mixtures were poured through holes in the floor and ignited. Thus, on March 1, the last Japanese resistance in the Agricultural Building came to an end.

On March 1, 1945, the Finance Building was the sole building in Manila remaining in Japanese hands. The preliminary bombardment began at 2.30 p.m. and lasted for two hours. On completion of the fire mission an invitation was broadcast to the Japanese to surrender and, unusually, 22 Japanese emerged under a white flag, leaving 74 to fight on. The bombardment resumed at 8 a.m. on March 2 for a further two hours. The assault of the 148th stopped in its tracks as three Japanese came out carrying a white flag. The Americans allowed their vigilance to drop as they pondered whether this was the sum of those to surrender or merely the advance guard of the total body. As the assault troops stood out in the open, the Japanese raked them with machine-gun fire. The infantry withdrew and took their revenge by resuming the bombardment. When it had concluded, the Finance Building 'seemed to be standing only from sheer force of habit.'[26] By 6 p.m. the Americans had taken the pile of rubble that had been the building, with the exception of a small outpost of resistance on the top floor. The pocket was removed early on March 3. After dealing with sporadic interference from Wallace Park, the whole of Manila was in American hands and the Japanese defeat was complete. That day General Griswold, from his Headquarters at Grace Park, sent a teletype message to General Krueger informing him that all organized resistance in the city had ceased.[27] The cost to the Americans of seizing the three buildings had been 10 killed and 145 wounded. Again, casualties were kept to a minimum on account of the ready availability and unreserved use of massive firepower.

Thus ended the battle for Manila; a battle which resulted in the destruction of the city. The tally of fatalities was 1010 Americans, 16,665 Japanese [counted dead] and 100,000 of Manila's inhabitants. The death toll in Manila compares with the 78,150 killed in Hiroshima and the 84,000 who died in the great fire raid on Tokyo, of March 9–10, 1945. The Japanese had not confined their bestiality just to Manila. The following Bills of Particulars arising during the course of General Yamashita's trial reveal the extent of the massacres:

(42) February 28, 1945 in Bauang, Batangas, 500 civilians massacred and property destroyed.

(43) February 16–18, 1945 in Lipa, Batangas, more than 2000 civilians massacred and property destroyed.

(44) February 19, 1945 in Cuenca, Batangas, 984 civilians massacred and property destroyed.

(45) February 20, 1945, San José, Batangas, 500 civilians massacred.

(47) February 16–March 19, 1945, Santo Tomás, Batangas, 1500 civilians massacred.

(55) In Calamba, Laguna, 7000 civilians massacred.

These are a few of the examples arising over a short period of time. The only reasonably effective method of determining approximately the number of Filipinos to die during the course of the Japanese occupation is to examine the claims for reparations at the war's end. Bearing in mind that the population of the Philippines in 1940 (census) was 16,356,000[28], the number of claims submitted for the death of Filipinos at Japanese hands between December 8, 1941 and September 2, 1945, was 1,111,938.[29]

The real surprise of the Battle for Manila was the manner in which the majority of the inhabitants stoically and philosophically accepted the decimation[30] of their families by American artillery and mortars. The manner in which hospitals and residential areas were systematically bombarded by US artillery is really indefensible. The desire of any commander to protect his men's lives is understandable; it is what is expected of him. Where the line is drawn is where the guns of war are loosed upon inhabited areas where the enemy is either not present at all or present in such small numbers as not to justify carpet bombardment. There comes a time when the civilian population, even when it is not of one's own nationality, has to be a key consideration in deciding on the means employed. To some degree the people of Manila were unfortunate that General

174

Beightler's admittedly heroic 37th Infantry Division was apportioned the lion's share of the fighting in Manila.

General Beightler wrote a short report of the activities of his division after the war.[31] In this report, he wrote that the Battle for Manila had been 'a hard battle, the most costly of the War for the 37th.' He recounts how the initial limitation of the use of artillery was partially responsible for the division's high casualties. What he says in his report is an indication of the nature of the man, a hint of arrogance, and the top-down attitude which reached the most lowly mortar fire controller. 'To me,' he wrote, 'the loss of a single American life to save a building was unthinkable.' That's fair enough, so long as the building that is sacrificed is not full of noncombatants at the time. He went on:

The 37th had always believed in the use of heavy fire power to the maximum and we had, therefore, picked up the reputation of being the most wasteful division in the theater in the expenditure of artillery ammunition. This reputation has certainly never bothered us, for we only point to the fact that we fought for more than two years and lost fewer men than other divisions with comparable fighting.

Here is a hint of an echo of MacArthur's assertion that good generals don't have casualties, something which a civilian-general is more likely to take literally than his professional peers. 'Lavish use of artillery played a big part in making this record possible.' Such a concept, which had been employed in the wide open spaces of Clark Field, was transferred with few concessions into the heart of the city of Manila. In fact, if 4.2-inch mortars are included, the declared expenditure of ammunition is broadly similar – 46,602 rounds for Clark Field (132 guns, 48 4.2-inch mortars) and 42,153 rounds for Manila (100 guns, 48 4.2-inch mortars). In rural environments, a large number of separate missions are fired against a large number of targets, while in urban areas there are multiple missions fired against a few targets.[32]

Beightler took his concerns about the restrictions placed on his artillery to his corps commander, General Griswold, 'a grand soldier.' Beightler's case had been persuasive. As a result, he was able to get 'restrictions lifted to permit both direct and overhead, or indirect fire. From then on, putting it crudely, we really went to town.' He was crowing while Filipinos were crying for their devastated city.

> We used these shells and plastered the Walled City until it was a mess. It fell to us with ease we never expected. We made a churned-up pile of dust and scrap out of the imposing, classic government buildings. Our bombers have done some pretty fine alteration work on the appearance of Berlin and Tokyo. Just the same, I wish they could see what we did with our little artillery on the Jap strongholds of Manila.

Perhaps they should also have seen areas such as Ermita and Malate, which were not 'Jap strongholds.' 'I have no apologies to make,' he continued,

> although I know there was plenty of weeping and wailing from property owners who saw their buildings disappear in the blasts of 240mm shells. If I could have had those dive bombers too, I might have made the big rubble into little rubble. So much for Manila. It is a ruined city – unhealthy, depressing, poverty stricken. Let us thank God our cities have been spared such a fate.

The obvious question is: was Beightler out of control? It appears not. The interchange of messages between the 37th Infantry and XIV Corps, on February 16–18, suggests that Beightler had intended to raze the whole of Intramuros. On 18 March, 1957 he denied this. However, the fact that the real American damage, necessary damage, occurred along the northeastern corner of the wall is perhaps indicative of the corps commander's intervention. After the fall of Intramuros the Americans demolished houses which had already been destroyed by the Japanese in order to create space for tented accommodation and supplies. Smith is of the opinion that 'it is certain that General Griswold believed it was Beightler's intent to raze all of Intramuros.'[33]

# NOTES

1  *Report After Action. XIV Corps. M-1 Operation 29 July 1945*, p. 114.
2  It is assumed that the actual crossing of the water obstacle would have been screened by smoke.
3  Robert Ross Smith, *United States Army in World War II. The War in the Pacific: Triumph in the Philippines* (Washington DC, 1963), p. 292.
4  Ibid., p. 293.
5  Ibid.
6  Ibid., p. 294.
7  Indirect fire means that the shells describe an arc from gun to target; direct fire means that there is a straight line between gun and target.
8  *Report After Action. XIV Corps*, p. 116.
9  *Sixth United States Army Report of the Luzon Campaign 9 January 1945–20 June 1945*, Vol. I (1945), p. 40.
10 *Report After Action. XIV Corps*, p. 119.
11 Glenn A. Steckel, 'The Role of Field Artillery in the Siege of Intramuros Manila P.I.,' Student Report, The Armored School, Fort Knox, Kentucky (May 1948), p. 9.
12 Stanley A. Frankel, *The 37th Infantry Division in World War II* (Washington DC, 1948), p. 288.
13 Stephen L. Garay, 'The Breach of Intramuros,' Student Report, The Armored School, Fort Knox, Kentucky (May 1, 1948), p. 10.
14 Smith, *Triumph in the Philippines*, p. 296.
15 General Clyde D. Edelman, 'The Clyde D. Edelman Papers. Drafts of Transcripts of Conversations with Clyde D. Edelman,' US Army Military History Research Collection (Unpublished).
16 Based on evidence given by Fr. Belarmino de Celis, Augustinian, to US Army, March 9, 1945.

17  Frankel, *The 37th Infantry Division in World War II*, p. 292.
18  Ibid.
19  *Report After Action. Operations of the 37th Infantry Division Luzon P.I., 1 November 1944–30 June 1945*, p. 81.
20  Smith, *Triumph in the Philippines*, p. 271.
21  'Philippine Area Naval Operations, Part IV, January 1945–August 1945,' *Japanese Monograph No. 114* (Military History Section HQ Army Forces Far East, 1952), p. 20.
22  Smith, *Triumph in the Philippines*, p. 301.
23  General Walter Krueger, *From Down Under to Nippon: The Story of Sixth Army in World War II* (Washington DC, 1953), p. 251.
24  *Report After Action. XIV Corps*, p. 127.
25  Smith, *Triumph in the Philippines*, p. 305.
26  Ibid., p. 306.
27  *Report After Action. XIV Corps*, p. 135.
28  W. Cameron Forbes, *The Philippine Islands* (1945).
29  These figures were declared in July 1951 by the Quirino Presidential Committee chaired by Secretary Salvador Araneta.
30  Here the word is used in its literal sense.
31  Major General Robert S. Beightler, *Report on the Activities of the 37th Infantry Division 1940–1945* (1945).
32  Kurt J. Sellers, *Artillery Ammunition Expenditures in Urban Combat: A Comparative Case Study of the Battles of Clark Field and Manila* (US Army Human Engineering Laboratory, Maryland, September 1989).
33  Smith, *Triumph in the Philippines*, p. 293, footnote 3.

# 7

# THE UNWANTED BATTLE: AN APPRAISAL

The Battle for Manila requires analysis. We need to know why the battle took place and whether it was avoidable, saving the enormous casualties inflicted. Next it is important to describe the way in which the battle was conducted by both the Japanese defenders and American liberators, to see if any useful lessons may be extracted in terms of urban fighting. Finally it is essential to place the battle in the wider context of the Philippines Campaign, which in turn must be seen in relation to the rest of the war in the Pacific Theater. Without such analysis, the battle becomes no more than a bloody and isolated incident, with little historical meaning. The dead deserve more than that as their epitaph.

At a strategic level, the reasons for the battle would appear to be straightforward. Manila was an understandable goal for the Americans, still smarting from the humiliations of 1941–2, and its liberation would symbolize their determination to smash the power of Japan in the western Pacific, while freeing Filipinos from enforced occupation. In addition, Manila was seen by many Americans, including MacArthur, as the key to the Philippines, representing what is known in modern military parlance as a 'center of gravity,' the loss of which would unhinge the Japanese defense of the islands as a whole. In other words, if Manila fell, the enemy would have no further reason to continue the fight. Such an optimistic analysis (which was soon to be proved wrong) was based on the undoubted significance of Manila as a superb port, surrounded by valuable airfields. If the next step on the Allied road to victory was to be

179

an invasion of the Japanese Home Islands, a mere 1800 miles away, control of both port and airfields would be vital.

But there was more to it than that. Manila was never the true center of gravity – that was the main Japanese army defending Luzon, situated outside the city – so other reasons for the battle need to be explored. Chief among these was clearly MacArthur's personal obsession with Manila as a symbol of his promised 'return.' Until he could hold a victory parade in the city and publicly hand power back to a Filipino Commonwealth government, his self-appointed task was incomplete.

Such a single-minded aim was manifested in a number of ways, all of which virtually guaranteed a battle for control of Manila. When the Sixth Army advanced south from Lingayen, MacArthur insisted on speed despite Krueger's understandable worries about Japanese counterattacks against his exposed flanks. The fact that no similar orders were given to those elements of the same army which faced Yamashita's main force to the northeast, implies that Manila was the only objective in MacArthur's mind. This is reinforced when it is realized that he was actively planning his victory parade before the city had been secured (see Appendix), and by his insistence on touring Manila while the fighting was going on. Indeed when US troops were about to assault the Manila Hotel on February 22, MacArthur appeared among them and assisted in the fighting, being among the first to enter his penthouse apartment after clearing operations floor by floor.[1] This was an extraordinary episode, reducing MacArthur to the role of squad leader and, of necessity, diverting his attention away from overall command of the Luzon Campaign. It was indicative of the depth of his obsession, summed up by his G-2, Major General Charles A. Willoughby, after the war was over:

> From the day of his confident parting message to the Filipinos, 'I shall return,' no deviation from MacArthur's single-minded plan is discernible. Every battle action in New Guinea, every air raid on Rabaul or PT-boat attack on Japanese barges in the Bismarck Sea, was a mere preliminary for the reconquest of the Philippines.[2]

Given that MacArthur viewed Manila as the key to victory in that campaign of reconquest, the city drew him like a magnet. It also appears to have clouded his military judgment, for his decision to surround the enemy, leaving no avenue of escape, ensured that Manila would be defended to the death. As the Chinese strategist Sun Tzu pointed out more than 2400 years ago, it is an integral aspect of the art of war to 'leave a way of escape to a surrounded enemy.'[3] Once the trap had been closed on February 12, 1945, Manila was doomed.

Such obsession at the top of the chain of command was sure to be reflected at lower levels, particularly as MacArthur's method of command precluded alternative proposals. Krueger, for example, seems to have favored a policy of bypassing Manila, leaving the Japanese garrison to 'wither on the vine' while the real threat from Yamashita was faced. This led him to advocate caution during the advance of XIV Corps from Lingayen, for he realized that his units were potentially vulnerable to counterattacks from both Kembu Group in the west and Shobu Group in the northeast. If these had materialized, XIV Corps could have been cut off from its supplies at Lingayen and forced to fight for its survival, probably in the vicinity of Clark Field. Yet he was reluctant to voice such fears too openly and proved susceptible to the pressures exerted by MacArthur for more speed in the drive toward Manila. It could be argued that, of all the American commanders, Krueger was the one who recognized most clearly that Manila was a false center of gravity, but there was little he could do once MacArthur had ordered him into the city, particularly when the ostensible reason for the advance was to rescue internees and prisoners of war at Santo Tomás and Bilibid. Once the 1st Cavalry and 37th Infantry Divisions were locked into the rescue plan, there was no way that a withdrawal could be countenanced or carried out. They had to fight for control of the city.

According to Eichelberger, there was another factor: Krueger's own ambition. It was strongly rumored that MacArthur had promised to appoint Krueger to command an army group in the eventual invasion of Japan, and although this was never officially documented,[4] it fitted exactly into MacArthur's preferred process of 'carrot and stick' when dealing with subordinate commanders. Whatever the truth, however, the implied criticism that Krueger chose to keep any reservations to himself rather than risk his career comes oddly from Eichelberger, who displayed all the symptoms of frustrated ambition himself during the advance on Manila. His letters to his wife ('Miss Em') are revealing. In them, he takes every opportunity to criticize Krueger, even going so far as to doubt his personal bravery, and catalogues every supposed slight against his own position as commander of the Eighth Army.[5] This may be understandable when it is realized that Krueger's Sixth Army was far better known to the American public than the Eighth – when Eichelberger was pulled out of Luzon to prepare for future operations, his satisfaction at having gained publicity for his command was apparent – but that does not excuse his high-handed actions during the 'race for Manila.' His insistence on treating the advance as a symbol of his superiority over Krueger led him, inevitably, to regard Manila as an objective that had to be forcibly occupied, preferably by elements of the Eighth Army, rather than bypassed.

Eichelberger's spearhead for the advance was the 11th Airborne Division, put ashore at Nasugbu on January 31, two days after a larger element of the Eighth Army – Major General Charles P. Hall's XI Corps – had landed further north at San Antonio. Yet Eichelberger chose to accompany 11th Airborne, leaving Hall to cut off and clear the Bataan Peninsula, chiefly it seems because the advance on Manila was likely to attract more publicity. This probably suited Hall, who conducted a successful (if largely unreported) campaign, but it must have made life difficult for the commander of 11th Airborne, Major General Joe Swing. He found that any command initiative he expected to enjoy was taken away, for Eichelberger stayed with him throughout, interfering at levels that were not appropriate to his position as an army commander and 'interpreting' orders from MacArthur in ways that jeopardized his airborne troops.

Eleventh Airborne was not well suited to a deep advance – it was small and not equipped with armor, heavy artillery or sufficient vehicles – and should have been devoted to securing the Tagaytay Ridge (its stated objective) until reinforced or relieved. Eichelberger chose to ignore this restriction, and although it can be laudable for commanders to display initiative, the results of such initiative must be worthwhile. As it was, 11th Airborne predictably bogged down as soon as it encountered determined enemy resistance around Nichols Field and began to take heavy casualties. At one point, Swing had to request artillery support from XIV Corps to the north, creating an unusual, and potentially dangerous, situation in which support fire was coming in from the front rather than the rear of the airborne forces. In addition, the division's supply lines, stretching back to Nasugbu, became overextended, making it difficult to sustain any operations. In the end the only tangible result was to ensure that the Japanese had no escape route out of Manila to the south, although it should be added that the airborne troops themselves fought with incredible bravery and undoubtedly diverted enemy resources that could have been devoted to the defense of Manila.

The outcome of all these command machinations was that both Krueger and Eichelberger were driven toward Manila, making a battle for control of the city inevitable. Krueger was under constant pressure from MacArthur and soon found himself committed to the northern suburbs; Eichelberger was determined to lead his troops into Manila to gain publicity and score career points. Behind both men was the driving force of MacArthur, obsessed with Manila as both a political and military objective.

But *was* there an alternative? The city could only have been bypassed if there was a reasonable chance that the Japanese garrison would accept its fate and surrender, presumably after suffering starvation and isolation from its own command chain. This had been the plan for Rabaul in 1943–4, but Manila was different in one key respect: it contained up to a million civilians who would by definition suffer even worse deprivations than the Japanese. Filipino guerrilla leaders were convinced that the civilian population would be held hostage or, far worse, massacred in large numbers to ensure Japanese survival in a siege situation, while Manila itself would be systematically destroyed.[6] MacArthur's G-2 staff was well aware of these fears, reinforced in early February when the Japanese set fire to the business district of Manila in response to Krueger's advance. Having experienced the fanaticism of Japanese defenders on islands from New Guinea to Saipan, the Americans understandably (and, as it turned out, quite rightly) assumed the worst in Manila. MacArthur's insistence on the rescue mission to Santo Tomás and Bilibid indicated a belief that internees and prisoners of war were about to be killed, and as XIV Corps pushed into the northern suburbs grim evidence of civilian massacres quickly came to light. In such circumstances, a battle to liberate Manila before its population was deliberately liquidated by the Japanese became essential on humanitarian grounds alone. There are those who believe that if the city had been bypassed, the civilian casualties would have been far higher.[7]'

In order to test the validity of this belief, it is necessary to look at Japanese plans and intentions. If there was a deliberate policy of destruction, the motives of MacArthur in pressing for an advance on the city become more laudable and the personality clashes between Krueger and Eichelberger less important. It does not alter the fact that command problems existed, and it certainly does not excuse some of the methods used by the Americans in securing the city, but it could make the reasons for the battle more understandable. Since 1945 it has been generally accepted, particularly in the United States, that Manila was destroyed principally by the Japanese, and that Yamashita, as overall commander, was responsible for ordering this to happen. Indeed it was one of the specific charges that Yamashita faced when brought before the American Military Commission in October 1945 and one of the reasons for the death sentence he received.[8] Legal arguments put forward in his defense may have pointed out that no evidence existed to suggest that he gave or signed specific orders for the destruction of the city or its population, but his role as overall commander, with responsibility for the actions of his troops, ensured his conviction and execution.

This is a simplistic view, based on an assumption that Yamashita actually enjoyed and exercised complete control. In reality the opposite was true. When he arrived in the Philippines in early October 1944 to take command of Fourteenth Area Army, he soon found that he was part of a complex command chain which seriously restricted his authority. His chief of staff, Lieutenant General Akira Muto, has left an account of events between October 1944 and September 1945 which makes it clear that Yamashita faced a number of persistent problems that were not taken fully into account at his trial.[9] Admittedly, Muto can hardly be described as a disinterested witness, but certain points he makes can be verified from elsewhere.

Chief among these is the fact that Yamashita was involved in a bitter debate about the Japanese response to American attacks on the Philippines, the first of which, on Leyte, occurred as Yamashita was settling into his new position. Field Marshal Count Terauchi, commander of Southern Area and headquartered in Manila until mid-November 1944, was surrounded by officers who believed firmly in 'the providential moment' – a precise time when American forces could be engaged in open battle and defeated – and were convinced that this would occur in the Philippines. In October 1944 these officers were excited by the prospect of seizing such a moment on Leyte, but were aware that it could not arise if the enemy was met on the invasion beaches, where naval and air bombardments would be severe. Far better, in their eyes, if the Americans could be drawn into a set-piece battle in the interior, fought at a time and place of Japanese choosing. Yamashita was not convinced, particularly if such arguments were extended to Luzon, preferring to inflict almost guerrilla-style damage while withdrawing into the mountains. His aim was to force the Americans to fight a long drawn-out campaign that would be time-consuming and costly, causing them to delay any assault on the Japanese Home Islands. When Terauchi withdrew his headquarters to Saigon, Yamashita seems to have taken the initiative and ordered his own strategy to be adopted. Units belonging to Fourteenth Area Army were withdrawn from Manila and Yamashita himself left the city to set up a command headquarters at Baguio, ideally placed for both counterattacks on possible landing beaches in Lingayen Gulf and, more importantly, delaying actions in the mountains. Manila itself was not to be defended, chiefly because it would tie down troops desperately needed elsewhere.

But Yamashita did not declare Manila an 'open city' (as MacArthur had done in December 1941), implying that he intended to maintain some troops and facilities in the area. His failure to withdraw completely from the city was cited at his trial as evidence of an intention to fight for its control, leading to destruction, although the real reason is probably far more mundane: he did not enjoy full rights of command over the troops involved. They belonged principally to the Navy and their commander, although ostensibly under Yamashita's operational control from the time of the American landings at Lingayen, looked to Vice Admiral Denshichi Okochi, commander of the Southwest Area Fleet, for his orders. According to Muto, Okochi readily accepted Yamashita's strategy, but many of his staff officers did not. They argued that Manila harbor was a vital facility that had to be denied to the Americans for as long as possible, partly through defending its approaches, partly through its destruction. Rear Admiral Sanji Iwabuchi, commanding the Manila Naval Defense Force, clearly believed the same and exploited the confusions of the command chain to ensure that he fought for control of the city.

Yamashita was aware of this – his repeated orders to Iwabuchi to pull out of Manila are well documented[10] – and for this reason he must be held partly to blame for the ensuing tragedy, but a plethora of practical problems meant that it was virtually impossible for him to exercise his authority. Communications between Japanese headquarters on Luzon were, at best, spasmodic, there was a chronic shortage of transport with which to move troops around, and guerrilla activity was disrupting the entire command infrastructure. Iwabuchi found himself in a position of unique freedom and wasted no time in exploiting it. The fact that most (if not all) the civilian massacres in Manila were perpetrated by Japanese marines under Iwabuchi's command reinforces the fact that the battle was essentially a naval affair.

The Battle for Manila therefore takes on the appearance of a Greek tragedy, with the main actors drawn inexorably toward a bloody climax by forces largely outside their control. On the American side, MacArthur's obsession with liberating the city closed his eyes to any alternative strategy and clouded his military judgment. Although there is evidence to suggest that bypassing the city would have led to even more destruction and loss of life than in fact occurred, the rivalry between Krueger and Eichelberger, deliberately exploited by MacArthur, undoubtedly contributed to the move to surround Manila rather than allow the Japanese an escape route. Neither commander was prepared to leave an open door in his sector, as this might suggest weakness and lack of resolve. Nevertheless, the actions of Iwabuchi in defying Yamashita's orders to evacuate Manila while there was still a chance to do so imply that the naval forces involved always intended to fight to the death. Yamashita's position in the command chain was never clear: he was unable to exercise authority over Iwabuchi and lacked support from Terauchi when he tried to do so. It was perhaps a little unjust to send Yamashita to the gallows, in part because of this, although it should be stressed that he was aware of the difficulties and appears to have made only halfhearted efforts to prevent the destruction of Manila. Caught in the middle was the civilian population, unable to avoid Japanese atrocities and forced to suffer the consequences of a battle that no one other than Iwabuchi actually wanted to fight. MacArthur would have preferred a victor's entrance into an undamaged city; Yamashita would have preferred to fight delaying actions in the mountains with all his forces available.

This was reflected in the conduct of the battle, which was fought by both sides on the basis of improvisation rather than carefully prepared tactical responses. Iwabuchi's Naval Defense Force may have created elaborate defenses, but they were ones that were put together quickly, implying an absence of long-term planning for an urban battle. Similarly, although some sources state that Beightler's 37th Division had been trained for fighting in built-up areas,[11] neither they nor the 1st Cavalry Division found it easy to deal with the realities of an advance through the city and had to experiment with their tactics as they fought. In such circumstances buildings were sure to be destroyed and civilians killed, often in ways that might have been avoided if more deliberate preparations had been made.

The Japanese units defending Manila were not a coherent force. To the north of the Pasig River, there were two Army detachments (about 3750 men), charged by Yamashita with the task of delaying any American advance from Lingayen while the evacuation of the city was completed. Designated the Manila Defense Force, they were commanded by Major General Takashi Kobayashi and were part of Lieutenant General Shizuo Yokoyama's Shimbu Group. They were expected to withdraw eastward, away from the city, once the Americans arrived, having destroyed bridges and carried out key demolitions. To the south of the river was Iwabuchi's Naval Defense Force, initially numbering no more than 3000–4000 men but steadily reinforced until, by late January 1945, it mustered a total of about 16,000 troops, some 2000 of whom were deployed onto islands in Manila Bay. They were drawn from a wide variety of units, principally Iwabuchi's own 31st Naval Special Base Force but including 'elements of naval flying units, crew members of both naval and merchant ships sunk or disabled in Manila Bay, and some civilian employees of the Naval Base.'[12] Iwabuchi intended to use them to hold Nichols Field and Cavite naval base, while mining Manila Bay and destroying any stores that remained. He interpreted this to mean that his main task was to fight the Americans to a standstill in and around Manila; he certainly seems to have had no intention to withdraw, arguing that he had 'no alternative but to carry out [his] primary duty of defending naval facilities.'[13]

Until late January 1945 the Japanese expected the main American advance on the city to come from the south or from the sea and organized their defenses accordingly, concentrating on the protection of Nichols Field, Fort McKinley and the harbor area. Iwabuchi was well aware that, if it came to a fight, his chief asset was control of the fortress of Intramuros, with an outer ring of defenses in the

Finance, Legislative and Agricultural Buildings, but when the threat from XIV Corps materialized, he had rapidly to shift his emphasis northward. Orders to this effect were issued on January 23,[14] giving the defenders about ten days in which to prepare positions that would delay the American advance. Thus, although Intramuros and the public buildings were well defended, having been subject to preparation for some time, other Japanese positions in the center and north of Manila were largely extemporized, using whatever was available at the time.

This does not mean that they were weak. The Japanese were adept at improvisation, exploiting all the opportunities presented by a city area. Street barricades were constructed quickly and effectively using anything from overturned vehicles to steel rails embedded in the ground or in concrete drums. Antitank and antipersonnel mines were deployed to protect the approaches to barricades and were sown, often indiscriminately, to impede movement over bridges, along roads or across open ground. In addition naval depth charges, taken out of store or recovered from vessels in Manila Bay, were concealed at key locations and electrically detonated as soon as American troops arrived, while ceramic mines, designed to avoid the normal methods of magnetic detection, were used as booby traps, occasionally on top of or around more conventional explosives. There were even cases of aerial bombs, recovered from crashed or disabled aircraft, being buried with a nose-impact fuse set close to the surface, requiring less than 50lb of pressure to set it off. The Botanical Gardens, for example, were described by the Americans as 'one vast minefield consisting of every type of obstacle from grenade booby traps to huge aerial bombs.'[15] In nearly all cases barricades and minefields were covered by machine-gun or rifle fire from protected positions.

Many such positions were pillboxes constructed from concrete, metal, wood and earth, depending on what was available and how long the defenders had to prepare. These were designed to absorb infantry fire and were normally protected by barbed wire as well as mines. Although buildings in the city often prevented the integration of pillbox defences – pillboxes were not always within sight of others around them and could not, therefore, provide supporting fire – some were connected by tunnels and trenches, allowing the defenders to move around even under American attack. In more open areas pillboxes were buried and camouflaged – in the Laloma

Cemetery, for example, three 25mm automatic cannon were dug in and disguised as burial mounds, 'complete with sod, flowers and statues or crosses.'[16] As the battle raged, many pillboxes gained additional protection from the rubble of buildings destroyed by American artillery fire or deliberately demolished by the Japanese themselves. As might be expected, bridges across the Pasig and other waterways in or around Manila were blown up, further impeding any American advance.

Effective use was also made of buildings, especially those such as private homes, churches and schools that had been designed to withstand the force of earthquakes. Approaches were covered by minefields, pillboxes and barricades, but it was inside the structures that some of the toughest defenses were found. The Japanese, drawn from different units and often left to their own devices, followed no set doctrine in the preparation of these defenses, although common sense often dictated the best policy. Corridors and room entrances were barricaded, pillboxes constructed and barbed wire deployed, usually on the ground floor but sometimes on every level including the roof. It was not unknown for artillery prices to be dragged into buildings and up stairways, nor for rooms and even blocks of buildings to be connected by tunnels. In addition, full use was made of basements or cellars as 'last-ditch' positions, from which the defenders could trigger explosive charges that demolished what was left of the building around the ears of the assaulting troops. Such techniques were more sophisticated in the government buildings protecting Intramuros, partly because the Japanese had spent more time preparing them, partly because the buildings themselves were strongly constructed to prewar American standards of earthquake protection and surrounded by open spaces. As a final bastion, the natural defenses of Intramuros were adapted to Japanese needs, with gun emplacements built into the surrounding wall, itself up to 40 feet thick in places. Indeed the Americans later described the defense of Intramuros as combining a 'fortress of the Middle Ages with the fire power of modern weapon.'[17]

The types of weapon deployed varied considerably, reflecting the improvised nature of the defense, but there was an emphasis on artillery and automatic weapons, capable of producing large volumes of fire over sustained periods. The Manila Naval Defense Force, denied access to Army weapons, scoured the city and its environs for anything that might be used. As a result, 12cm naval guns and antiaircraft guns were recovered from damaged ships in Manila Bay, and 20mm cannon were taken out of aircraft destroyed in American air-strikes. All were converted into ground weapons. In addition 25mm automatic cannon – the standard naval antiaircraft gun – appeared in large numbers, adapted to the ground role. Capable of firing 250 rounds a minute using high explosive (HE), HE tracer and armor-piercing (AP) ammunition, the 25mm proved to be an effective weapon, although its muzzle blast could give its position away. Equally effective (and more difficult to spot) was the 75mm field gun, examples of which were mounted on trucks which could move rapidly into position, fire a few rounds and then disappear. Other artillery pieces encountered by the Americans included 40mm antiaircraft guns, 47mm antitank guns and, for the first time in the Pacific Theater, large numbers of 200mm and 447mm rockets, fired from tubes, open troughs or rail launchers. The rockets proved to be frightening rather than destructive, affecting the morale of American troops because of the 'tremendous concussion, the noise, and the long time of flight.'[18] Artillery fire throughout the battle tended to be indiscriminate or pre-registered against road junctions, bridges and buildings that might be used by the Americans, reflecting a lack of observers and poor communications. In some cases, however, artllery tactics were quite sophisticated: as the battle developed, Japanese gunners learnt to fire airburst incendiary shells against American-held buildings, followed a few minutes later by HE shrapnel to catch fire-fighters in the open. There does not appear to have been a shortage of ammunition.

Mortars were often used in conjunction with the artillery, with the added advantage of being easy to hide, often behind buildings or barricades. The usual calibers were 81mm and 90mm, although 15cm versions were encountered. Some 50mm grenade-launchers were available, proving particularly devastating in the close confines of defended buildings, but the most effective weapon was undoubtedly the machine-gun. Large numbers of 13mm, 7.7mm and 7.92mm examples were deployed in pillboxes, behind barricades and inside buildings, capable of laying down such a weight of sustained fire that American advances were reduced to a crawl. Most of the Japanese defenders also had rifles, including a variety of American designs captured in 1942, and hand grenades seem to have been freely available. Molotov cocktails – petrol-filled glass bottles that were ignited using red phosphorus – were manufactured on a local basis and dropped into the streets from the windows of buildings or thrown room to room once the Americans had entered. Other extemporized weapons included cakes of explosives with an igniter attached, pole-charges comprising 10-foot-long pieces of wood with mines on the end (used principally against vehicles in suicide attacks), small aerial bombs dropped from high buildings, and even improvised spears made by fixing a bayonet to a shaft of wood. The only major weapon missing from the Japanese inventory was the tank, although the Americans did report having destroyed one such machine on Padre Faura on February 16. It should also be noted that no air support was available to the defenders.

When the Americans entered Manila in early February, therefore, they faced a formidable array of defensive capability. The Japanese troops may not have been particularly well trained for urban fighting – many of their positions were isolated, with poor communications and a lack of integration – but they made up for it by means of impressive improvisation and a fearsome dedication to their task. The ease with which they transformed buildings into strongpoints indicates how quickly and effectively a city can be defended, even by second-rate units. When those units include large numbers of men who are prepared to continue fighting literally to the death, firing from within piles of rubble and mounting suicidal counterattacks regardless of the odds, the task of rooting them out becomes infinitely more time-consuming and costly. Without fully realizing the fact, the men of XIV Corps in early February 1945 were entering a nightmare.

According to the American Field Manual that dealt with urban fighting (FM 31–50, revised in 1944), the capture of a defended city required a great deal of forward planning. As ground forces advanced toward the city, commanders were expected to produce an 'estimate' of the situation facing them, integral parts of which would comprise detailed descriptions of the area and of the enemy dispositions. Once the attack began, the primary aim would be to seize key locations, partly to deny them to the enemy, partly to give the attackers positions from which to observe defenses and call in supporting artillery or air-strikes. Then, and only then, would the infantry, backed by armor and artillery, push into the city, driving toward observed enemy strongpoints that would be softened up beforehand. Enemy defenses could be bypassed, but only if follow-on units were available to deal with them before their occupants mounted counterattacks. The key to success was seen as the creation and maintenance of momentum, denying the enemy any opportunity to consolidate.

This was very theoretical. Urban fighting had not figured large in the Pacific Theater before February 1945, and although Major General Beightler, commander of the 37th Division, implied in his post-battle report that his men had been trained in 'street fighting' before the Luzon Campaign began,[19] there is little evidence of this in the early stages of the Battle for Manila. The main problem appears to have been a lack of accurate information which could be transformed into usable tactical intelligence. Although the Americans possessed detailed prewar knowledge of the city and of individual buildings within it, they had an extremely limited awareness of the Japanese dispositions in early February and no clear idea of how Manila was to be defended. Maps of the city were inadequate – the Americans were using general area maps on a scale of 1:50,000 – and aerial observation, which should have provided an advantage, often failed to locate carefully camouflaged Japanese positions, especially once the city was covered in smoke from demolitions and from the battle itself. In addition the advance into the northern suburbs happened quickly, in response to the need to rescue internees and prisoners of war, leaving commanders little time in which to prepare their plans. Just as the Japanese needed to improvise their defense, so the Americans had to improvise their assault.

But American problems went deeper than this. MacArthur and his subordinate commanders were aware that the city contained a large population, the safety of which had to be taken into account. For this reason the initial attacks into northern Manila were infantry affairs, with quite rigid restrictions imposed on the use of artillery, tanks and aircraft. As American military casualties increased, the artillery restrictions were lifted, leading to significant civilian losses and the razing of entire city blocks, but MacArthur never relaxed the rules concerning air power. Individual air-strikes did occasionally take place – SDBs from Lingayen bombed parks along Dewey Boulevard and in the vicinity of Burnham Green on February 13[20] – but when Lieutenant General Griswold, commanding XIV Corps, formally requested air-strikes on Intramuros on February 16, his request was firmly rejected by the Supreme Commander.[21] This does little to excuse the excessive use of artillery in the city – indeed the devastation could hardly have been greater if air-strikes had been authorized – but it does identify a major constraint on American operations.

Thus, when the men of the 1st Cavalry and 37th Infantry Divisions entered Manila, they were operating blind and were denied the fire support they knew was available. At first their advance was relatively straightforward – Japanese Army units to the north of the Pasig fought hard, yet were always aware of their orders from Yamashita to withdraw – but it was soon apparent that the rest of Manila, centered on Intramuros, was well defended. A decision was made to outflank the city by sending the 1st Cavalry on a wide sweeping movement to the east before striking toward the Port district, while elements of the 37th Division crossed the Pasig and advanced westward against Intramuros. This was a mistake. Not only did the two divisions lose contact, so that when they moved into the city they inevitably left substantial Japanese pockets untouched in the area between their respective boundaries, but the initial objectives – the power-generating plants on Provisor Island and the water resources of the Novaliches Dam and San Juan Reservoir – were not vital to the forthcoming battle. It was the sort of breathing space the enemy should not have been allowed.

To offset such problems, however, the Americans did enjoy some advantages. Although neither of the attacking divisions was up to full strength at any time during the battle,[22] both were highly experienced and contained veterans of previous campaigns. Command arrangements within the divisions were therefore quite smooth and coordination of constituent units well practised. The latter consideration was important, for one thing the Americans had learned from more than three years of war was the inestimable value of all-arms cooperation. The lack of air support and, initially, the restrictions on the use of artillery meant that key elements of the all-arms 'team' were not available in Manila, but in other respects coordination was slick. Infantry and 'dismounted' cavalry units involved in the battle operated well, effecting or improvising tactical responses; engineer companies attached to the assaulting troops quickly learned how to deal with Japanese mines and booby traps; artillery battalions ensured that fire support was on call at all times; medical and logistic units provided invaluable backup to the fighting men. In addition, once temporary bridges were erected over the Pasig (another engineer task), tanks, tank destroyers and self-propelled guns accompanied the infantry in clearing operations, providing the sort of close fire support so desperately needed. Without this 'mix' of capabilities, the battle would have been even more desperate and costly to the Americans.

Equally important were the weapons available to the attacking troops. Some proved to be less effective than expected – the 4.2-inch mortars in the infantry units were incapable of penetrating concrete and the 75mm or 76mm guns on the tanks and tank destroyers experienced similar problems – but compared with the Japanese, the Americans were superbly equipped. Their chief strength lay in artillery, particularly when restrictions were lifted and the full power of XIV Corps' assets was deployed. According to a recent study, these assets comprised 'five battalions of 105-mm, three of 155-mm, more than a battalion of 4.2-inch mortars and several batteries of 8-inch and 240-mm howitzers;' when the self-propelled 105mm M7s in the infantry regimental Cannon Companies were added, this represented a total of 'well over 140 cannons and heavy mortars.'[23] Altogether, they were to use 42,153 rounds during the Battle for Manila, creating a weight of fire that was often devastating.[24] In addition the 37th Division had within it the 754th Tank Battalion, equipped with Shermans, and the 637th Tank Destroyer Battalion, equipped with M10s. Within the infantry and cavalry units individual soldiers were issued with semiautomatic carbines, .3-inch and .5-inch machine-guns, flamethrowers and grenades. There appears to have been no shortage of ammunition during the battle, despite the fact that it had, in most cases, to be brought forward from the Lingayen logistic base.

But none of this tells us how the battle was fought and whether or not the Americans could have conducted it in a less devastating way. There is no doubt that during the early stages the infantry (including 'dismounted' cavalrymen) were reacting to events, probing Japanese defenses without the benefit of full support. During the 37th Division's crossing of the Pasig and its assault on Provisor Island, for example, casualties mounted significantly as foot soldiers tried to carry out assigned tasks virtually on their own. Indeed February 9 was the most costly day of the entire battle for Beightler's men, when they lost 19 dead and 216 wounded,[25] chiefly because they assaulted enemy strongpoints head-on, often without the benefit of prior reconnaissance or heavy artillery support. The situation was not helped by the fact that tanks and tank destroyers could not cross the Pasig until February 13 – the temporary engineer-built bridges were not strong enough to take the weight until then – but the real problem lay in the lack of intelligence about enemy positions. As the area south of the Pasig degenerated into 'a fantasia of death and destruction,'[26] infantrymen discovered to their cost that every street, house and open space had been transformed into a death trap.

It took time for the attacking units to sort out effective responses; in the meantime the casualties continued to mount. By the end of the battle the Americans had lost 1010 men dead and 5565 wounded,[27] and although this figure may seem small when set against comparable losses during other urban battles in World War II – the Soviets, for example, lost over 100,000 men during the taking of Berlin in April-May 1945 – it does need to be placed in the context of American war-fighting experience. The heavy losses suffered by both sides during the Civil War of the 1860s had led to a conscious policy of avoiding large casualty lists, principally by ensuring that so much firepower was available that the enemy would be decisively weakened before the infantry and their close-support units were committed. During the Pacific Campaign prior to Manila this had been manifested in massive naval and air bombardments, followed by concentrated artillery fire, effectively substituting technology for manpower on the battlefield. But it presupposed that the enemy was the only other occupant of that battlefield, something which may have been true on isolated Pacific islands but was patently not the case in Manila. To begin with, local commanders such as Beightler appear to have accepted the restrictions imposed by MacArthur, but the steadily rising casualty returns, day after day, soon had them demanding their usual fire support. In Beightler's case, moreover, there was probably the added pressure that his division was locally raised, principally in Ohio, and although many of the original National Guardsmen had been replaced by early 1945, he must have been aware that he would have to face hostility back home if he allowed his units to be destroyed.

The result was a loosening of the restrictions concerning artillery fire inside the confines of Manila, a decision which contributed significantly to the devastation and loss of civilian lives. A balanced view must be maintained – after all, the Japanese began to destroy large areas of the city well before the American restrictions were lifted, and there can be no doubt that many more civilians were killed by Japanese than American actions – but the deployment of artillery onto the streets constituted a key change in American

tactics. By February 15, every infantry assault was being presaged
by heavy weights of artillery fire, often delivered at very close range.
The Americans soon discovered that the 105mm howitzer, normally
used for infantry support fire, was not particularly effective against
well-constructed buildings, but that the 155mm was far more useful.
As a result, 155s were often brought to within 200–400 yards of
the target, which would then be pounded with unfused shells to
open cracks in the structure, followed by delay-fused ammunition
to create a breach for the infantry to exploit. If the building was to
be stormed, the bombardment would be directed at the top floor
first, the aim being to drive the defenders down into the path of
the assaulting infantry; if it was just to be destroyed, the fire would
concentrate on the bottom floor to collapse the structure. In extreme
cases, such as the assault on Intramuros on February 23, 8-inch and
240mm howitzers could be brought into play, lobbing 240lb or 360lb
shells into enemy positions from ranges as close as 800 yards.

The results were devastating, particularly when it is borne in
mind that the artillery was often joined by tanks, tank destroyers
and self-propelled M7s (105mm howitzers mounted on tank bodies.
During the attack on the Manila Police Headquarters of February
13–20, for example, more than 680 rounds of 155mm ammunition
were fired in support of the infantry assaults, while the 10-day battle
for the Philippine General Hospital and University campus complex,
beginning on the 14th, involved a staggering total of 3400 rounds
of 105mm and 155mm fire. On February 22, during the assault on
the City Hall, two 155mm howitzers of the 136th Field Artillery
Battalion were brought to within 250 yards of the target, the east
wall of which was hit by 145 rounds before the infantry went in.[28]
The attack on Intramuros has been described in an earlier chapter,
but it is worth noting that between 0730 and 0830 hours on February
23 a total of 7896 rounds (185 tons) of HE, AP and white-phosphorus
(WP) shells were fired by a mixture of artillery, tanks and tank
destroyers, plus a further 1900 rounds (45 tons) of HE and WP fired
by 4.2-inch mortars, all into an area of little more than 3 square
kilometers.[29] It was inevitable that civilians would be hit. In their
overwhelming desire to minimize infantry casualties, the Americans
lost sight of the need to protect the Filipino population. Indeed, if
Beightler's post-battle report is typical, the general feeling appears
to have been that civilians were unwelcome bystanders; he makes
no mention of the Filipino casualties.[30]

But artillery could never operate alone. Because of the buildings in Manila, indirect fire was difficult – the guns did not have the trajectory to fire over tall structures and, in the interests of accuracy, could not 'stand off' from the city. In addition the infantry demanded the sort of close support that could only be provided by moving the guns deep into the urban complex. This raised problems, not least in terms of clearing routes through the streets to allow particularly the larger-caliber weapons to be deployed. In some areas this entailed bulldozing rubble to one side while the infantry battle was progressing, although the main obstacle to movement was undoubtedly Japanese mines. Throughout the fighting south of the Pasig, at least two companies of engineers were attached to each infantry regiment, tasked with mine-clearing. Because the rubble of demolished buildings invariably contained large quantities of metal, magnetic mine detection proved impossible, although this did not prevent the development of effective techniques. Among the most interesting of these involved close cooperation with a tank:

A length of cable was attached to the front of a medium tank and coiled on the back. A tank would move forward through a swept lane followed by three engineers behind it. Upon arrival at a mine an engineer would jump out from behind the tank, run up to the mine, unscrew the fuse, loop the cable around it, and duck back behind the tank, which would then back away pulling out the mine. This procedure was refined into a matter of seconds . . .[31]

When it is realized that the process was almost always carried out under enemy fire, the bravery involved may be appreciated.

Nor was such bravery confined to the engineers. American success in Manila depended, first and foremost, on the courage and tenacity of infantry or cavalry soldiers as they moved through streets swept by murderous fire to assault enemy-held buildings. Their tasks were by no means enviable. As the battle progressed, the conditions deteriorated: enemy resistance grew more desperate the closer the Americans came to Intramuros, casualties mounted steadily and, with water and power to Manila cut off, fires raged uncontrollably around the attacking troops. In addition the large numbers of bodies, many of them covered by rubble, began to rot, adding an indescribable stench to the nightmare scene.

Yet the soldiers persisted with their assaults, refining their techniques as they gained experience. According to FM 31–50, buildings had to be cleared from the top floor down so that the enemy could not drop grenades or fire onto the attacking troops, but this proved difficult. Some squads advanced across the roofs of neighboring buildings, but the normal technique was to use tanks or artillery to blast a way in, allowing the soldiers to rush forward to secure stairways or to climb upward across the rubble. This did not always produce success, chiefly because the compilers of FM 31–50 had taken no account of Japanese fanaticism. Machine-gun fire would continue to issue forth from the ruins of even the most comprehensively demolished structures, while inside enemy troops would defend each floor and room to the death. Indeed in some cases they would move from floor to floor using specially constructed passages, leaving the Americans unsure whether they had cleared the building or not. In such circumstances, it was not unknown for the infantry to be pulled back so that even more artillery fire could be poured in. On February 20, for example, Company K, 145th Infantry withdrew from the City Hall despite having secured a foothold, so that M7s of Cannon Company could mount another bombardment. Even then, however, the building still had to be cleared, a process involving hand-to-hand fighting using infantry weapons. Carbines, BARs and machine-guns were of only limited use in the dust and smoke of a small room containing an unknown number of enemy troops; in the end the infantry came to depend much more on grenades, flamethrowers and, if the defenders sought refuge in enclosed spaces such as basements, explosive charges designed to seal them in. One overriding lesson was learned early on – in any attack on a defended building, the key was to go in firing with every weapon available. The alternative was just to stand off and allow the artillery to demolish the structure brick by brick, burying the Japanese in the ruins.

These techniques, shown in their most effective form during the attacks on Intramuros and the government buildings in late February, inevitably became the new doctrine of urban fighting, refining many of the details in FM 31–50. In the aftermath of the Manila battle XIV Corps compiled a detailed report on their experiences, principally to ensure that any points of value in the anticipated attacks on Japanese cities were widely disseminated.[32] In the event, those attacks did not take place, although the experience of Manila was not forgotten. When the Americans found themselves involved in urban fighting in Vietnam – not least in the aftermath of the 1968 Tet Offensive – many of the techniques employed would not have been unfamilar to veterans of Manila. Artillery and tank fire was used to prepare the way for infantry attacks, producing widespread devastation and civilian casualties; buildings were cleared using grenades, flame throwers and explosives. The only difference was that in 1968 there were few restrictions on the use of airpower, particularly helicopter gunships. American losses, although severe, were minimized by substituting technology for manpower wherever possible; little remorse was shown when ancient towns and urban areas were razed to the ground. As an unnamed American major reportedly said to the journalist Peter Arnett as they surveyed the ruins of Ben Tre in the Mekong Delta in February 1968, 'It became necessary to destroy the town to save it.'[33] It was a sentiment that many Filipino survivors of Manila would have found chillingly familiar.

But what, in retrospect, should have been learned from the Battle for Manila in terms of urban fighting? The first lesson must be that the defense of cities is not difficult. If the Manila Naval Defense Force is anything to go by, even an *ad hoc* formation of essentially second-rate troops can quickly transform a city into a veritable fortress, simply by exploiting the advantages provided by streets, parks and buildings. Fanaticism certainly helps to ensure a long drawn-out battle, but if the intention is to delay or divert an enemy, denying him momentum even in the short term, then virtually any armed force should be able to do the job quite adequately. The opposite is the case with the attackers, for the second major lesson from Manila is that seizing a defended city is time-consuming and costly, requiring forces that have been trained specifically for the task rather than merely thrown into it because they are acting as the spearhead of an advance. Much of what FM 31–50 had to say in 1945 was valid – the commander of an attacking force must have good intelligence about the city and its defenders; he must make a realistic 'estimate' based on such intelligence; and he must be able to identify key objectives that, once taken, will unhinge the enemy defense. Unfortunately these were the very factors that were absent from the American response in Manila. Neither Krueger nor Elchelberger was prepared for an urban battle, information about Japanese defenses was sparse, the attacking divisions were neither trained nor configured for urban fighting, and the initial objectives –

Santo Tomás, Bilibid, Provisor Island, and the Novaliches Dam and San Juan Reservoir – were, in reality, of only secondary importance. The third lesson is even more mundane: never surround a city entirely, but always leave an escape route so that the enemy is not forced to fight to the death. Again, the Americans failed to bear this in mind.

In the end, if these lessons are not recognized, the fight for control of a city will be bitter and bloody, leading to heavy losses among both soldiers and civilians and to widespread destruction of urban facilities. If the attackers are not trained to deal with the situation confronting them, they will inevitably demand greater fire support in an effort to blast their way out of the problem, particularly if there is pressure on their commanders to keep casualties to a minimum. In such circumstances, the civilian population – whether 'friendly' or not – will be seen as a nuisance and their suffering ignored or underplayed. Throughout American accounts of the Battle for Manila, the fate of ordinary Filipinos does not figure large. Occasional references are made to the need to rescue refugees from the fighting, and MacArthur did at least acknowledge that air attacks would increase civilian losses, but it is far more common to find American participants dismissing Filipinos as 'collaborators' or 'looters', or blaming the Japanese entirely for civilian deaths.[34]

This should not be misunderstood – in the heat of battle, when their own survival is taking precedence, soldiers tend to become both introspective and ruthless – but in Manila the situation was compounded by the fact that none of the American units involved had expected or trained for the nightmare that confronted them. Nor should these comments detract from the very real bravery displayed by the attacking troops. Their task was one of the most difficult in the military lexicon, and although it took time for them to adapt, their seizure of the city from dedicated and fanatical Japanese was a major achievement in its own right.

Manila may have been devastated – indeed of all the Allied capitals in World War II only Warsaw equals it in terms of death and destruction[35] – but this can hardly be blamed on the ordinary soldiers who fought for its liberation. The fault lies with the commanders who had not prepared their troops for such a battle and who, once presented with the need to take the city by force, preferred to solve the problem with firepower. It must also be remembered that if the Japanese had obeyed Yamashita and withdrawn from Manila, or if they had listened to the American radio broadcasts demanding their surrender, the battle would have been avoided. After all, they were the aggressors; without their attacks on the Philippines in 1941, the liberation of the islands three years later would have been unnecessary. As it was, some 16,000 Japanese died in and around Manila in a last-ditch attempt to preserve an illegal and unjustified occupation.

What was the effect of this battle on the victors as individuals? Some had been directly affected by the appalling losses. Lieutenant Colonel McMicking had lost his mother, his brother and his two sisters. Sergeant Rogers saw him the day he found their bodies in the Masonic Temple. McMicking's eyes were 'red with tears that welled up and flowed down a face torn with anguish.'[36] Rogers himself started to fall to pieces. He remembered 'there was an overpowering stench of death and decay. It prevaded the air, and there was no escape . . . This was not Manila. It was simply hell.'[37]

Senior officers, those who had to make the decisions, also suffered. Sutherland was already under great strain and the experience of Manila seems to have pushed him over the edge. He became an automaton, performing his duties in a lifeless and mechanical manner. MacArthur, too, was shattered. Courtney Whitney watched him prepare to speak at Malacañan Palace on February 27 at a ceremony marking the reestablishment of the Commonwealth government. Whitney observed that 'the mask he was able to wear at times of danger and the eve of great battles did not serve him now.' MacArthur spoke hesitantly, unable to control his emotions. When he talked of Manila, the cruelly punished citadel of democacy, he broke down completely and was unable to continue for some moments. A few days later MacArthur reacted with anger at the sight of the banner headline 'Manila Is Dying' in a correspondent's report. He instructed his military censor, Legrand Diller, to prohibit any reference to the death of Manila.[38]

On March 2 MacArthur went to Corregidor for a more triumphal ceremony. The monument – approved by MacArthur – which was eventually erected on the island listed all the battles of the Pacific War except one. There had not, it appeared, been a Battle of Manila. It was just possible that the Americans had deleted the reference to Manila because they considered it was not a very important battle. How important was it? In one sense the destruction of the city achieved little: the number of Japanese soldiers caught up in the battle was relatively small and the real enemy lay elsewhere, in northern Luzon, to the west of Clark Field and to the east and south of Manila. In addition Manila itself was only valuable in strategic terms as a port, the use of which was dependent on seizing the Bataan Peninsula as well as the small islands that protected the South Channel – Corregidor, Cabalo, Carabao and El Fraile ('Fort Drum'). Until they were safely in American hands, transport ships could not use Manila Bay, while the destruction of the Port district by the Japanese meant that, even when ships did start to arrive, offloading facilities were severely limited. In addition American troops (chiefly of the 37th Division) were tied down in Manila for some time after the battle was over. They had to restore a semblance of order to the shattered city, looking after refugees, clearing some of the worst devastation and making safe the enormous amounts of unexploded ordnance strewn around the streets. It is amazing how quickly parts of the city did recover – the Americans began to enjoy the benefits of markets and even entertainment soon after the end of the fighting[39] – but the people of Manila needed to be protected and fed. Fortunately, by 1945 the Americans could afford to meet such demands.

In order to appreciate its true significance, the Battle for Manila must be placed in the context of the Philippines Campaign. While XIV Corps was struggling to liberate the city, American and Japanese soldiers were locked in combat in a wide variety of other areas.[40] On Luzon itself, Krueger had two priorities – the clearing of Manila Bay and the destruction (or, at least, neutralization) of the rest of Yamashita's Fourteenth Area Army. Hall's XI Corps, having landed to the north of the Bataan Peninsula on January 29, cut across the northern approaches and, on February 14, began to push down the east coast road. The following day, elements of the 38th Infantry Division landed at Mariveles, on the southern tip of the peninsula, before driving north to link up. On February 16 the 503d Parachute Regimental Combat Team (RCT) carried out a dramatic airborne landing on Corregidor, closely followed by a seaborne landing by men of the 24th Infantry Division. Although the fighting for the island was to take until February 28 and cost nearly 1000 American casualties, it did mean that one of the main obstacles in the approaches to Manila Bay had been seized while the Battle for Manila itself was still raging. Caballo, El Fraile and Carabao were not finally cleared until April 18, by which time

American engineers had cleared hundreds of mines and destroyed or raised nearly 350 ships that were blocking the harbor. By May 1 the port was operational, relieving pressure on the logistic base at Lingayen. Without this advantage – itself a direct result of having cleared Manila – the Americans would have found the liberation of the rest of Luzon, and the Philippines as a whole, extremely difficult.

As it was, the campaign quickly built up an unstoppable momentum. From late January, the 40th Infantry Division concentrated on the remnants of Kembu Group to the west of Clark Field, breaching the enemy defense line toward the end of the following month. The 40th was replaced by the 43d Infantry Division, which in turn was relieved by the 38th, who between them cleared the area of all but a few scattered groups by April 6. Further east, where the remains of Yokoyama's Shimbu Group were holding strong positions, XIV Corps (now comprising the 1st Cavalry and 6th Infantry Divisions) attacked between Antipolo and Wawa Dam on March 8. Here the fighting was heavy as American troops advanced slowly into difficult terrain well defended by the Japanese; it was not until May 28 that Wawa Dam was finally seized by elements of the 38th Division. By then, other American units had struck south toward Laguna de Bay; as early as February 23, men of the 11th Airborne Division, with Filipino guerrilla support, carried out a daring 'raid' to rescue over 2000 internees at Los Baños, but the main attacks to clear the region, carried out by the 1st Cavalry and 43d Divisions, took place in March and April. On April 1 the 158th RCT landed at Legaspi on the southeastern tip of the Bicol Peninsula, driving north to link up with the 1st Cavalry by May 2.

This effectively cleared southern and central Luzon, but Yamashita's Shobu Group, containing more than 110,000 men, was still at large in the north, defending the mountainous approaches to the fertile Cagayan Valley. American attacks into this region began as early as February, when the 33d Infantry Division pushed toward Yamashita's headquarters at Baguio, with the 25th and 32d Divisions aiming for Bambang. This turned out to be the toughest part of the Luzon Campaign, conducted over impossible terrain in rapidly deteriorating weather. In mid-April, the 37th Division arrived from Manila as reinforcement, but despite the seizure of Baguio on April 26, it was to take until late May for the Americans to force an entrance into the Cagayan Valley. Even then, the fighting was not over: in late June elements of the 11th Airborne carried out a parachute and glider assault at the northern end of the valley in an attempt to clear it by advancing to make contact with the 37th Division, but Yamashita (still with about 65,000 men) fell back to an area to the south of Bontoc. He was still there, impotent but posing a potential threat, in mid-August, when the Japanese surrendered.

Nor was this the full extent of the American commitment, for while Krueger was clearing Luzon, Eichelberger was under orders to liberate the rest of the Philippines. His first priority was to secure the islands that dominated the Visayan Passages (the San Bernardino Strait, Sibuyan Sea and Verde Island Passage), so that they could be used by Allied shipping convoys. He began the process as early as February 19, with landings on the northwest coast of Samar. Other landings, many of them unopposed, cleared a number of smaller islands, allowing Eichelberger to claim that his task was complete by April 5. By then his forces had widened their remit, taking on Lieutenant General Sosaku Suzuki's Thirty-Fifth Army throughout the central and southern Philippines. Between the end of February and mid-April, units of Eichelberger's Eighth Army, cooperating closely with Filipino guerrillas, carried out a total of 14 major and 24 minor amphibious landings (an average of nearly one a day) to complete the liberation of the Philippines. On February 28 Palawan was invaded, followed on March 10 by landings at Zamboanga on the western tip of Mindanao. On March 18 Panay was assaulted; on March 26 it was the turn of Cebu; on March 29 landings took place on the northwest coast of Negros. On April 11 Bohol was invaded and on the 17th the main portion of Mindanao was attacked. In nearly all cases, fighting occurred – Japanese defenders on Negros, for example, put up a stubborn resistance in the northern mountains for six weeks, while the battle for Mindanao absorbed the best part of three American divisions until late July – but most degenerated into extensive (and occasionally quite nasty) mopping-up operations. Some Japanese pockets were still holding out when the war ended in August.

By then the Japanese had lost 255,795 soldiers killed since January 9; a further 125,755 surrendered either during the battles or at the end of hostilities. American ground forces suffered 10,380 killed and 36,550 wounded during the same period.[41] In the process, the Americans achieved all of their strategic objectives. By as early as April, they held the naval and air bases they needed on Luzon for the projected invasion of the Japanese Home Islands, and by August the buildup for that invasion had begun. The fact that it did not need to be carried out is immaterial; in strategic terms the Philippines Campaign was a major success. At the same time, of course, the Filipino population had been liberated from Japanese occupation and a Commonwealth government restored. The Battle for Manila may have been costly and, at times, conducted with excessive force by the Americans, but it was a vital part of the campaign, securing a base from which future operations could be mounted.

# NOTES

1. Alfonso J. Aluit, *By Sword and Fire. The Destruction of Manila in World War II, 3 February-3 March 1945* (Manila, 1994), pp. 349–350.
2. Major General Charles A. Willoughby, *MacArthur 1941–1951* (New York, 1954), p. 209.
3. General Tao Hanzhang, *Sun Tzu's Art of War: The Modern Chinese Interpretation* (Ware, Hertfordshire, 1993), p. 116.
4. Paul Chwialkowski, *In Caesar's Shadow. The Life of General Robert Eichelberger* (Westport, 1993), p. 123, notes the existence of 'rumors' to this effect in late February 1945.
5. Ibid., pp. 116–129, *passim.*
6. Major General Charles A. Willoughby, *The Guerilla Resistance Movement in the Philippines 1941–1945* (New York, 1972), p. 29.
7. See above, Chapter 4, Note 3.
8. Arthur Swinson, *Four Samurai: A Quartet of Japanese Commanders in the Second World War* (London, 1968), Chapter 7.
9. Lieutenant-General Akira Muto, 'Battle Report of General Muto' (sometimes referred to as the 'Muto Memoirs'), G-2 GHQ FEC, *Translations of Japanese Documents*, Vol. II, Item 20; copy provided by the Office of the Chief of Military History, Washington DC.
10. Ibid., p. 30; also Swinson, *Four Samurai*, pp. 211–212.
11. 'Japanese Defense of Cities as exemplified by The Battle for Manila,' *A Report by XIV Corps* (HQ Sixth Army, July 1, 1945), pp. 21–22, states that 'Prior to the Luzon operation the 37th Infantry Division had undergone an extensive training program whereby each rifle company had a team of platoon size well versed in the technique of assaulting fortified positions.' By comparison, Stanley A. Frankel, *The 37th Infantry Division in World War II* (Washington DC, 1948), p. 250, states that the division had been trained for jungle and mountain fighting only.

12. 'Japanese Defense of Cities,' p. 3.
13. Quoted in Robert Ross Smith, *United States Army in World War II. The War in the Pacific: Triumph in the Philippines* (Washington DC, 1963), p. 243.
14  'Japanese Defense of Cities', p. 2.
15  Frankel, *The 37th Infantry Division in World War II*, p. 286.
16  'Japanese Defense of Cities', p. 9.
17  Ibid., p. 4.
18  *Report After Action. Operations of the 37th Infantry Division Luzon P.I., 1 November 1944–30 June 1945*, p. 162.
19  Major General Robert S. Beightler, *Report on the Activities of the 37th Infantry Division* (1945).
20  *Operations of the 37th Infantry Division*, p. 57.
21  Aluit, *By Sword and Fire*, p. 315.
22  *Operations of the 37th Infantry Division*, p. 238; also Major John Gordon IV, 'Battle in the Streets – Manila 1945', *Field Artillery*, August 1990, p. 25.
23  Ibid.
24  Kurt J. Sellers, *Artillery Ammunition Expenditures in Urban Combat: A Comparative Case Study of the Battles of Clark Field and Manila* (US Army Human Engineering Laboratory, Maryland, September 1989).
25  Frankel, *The 37th Infantry Division in World War II*, p. 274.
26  Ibid., p. 277.
27  Smith, *Triumph in the Philippines*, p. 307 Table 5.
28  All figures taken from Gordon, 'Battle in the Streets.'
29  Figures from Aluit, *By Sword and Fire*, p. 355. Gordon, 'Battle in the Streets,' cites a larger total of 11,237 rounds fired but uses the same tonnage figures.
30  Beightler, *Report on the Activities of the 37th Infantry Division*.
31  *Operations of the 37th Infantry Division*, p. 59.
32  'Japanese Defense of Cities;' see Note 11, above.
33  Don Oberdorfer, *Tet!* (New York, 1971), pp. 184–185. There is some controversy about whether the statement was ever made, but it does sum up a basic dilemma facing any army in urban combat: how do you protect or take a city without inflicting damage?
34  See particularly Frankel, *The 37th Infantry Division in World War II*, p. 298, and Beightler, *Report on the Activities of the 37th Infantry Division, passim*.
35  The Battle for Manila lasted a month and led to 100,000 civilian deaths; the Battle for Warsaw in 1944 lasted two months (August 1–October 2) and caused 200,000 civilian deaths. In both cases little was left of the original city by the end of hostilities. It is worth adding, however, that Warsaw was not being liberated: it

was destroyed by German troops in the process of putting down an uprising by the Polish Home Army.

36 Paul P. Rogers, *The Good Years: MacArthur and Sutherland* (New York, 1990), p. 263.

37 Ibid., p. 265.

38 D. Clayton James, *The Years of MacArthur, 1941–45*, Vol. II (Boston, Mass.), p. 648.

39 Frankel, *The 37th Infantry Division in World War II*, pp. 297–303 covers the 37th Division in the immediate post-battle period. One of the unexpected problems associated with the recovery of city life was a sudden rise in venereal disease among American troops, *Operations of the 37th Infantry Division*, p. 215.

40 For full details of the Philippines Campaign, see Smith, *Triumph in the Philippines*, pp. 309–658. Other readable histories include Stanley L. Falk, *Liberation of the Philippines* (London, 1970) and William B. Breuer, *Retaking the Philippines. America's Return to Corregidor, Manila and Bataan: October 1944-March 1945 (New York, 1986)*.

41 Smith, *Triumph in the Philippines*, pp. 692–694, Appendix H-1 and H-2.

# APPENDIX

## GENERAL HEADQUARTERS
## SOUTHWEST PACIFIC AREA

ADVANCE ECHELON
2 February 1945

### PLAN FOR ENTRY OF THE COMMANDER-IN-CHIEF
### AND OFFICIAL PARTY INTO THE CITY OF MANILA

1. The Commander-in-Chief and official party will enter the City of Manila and make a tour of the City along the route of Rizal Avenue – Taft Avenue – Calle Vito Cruz – Dewey Boulevard – around Burnham Green, keeping same to the right – P Burgos to the Legislative Building, arriving thereat for the official ceremony at 1100/I on D-day.

2. Appropriate detachments of selected troops from available combat divisions, totalling approximately the strength of one division, will be assembled in mass formation in front of the speaker's stand (as near as possible) prior to the arrival of the Commander-in-Chief.

3. After the arrival of the Commander-in-Chief at the Legislative Building, and as the Commander-in-Chief approaches the speaker's stand, four ruffles and four flourishes will be sounded, followed by the 'General.' Upon completion of the honors the Commander-in-Chief will make an address.

4. After the Commander-in-Chief has completed his address and the applause has subsided, President Osmena will move toward the side of the Commander-in-Chief, and as he reaches position

beside the Commander-in-Chief four ruffles and four flourishes will be sounded, followed by a few bars of the Philippine National Anthem. President Osmena will then make an address.

5. Upon completion of President Osmena's address, and following applause, while both President Osmena and the Commander-in-Chief are still standing at the microphone, the band will render the United States National Anthem. At the first note troops will execute 'present arms' and the color guard will raise the United States National Flag smartly to the top of the flagpole. Upon completion of the playing of the United States National Anthem, and after the troops have returned to 'order arms' the Constabulary Band (if present) or, in its absence the United States Army Band, will render the Philippine National Anthem. At the first note of same the color guard will smartly raise the Philippine National Flag.

6. Upon completion of the playing of the Philippine National Anthem, and after the troops have returned to 'order arms', the Commander-in-Chief, followed by the official party, will withdraw from the stand, 'remount' jeeps (in same order as arriving) and leave the city by the most direct route to the north.

## DETAILED INSTRUCTIONS RELATIVE TO THE PLAN FOR ENTERING THE CITY OF MANILA BY THE COMMANDER-IN-CHIEF AND CEREMONY AT THE LEGISLATIVE BUILDING ON D-DAY

1. The Headquarters Commandant will be responsible for the formation and movement of the General Headquarters column to Manila and its return as outlined below:

a. The column will be composed of members of General Headquarters, Army, Corps and Divisions, as designated by the Military Secretary.
b. The General Headquarters section will assemble along the road by Headquarters Building, facing north, with the leading jeep at the Headquarters Building, prepared to move at 0700/I on D-day. The

officers making up the General Headquarters section of the column will be designated by the Military Secretary, General Fellers, who will inform the Headquarters Commandant and all concerned 24 hours prior to H-hour of the names of the officers selected, the number of vehicle to which assigned (3 per jeep) and the position of the vehicle in the column. In addition, the Military Secretary will be responsible for notifying selected Army, Corps and Division officers, and other guests, to be at the Bonifacio Monument at 1000/I on D-day, and will inform the Headquarters Commandant and those concerned of the position to be assigned to their vehicles in the column. The General Headquarters section, less the Commander-in-Chief's jeep, will proceed toward Manila on Highway 3, halting at the Bonifacio Monument approximately three miles north of Manila. At this point the column will be joined by the Commander-in-Chief and other members from the Army, Corps and Divisions. The entire column will be prepared to promptly resume movement upon the arrival of the Commander-in-Chief's jeep at 1015/I. Prior to departure each jeep will be numbered to facilitate assignment.

c. As the column moves toward Manila from the Bonifacio Monument, with the Commander-in-Chief and his two Aides in the leading jeep, it will be preceded by a motorcycle escort and two armored cars.

d. The route to Manila will be along Highway 3 to the outskirts of the City, thence Rizal Avenue – Taft Avenue – Calle Vito Cruz – Dewey Boulevard – around Burnham Green, keeping same to the right, thence along P Burgos to the Legislative Building. (See sketch map attached.) Column will pass in front of the Legislative Building and will move slowly in front of troops before turning right into the driveway where jeeps will close up and passengers dismount. As soon as passengers are discharged the convoy will move south, down the ramp, turn left at the south end of the grounds, circle the Legislative Building, and park the column with the leading jeep at the northwest corner of the Legislative Building. Further details, if necessary, will be announced later, after the preliminary reconnaissance. (Note: Route through the City of Manila will be dependent upon the condition of bridges at the time, and route will be varied accordingly, but it is essential that the column approach the City from the vicinity of Ford Abad (old Spanish Fort), thence along Dewey Boulevard – P Burgos to the Legislative Building. In addition to the jeeps referred to above, the necessary jeeps will be provided for War Correspondents and photographers as arranged with Colonel Diller. If desirable, all photographers may be located, as directed, at the Legislative Building prior to arrival of party.

e. Arrange with Sixth Army for the security and control of traffic along the road from San Miguel to the Bonifacio Monument during the . . . [indistinct] . . . and from Manila.

2. General Dunckel will be in charge of the ceremony at the Legislative Building and responsible for all details in connection therewith, to include the following. Pending the arrival of General Dunckel, Colonel Bullock, with Major Burton and such other assistants as he may select, will make all preliminary arrangements.

a. When notified by the Chief of Staff as to the division troops to be represented at the ceremony, arrange for their movement to the City of Manila at such times and in such manner as to insure that all units are in their prescribed position in front of the Legislative Building prior to the arrival of the Commander-in-Chief (1100/I), and commanders thereof instructed in detail of procedure to be followed on arrival of Commander-in-Chief. In general troops will appear in combat uniform – clean and neat – but no 'spit and polish,' and armed with individual weapons only. Troops will be transported in trucks to Manila. Trucks will be parked at a reasonably close distance from the Legislative Building so that the troops will not be required to march any further than absolutely necessary.

b. Arrange for at least two bands to be present, preferably a band per division represented, and the Constabulary Band, if available. Issue detailed instructions covering honors to be rendered as the Commander-in-Chief approaches the massed troops in front of the Legislative Building, including necessary coordination of signals, for the rendering at the proper time of the United States National Anthem and the Philippine National Anthem. Similar arrangements for the field music and instructions as to the timing and coordination in rendering of honors at the proper moment. Note: Both the Commander-in-Chief and President Osmena are entitled to four ruffles and four flourishes.

c. Obtain flags of both the United States and the Philippines and be responsible for instruction of the color guards selected for their raising at the proper time. In this connection, upon arrival, prior inspection should be made to verify that the flagpoles and halyards, including snaps, are in serviceable condition, and that each flag is properly folded for raising.

d. Allot space on the speaker's stand in rear of the Commander-in-Chief for the official party according to the plan to be furnished by the Military Secretary.

e. Arrange with local police and other appropriate authorities, including the Provost Marshal of the City of Manila, for security and the control of spectators along the route of march in the City of Manila, as well as close-in security and traffic control at the Legislative Building.

3. Military Secretary – General Fellers:

a. Furnish Headquarters Commandant with list of officers and official guests to accompany the Commander-in-Chief not later than 24 hours prior to H-hour. This list should include the name of the individual and assignment to a specific jeep in the column (3 per jeep); furnish an additional list of those expected to be present from the Army, Corps and Divisions.

b. Arrange for the representatives of the Army, Corps and Divisions to join the column at the Bonifacio Monument and notify the Headquarters Commandant as to the number of jeeps and the position to which each jeep will be assigned in the column.

c. Furnish Colonel Bullock with the list of officers and guests to be present on the platform with the Commander-in-Chief at the ceremony at the Legislative Building. This list should be furnished preferably in the form of a chart prescribing the exact position each individual is to be assigned in the line, or lines, to be formed in rear of the Commander-in-Chief.

d. Arrange for the wide distribution and dropping of leaflets of the Commander-in-Chief's address in the form of a proclamation at a date later than that of the ceremony.

4. PRO – Colonel Diller:

a. Arrange for the broadcast and reception coverage in the United States and Philippines of the ceremony at the Legislative Building.

b. Arrange for the publication in local newspapers and re-broadcast to the Philippine Islands of the Commander-in-Chief's address in the form of a proclamation.

c. Arrange with Headquarters Commandant for the necessary

transportation and instruction of News Correspondents and photographers, and for their assignment to positions in the column and at the Legislative Building.

5. Assistant to the Military Secretary (Colonel Soriano) will be responsible for the following:
a. Notify general public of route of march through the City of Manila, and place and time of ceremony at the Legislative Building. Use all available means such as newspapers, radio and sound trucks.
b. Notify and direct local city government to declare D-day an official holiday.
c. Secure the services of the Constabulary Band, if available, for the official ceremony at the Legislative Building; coordinate with Colonel Bullock in connection with their instruction and time and place of reporting.

6. Colonel Wheeler:
Will be in charge of the arrangements for the official entrance to the City of Manila by the Commander-in-Chief and the ceremony at the Legislative Building on D-day.

7. Colonel Ballantyne:
Will act as assistant to Colonel Wheeler, and will arrange for a display of the Air Forces over the City of Manila for approximately one hour at the conclusion of the ceremony at the Legislative Building.

8. Signal Officer:
Will be responsible for the installation of an adequate public address system at the Legislative Building prior to 100/I on D-day. The location of both microphone and outlets will be coordinated with the PRO. Such assistance as may be necessary will be furnished the . . . [indistinct] . . . sure that the broadcast facilities and the . . . [indistinct] . . . facilities are adequate.

By command of General MacARTHUR
R.K. SUTHERLAND,
Lieutenant General, U.S. Army,
Chief of Staff.

# BIBLIOGRAPHY

Allen, Robert Coleman, 'Philippine War Diary. A Prison Camp Saga' (Washington DC, 1991)

Aluit, Alfonso J., *By Sword and Fire. The Destruction of Manila in World War II, 3 February-3 March 1945* (Manila, 1994)

'Armor on Luzon,' Research Report, The Armored School, Fort Knox, Kentucky 1949–1950)

Baclagon, Uldario S., *Philippine Campaigns* (Manila, 1952)

Beightler, Major General Robert S., *Report on the Activities of the 37th Infantry Division 1940–1945* (1945)

Breuer, William B., *Retaking the Philippines. America's Return to Corregidor, Manila and Bataan: October 1944-March 1945* (New York, 1986)

Buencamino, Victor, *Memoirs of Victor Buencamino* (Manila, 1977)

Caro Wilson, Isabel, 'Chronology of Events – Last Days of the Liberation of Manila, 3–27 February 1945' (Unpublished)

Chwialkowski, Paul, *In Caesar's Shadow. The Life of General Robert Eichelberger* (Westport, 1993)

Cook, Haruko Taya and Theodore F., *Japan at War – An Oral History* (New York, 1992)

Devlin, Gerard M., *Paratrooper!* (New York, 1979)

Devlin, Gerard M., *Back to Corregidor: America Retakes the Rock* (New York, 1992)

Edelman, General Clyde D., 'The Clyde D. Edelman Papers, Drafts of Transcripts of Conversations with Clyde D. Edelman', US Army Military History Research Collection (Unpublished)

El Secretario de Kebajada, *Encargado de la redacción del Inventario de pérdidas españolas en Pilipinas durante la ocupación japonesa* (Manila, June 19, 1946)

Estebán, Luis R., 'My War. A Personal Narrative' (Unpublished)

Falk, Stanley L., *Liberation of the Philippines* (London, 1970)

Falk, Stanley L., *Seventy Days to Singapore. Malayan Campaign 1941–1942* (London, 1975)

Flanagan, Edward M., *The Angels. A History of the 11th Airborne Division 1943–1946* (Washington DC, 1948)

Frankel, Stanley A., *The 37th Infantry Division in World War II* (Washington DC, 1948)

Garay, Stephen L., 'The Breach of Intramuros,' Student Report, The Armored School, Fort Knox, Kentucky (May 1, 1948)

GHQ SWPA Military Intelligence Section, 'Report on Conditions in the Philippine Islands' (June 1943)

Gonzalez, Andrew, and Reyes, Alejandro T., *These Hallowed Halls* (Manila, 1982)

Gordon, John, IV, 'Battle in the Streets – Manila 1945,' *Field Artillery*, August 1990

Greenfield, Kent Roberts (ed.), *United States Army in World War II. The War Against Japan: Pictorial Record* (Washington DC, 1952)

Guerrero Nakpil, Carmen, *A Question of Identity. Selected Essays* (Manila, 1973)

Hall, Consuelo, Unpublished letters to her husband in Santo Tomás internment camp

Hartendorp, A.V.H., *A Few Poems and Essays* (Manila, 1951)

Hartendorp, A.V.H., *The Japanese Occupation of the Philippines*, Vol. II (Manila, 1957)

Hartendorp, A.V.H., *The Santo Tomas Story* (New York, 1964)

James, D. Clayton, *The Years of MacArthur, 1941–1945*, Vol. II (Boston, Mass., 1975)

'Japanese Defense of Cities as exemplified by The Battle for Manila,' *A Report by XIV Corps* (HQ Sixth Army, July 1, 1945)

Joaquín, Nick, *Manila my Manila* (Manila, 1990)

# BIBLIOGRAPHY

José, Ricardo T., *The Japanese Occupation of the Philippines – Sources and Directions* (Manila, 1988)

Krohn, Edgar, and Kühne, Walter, *The German Club 1906–1986. A History of the German Community in the Philippines* (Manila, 1986)

Krueger, General Walter, *From Down Under to Nippon: The Story of Sixth Army in World War II* (Washington DC, 1953)

Leary, William M. (ed.), *We Shall Return! MacArthur's Commanders and the Defeat of Japan* (Kentucky, 1988)

MacArthur, General Douglas, *Reminiscences* (London, 1964)

McMahon, Perry R., 'Retaking the Harbor Defenses of Manila and Subic Bays,' *Coast Artillery Journal*, July–August 1945

Montgomery, William H., 'I Hired Out to Fight. The Military History of William H. Montgomery. November 1927-November 1947,' US Army Military History Research Collection (Unpublished)

Morison, Samuel Eliot, *History of United States Naval Operations in World War II. The Liberation of the Philippines 1944–1945 (Boston, Mass., 1959)*

Muto, Lieutenant General Akira, 'Battle Report of General Muto' (or 'Muto Memoirs'), G-2 GHQ FEC, *Translations of Japanese Documents*, Vol. II, Item 20 (Washington DC, 1948)

Ooka, Shohei, *Nobi* (Tokyo, 1973)

Owens, William A., *Eye Deep in Hell. A Memoir of the Liberation of the Philippines 1944–45* (Dallas, 1989)

'Philippine Area Naval Operations, Part IV, January 1945–August 1945,' *Japanese Monograph No. 114* (Military History Section HQ Army Forces Far East, 1952)

Picornell, Pedro, 'The Remedios Hospital 1942–1945. A Saga of Malate' (Unpublished)

'Plan for entry of Commander-in-Chief and official party into the city of Manila' (GHQ SPA, February 2, 1945)

Potter, John Dean, *A Soldier Must Hang – the biography of an oriental general* (London, 1963)

Price, Fr. Arthur, 'Matale Martyrs. The Columban Fathers in Manila before and during the Japanese Occupation 1942–1945' (Unpublished paper)

Prising, Robin, *Manila, Goodbye* (Boston, Mass., 1975)

Pritchard, R. John, and Zaide Sonia, Magbanna, *The Tokyo War Crimes Trial* (New York and London, 1981)

Reel, A. Frank, *The Case of General Yamashita* (Chicago, 1949)

*Report After Action. XIV Corps. M-1 Operation 29 July 1945*

*Report After Action. Operations of the 37th Infantry Division Luzon P.I., 1 November 1944–30 June 1945*

*Report After Action with the Enemy. 11th Airborne Division. Operation Mike VI, Luzon Campaign, January 1946*

*Reports of General MacArthur*, Vol. I 'The Campaigns of General MacArthur in the Pacific' (Washington DC, 1966)

*Reports of General MacArthur*, Vol. II, Part II 'Japanese Operations in the South West Pacific Area' (Washington DC, 1966)

Reyes, Pedrito, and Grau-Santamaria, *Pictorial History of the Philippines* (Manila, undated)

Romulo, Beth Day, *The Manila Hotel* (Manila, 1987)

*Sack of Manila*, US Senate Committee on Military Affairs (1945)

Sams, Margaret, *Forbidden Family. A Wartime Memoir of the Philippines 1941–1945* (Wisconsin, 1989)

Savary, Gladys, *Outside the Walls* (New York, 1954)

Sellers, Kurt J., *Artillery Ammunition Expenditures in Urban Combat: A Comparative Case Study of the Battles of Clark Field and Manila* (US Army Human Engineering Laboratory, Maryland, September 1989)

Shortal, John F., *Forged by Fire. General Robert L. Eichelberger and the Pacific War* (Columbia, 1987)

# BIBLIOGRAPHY

*Sixth United States Army Report of the Luzon Campaign 9 January 1945–20 June 1945*, Vol. I, 1945.

Smith, Robert Ross, *United States Army in World War II. The War in the Pacific: Triumph in the Philippines* (Washington DC, 1963)

Spector, Ronald H., *Eagle Against the Sun. The American War with Japan* (New York, 1985)

Stauffer, Alvin P., *United States Army in World War II. The Technical Services. The Quartermaster Corps: Operations in the War Against Japan* (Washington DC, 1956)

Steckel, Glenn A., 'The Role of Field Artillery in the Siege of Intramuros Manila P.I.,' Student Report, The Armored School, Fort Knox, Kentucky (May 1948)

Stevens, Frederic H., *Santo Tomás Internment Camp* (Manila, 1946)

Swinson, Arthur, *Four Samurai: A Quartet of Japanese Commanders in the Second World War* (London, 1968)

Taylor, Lawrence, *A Trial of Generals* (Indiana, 1981)

'The War with Japan, Part 3, January to August 1945,' Department of Military Art and Engineering, United States Military Academy, West Point, 1951

Trudeau, Lieutenant General Arthur G., *The First Team* (Dallas, 1984)

Ward, Ian, *The Killer they called a God* (Singapore, 1992)

Willmott, H. P., *Empires in the Balance* (Annapolis, 1982)

Willmott, H. P., *The Barrier and The Javelin* (Annapolis, 1983)

Willoughby, Major General Charles A., 'The Liberation of the Philippines,' *Military Review*, Vol. XXVI, August 1946

Willoughby, Major General Charles A., *MacArthur 1941–1951* (New York, 1954)

Willoughby, Major General Charles A., *The Guerilla Resistance Movement in the Philippines 1941–1945* (New York, 1972)

Wright, Bertram C., *The First Cavalry Division in World War II* (Tokyo, 1947)

Yu-Jose, Lydia N., *Japan Views the Philippines 1900–1944* (Manila, 1992).

# INDEX

Page numbers in *italics* refer to photo captions